PRAISE FOR *Everything Is Perfect When You're a Liar*

"Oxford's writing is marked by the same wry voice that's made her a social media sensation."
—*Los Angeles Times*

"Kelly Oxford is the new cool kid in Hollywood. . . . [In] *Everything Is Perfect When You're a Liar* Oxford displays the comic relief that's been drawing celebrities like Jimmy Kimmel and Jessica Alba to her Twitter feed since 2009."
—*Daily News* (New York)

"[Oxford's] new book is full of humorous stories about growing up, making mistakes, stalking Leonardo DiCaprio, and braving Disneyland. . . . It's funny but also surprisingly touching . . . a coming-of-age story . . . just a hell of a lot funnier."
—*Forbes*

"One of the funniest voices ever to hit the Internet uses her trademark blend of biting wit and self-deprecation to find hilarity in everyday life."
—NPR.org

"A hilariously mortifying memoir. . . . Oxford plumbs her past for painful moments and turns them into slyly funny stories. . . . These vignettes are vulnerable and powerful—they make us feel less freakish by comparison. Effortlessly cool, offbeat, devilish, dramatic Oxford makes sense and smart humor from her adventures."
—*Interview*

"*Everything Is Perfect When You're a Liar* is personal without being exploitative, smart but utterly unpretentious, and a complete delight to read. I'm not lying when I say this book is damn near perfect."
—The Frisky, named "The Funniest Memoir You'll Read This Year"

"Kelly Oxford in one hundred and forty characters seems like small doses of a great drug. We want more! Thanks to her new book, we've got it."
—Lifestyle Mirror

"[Oxford's] first book of humorous essays and we can officially confirm: They are indeed humorous."
—E! Online

"Here is a funny, fantastic writer. . . . For someone trained in a hundred-and-forty-character quips, Kelly Oxford has proven her abilities as a complex and gifted memoirist. *Everything Is Perfect When You're a Liar* is worth following as a new model ⎮⎮⎮⎮⎮⎮⎮⎮⎮⎮⎮⎮⎮ be an a-hole, as long as you're this funny
—*National Post*

EVERYTHING IS
PERFECT
WHEN YOU'RE A
LIAR

KELLY OXFORD

*it*books

AN IMPRINT OF HARPERCOLLINS*PUBLISHERS*

it **books**

HarperCollins books may be purchased for educational, business, or sales promotional use. For information please e-mail the Special Markets Department at SPsales@harpercollins.com.

A hardcover edition of this book was published in 2013 by It Books, an imprint of HarperCollins Publishers.

FIRST IT BOOKS PAPERBACK EDITION PUBLISHED 2014.

Designed by Paula Russell Szafranski

Grateful acknowledgment is made to the following for permission to reprint copyright material: "Both Sides Now." Words and Music by Joni Mitchell. © 1967 (Renewed) Crazy Crow Music. All Rights Administered by Sony/ATV Music Publishing. All Rights Reserved. Used by Permission of Alfred Music Publishing.

The Library of Congress has catalogued the hardcover edition as follows:

Oxford, Kelly.
   Everything is perfect when you're a liar / Kelly Oxford.—First edition.
     pages   cm
     1. Oxford, Kelly.   2. Mothers—United States—Biography.
   3. Mothers—United States—Anecdotes.   4. Mothers—United States—Humor. I. Title.
    HQ759.O94   2012
    306.874'3—dc23   2012045190

ISBN 978-0-06-210223-2

14 15 16 17 18 DIX/RRD 10 9 8 7 6 5 4 3 2

This book is dedicated to my childhood glasses.

You made me who I am today.

CONTENTS

Contents

INTRODUCTION

KELLY: I need to write an introduction for my book.

SALINGER, AGE ELEVEN: Like what?

KELLY: An introduction for my book. Like, a "Hey, what's up, I'm Kelly's book."

HENRY, AGE EIGHT: Your book, *How I Molest Your Mother*?

SAL: Can I be in the introduction?

KELLY: I'm not calling the book *How I Molest Your Mother*, Henry.

SAL: Just say, "Buy this book, it's hilarious." There. That's an introduction.

HENRY: Write this down, say, "My stupid kids are in this, it's hilarious. Buy it today."

KELLY: Don't you want to know what the book is about?

HENRY: *How You Molest Your Mother*? Okay, okay, fine. I'll stop making that joke.

SAL: Can I read the book?

KELLY: Yes.

SAL: Who are you dedicating it to? Your beautiful children? Your loving husband? Angela? Aimee? Your sister? Your editors?

KELLY: I don't know. Does that make me a bad writer?

SAL: Yes. NO . . . I thought you were going to say, "Does that make me a bad person?" It makes you a bad *person* but not a bad *writer*.

KELLY: So how do I get people to buy the book?

SAL: Put it on sale, like normal people do. Or dedicate it to everyone in the world so people feel like it's about them.

KELLY: Henry, quit watching *Adventure Time*.

SAL: It's the *Regular Show*. Know the difference.

KELLY: Bea, why are you sitting on the other side of the room? Come talk to me about my book.

BEATRIX, AGE FOUR: I'd better not be in the book. I don't want to be in it at all. I'm going to see Dad.

KELLY: Maybe I should write the introduction about how some people try to make their lives seem perfect but end up just filtering out all the good stuff.

HENRY: Like Britney Spears, but her life sucks.

SAL: Morgan Freeman seems perfect. He sounds perfect.

HENRY: Martha Stewart, but she went to jail. Rihanna.

SAL: Rihanna was punched by Chris Brown.

KELLY: Do you think that maybe some people have boring lives because they don't take risks?

HENRY: Martha Stewart.

KELLY: Her life doesn't seem boring.

HENRY: The hoarder guy in the Speedo who lives across the street from us. His house is full of garbage.

SAL: Henry, he stands outside in a Speedo. He's a risk taker.

HENRY: You're right. Mom, if I see someone pick up your book in the bookstore, I'm gonna whisper, "Buy it, buy it." Okay, I want to watch TV.

KELLY: But I need ideas.

HENRY: Only if I get some of that Coke.

KELLY: Fine.

SAL: I need some too. Now what?

KELLY: What do you think a perfect life is?

SAL: Like the lady in *Troop Beverly Hills*, only if she wasn't getting a divorce.

KELLY: Right, and if she left out the part where she was getting a divorce she'd be lying, but her life would be totally perfect.

SAL: Uh, yeah.

KELLY: But a lot of my life sounds like a lie because I'm not perfect and I do a lot of weird and stupid things.

SAL: What? Too deep.

KELLY: Sal, quit reading that magazine.

HENRY: Shh, one more thing . . . [Henry farts.]

KELLY: I think the stories in the book are basically about how you can't and shouldn't sugarcoat things.

SAL: You don't sugarcoat anything.

BEA: I'm back, and I have two spoons in my chocolate milk.

HENRY: I think Christina Aguilera's life is perfect. Wait. Maybe not. She has lots of sad songs and lots of weird ones, like the one where she is in a bra in a cage and singing with mud on her. Man, I love when you drink a Coke then hit your stomach and you can hear the Coke in there. Can I have chips? A peanut butter cup? Otherwise I'm watching my show and doing homework.

KELLY: Fine.

HENRY: Sounds like you really need us. How's life?

KELLY: I'm stressed. What can I tell people about me?

SAL: You like Coke.

HENRY: You're obsessed with Coke . . . You're fat! Tell them you're fat.

SAL: She isn't fat, Henry.

HENRY: Tell them to look for you on Twitter and see how funny you are there. DONE. BOOM. That's a good one, write that down. Can I just un-pause the TV to see this one thing?

KELLY: NO! I GAVE YOU CANDY!

HENRY: Did you write this book to make dough?

KELLY: Yeah, when you were little we lived in a basement apartment and drove a Sunfire.

SAL: OMG and look, now you and Taylor Swift have the same shoes. Taylor Swift's housekeeper says she's a crazy cat lady. She leaves milk out for strays.

HENRY: Cats get diarrhea from milk.

SAL: This says Britney Spears hides burgers under her bed.

HENRY: I *knew* her life was perfect.

EVERYTHING IS
PERFECT
WHEN YOU'RE A
LIAR

QUEEN
OF THE
WORLD
OR SOMETHING

"DAMON!" I shouted, my smaller-than-average, tiny six-year-old hands cupped over my mouth. I pushed my giant plastic-framed glasses back up on my nose, re-magnifying my eyeballs, restoring my resemblance to a cartoon character.

Damon's mom, Karen, opened the gate. She was tiny with an odd blond bowl cut, and she had a loud, gravelly voice I was obsessed with. My voice was completely average. I wanted a weird voice like hers; I wanted everyone to have a weird voice like hers. *My* mom, Gaye, was a total weirdo and yet she sounded completely normal, with a completely average voice. I like the idea that we can contain our weirdness, but I prefer it when we wear it all over ourselves.

"Honey! Come in. Damon is just in the house. You want some cookies? You want to watch *Dukes of Hazzard*?"

"I just wanted to know if Damon would come over and audition for my play."

"Kelly! You wrote a play? What's it called?"

"It's called *Star Wars*."

"Honey," she said, smiling the smile of the kindly patronizer, "you didn't write *Star Wars*, did you?"

"I've *adapted* it, for the stage. It's my best play ever. And I think Damon's a natural Darth Vader."

The front door opened, and there was Damon—working a brown velour jumpsuit, his cowlicks sticking straight up. He looked like a tiny Tony Soprano. With the back of his hand, he wiped a smear of peanut butter and crumbs off his face. Even at the age of six, I knew Damon was a natural entertainment agent, or morning radio DJ.

"Kelly, I don't hang out with *girls* anymore," he said. "I'm not playing with you."

Karen marched up the steps and slapped the back of Damon's head. "Damon! What did I tell you about manners? Damon?! Look at me."

Damon looked up at Karen, who wasn't that much taller than he was. "*Whaaat?*" He shrugged, feigning confusion.

Karen looked at me and sighed, shaking her head. "My boy has ze-ro manners, Kelly. ZE-RO." She turned back to Damon. "What's wrong with you?"

"GIRLS SUCK! THEY THINK THEY'RE SO GREAT!"

Karen flung a single finger at her son, like a switchblade aimed at Damon's fat peanut-buttery face. "You keep saying things like that and one day you'll wake up and YOU WILL BE A GIRL, Damon! YOU WILL WAKE UP WITH A VAGINA!"

"Okay!" I said, hopping off my bike and running up the path to their house. I reached into my Aztec-print knapsack, pulled out a flyer, and handed it to Damon. "If you change your mind about girls, come over at two o'clock."

"He'll be there." Karen smiled and put her arm around Damon's shoulder. "He'll be there."

He rolled his eyes on cue.

"Damon," I said, climbing back onto the banana seat of my

2

bike. "You could be an awesome Darth Vader." I paused a minute, for effect, and looked past him, up toward some distant point in the sky. "Not sure how many other kids are going to be competing for the part, though. Maybe a lot. You might want to get there early."

I rode off, thinking about the morning of the play's opening. We'd have a penny carnival, maybe some sexy cancan girls. Around midday, the kids would perform *Star Wars*. After that, we'd go back to the penny carnival and I'd rake in the cash. Cash, however, wasn't my main motive. That would just be a tangible demonstration, to any skeptical adults, that I was indeed a prodigy to behold and a burgeoning success within the entertainment industry.

For the moment, though, I had a problem: no cast.

I needed to get serious.

After my little visit with Damon and his mom, my second stop was Jordan's house. Jordan was a nice enough kid; he had a lot of toys and we never fought over them and that's pretty much the foundation for any successful friendship. Jordan's mom was Venezuelan, and everything that went on in his house was straight out of my personal fantasy world. His mom let her kids put chocolate milk in bottles and DRINK OUT OF THE BOTTLES. She gave them an Easy-Bake Oven, a hamster, a polar bear fur rug, and the "Chicken Dance" record. They even had a fish tank full of guppies. My mom wouldn't let me have any of these things; she thought they were fine for other people but disgusting in her own home. "Hamsters are breathing balls of pee, fur, and disease." Even though she grew up on a farm and we were a middle-class family in one of the least respected cities in Canada, my mother acted as though we were all Ladies and my father was the Duke of Wellington.

When I got there, the kids were all out on the front lawn: Jordan, Ian, and Troy. I pulled up on my bike and grabbed a handful of the pamphlets from my backpack.

"You guys want to be famous?"

"What's this for?" Jordan asked, taking a pamphlet.

"FAME, Jordan! I wrote a play, and everyone's going to perform it in my yard. There's going to be a penny carnival. All we have to do is cast it first. Be at my house at two o'clock!"

Ian—a freckly, buck-toothed kid—looked up from my handout. "*Star Wars* is the greatest movie of all time. It's not a play. How are you going to *make a light saber*?!"

I stood back and held my arms out in front of me. "Imagine a light saber made out of the most amazing cardboard you've ever laid your eyes on. *Meeerrrrrr! Merrrrrrrr! Merrrrrrrrr!*" I said, swinging my imaginary saber back and forth across Ian's and Jordan's throats, decapitating the boys.

"Is that the saber sound we're going to use?" Jordan said. "Amateur. How many plays have you done?" He didn't look impressed.

My light saber sound was epic, actually. But my playwriting skills were juvenile. I tried to sway Jordan. "I wrote one play. It was called *The Kids of the Haunted Tree Hole*. But it really wasn't as good as *Star Wars*. So I've written out the best parts of *Star Wars*, like Jabba and the Death Star stuff, and we can act that out. I can make a metal bikini out of tuna cans."

It wasn't just plays. I'd also attempted to write truthful stories of living with my actual family—my Pooh Bear of a real estate mogul father, my annoyingly sweet younger sister, and my lovingly neurotic mother, a nurse who would bring me in to the doctor's office at least once a week, convinced that this was the week I'd inevitably developed leukemia, heart damage from undiagnosed strep throat, or some viral hemorrhagic fever from accidentally touching blood in a public bathroom.

But while I was watching *Star Wars*, I was moved. I wanted to see my friends as those characters. They were more exciting than my family. I didn't give a shit about Harrison Ford. But I cared a lot about my friends, and I wanted them to have the chance to be stars.

Ian started swinging his imaginary light saber. No sound. "Where are you going to put on your play? School? That's not gonna happen."

"I'm gonna get my dad and his friend to build me a stage, you know-it-all. Like Doozers. They're going to build it and then we'll have a penny carnival and make some money."

Jordan perked up. "How much money do I get?"

"Uh—NONE," I said. "It's my idea! IT'S MY YARD!"

Jordan looked at the sheet, then handed it back to me. "I don't want to be in a play."

"What the heck are you talking about? You'd rather chicken dance for no one?"

Jordan just stood there, running his fingers through his half-Venezuelan, half-Jewfro hair.

I looked him square in the eye. "It's *STAR WARS*, Jordan! Look at you—you're Han Solo if I ever saw him. Now, I'm not guaranteeing you're going to get the part, but I'm just saying . . . *I see you as Han*." I winked.

Troy, the kid who inhaled a piece of banana and almost died a few months prior, spoke up. "How many other kids are auditioning?"

I sighed dramatically and looked off into the distance again for effect. The kids all turned to see what I was looking at.

"Hmm. *Dozens*," I said, stalling for time. Then I had an idea.

"Hey, can you guys take some of these down to the park and give them to any kids who are playing there?" I passed them the rest of the sheets. I wasn't allowed to go to the park without an adult, but they totally were. I got on my bike, rode to the end of the street, got off the bike, walked it across the street after looking both ways and behind me, got back on the bike, and headed home.

I spent the rest of the morning lining up chairs in our living room, my makeshift waiting room for the auditions. Then I went to see my dad.

"Dad. We need to go to the 7-Eleven to rent the camera again!"

Dad's large eyebrows went up, and he quickly stroked his lifelong Burt Reynolds mustache as he looked up from his desk in the tiny room my parents used for their computer. This was his "newspaper desk": he would stand at the desk and read through the paper while watching TV. He never sat down. He was always ready to run out the door and into the action, like a superhero. A superhero, that is, who once owned a pair of gravity boots and threw his back out for life while doing inverted sit-ups.

"What do you need the camera for this time?" he asked, his voice lifting with excitement.

One of Dad's greatest memories was from when he was sixteen: "Now, don't ever do this, but when I was sixteen my parents went away for a week and me and John Walt stole their car and drove to California. We surfed, we went to the studios, and they told me at MGM that I had a face for the screen. *The screen.* Of course, we had to come back to Canada. Don't ever do that." After this secret confirmation of potential fame, my dad drove his parents' car back to Canada and became a property manager. My desire to be a part of the entertainment world would always spark that lingering ache for famous-screen-face that my dad still fantasized about.

"I'm holding auditions for my play. I need to record them for review. Also? You're going to need to build me a stage."

We went down to the 7-Eleven to rent the camera. When we got home, I set it up on a table in the computer room, which I'd commandeered for our audition room. Then I sat down, wrote out all the lines I wanted the kids to read for their auditions, put them in a big black binder, and kicked back with a Capri Sun.

At around two o'clock, just as I'd planned, the kids started filing in.

Besides all the kids I'd visited earlier that morning, others showed up *solely on the basis of my awesome flyers.* There were ten kids. With my sister and me, that was the dozen I'd been looking for.

I clutched my black binder to my chest and jovially rubbed Jordan's hair—mostly out of half-Jewfro curiosity, but also because I was proud of him for coming.

"I'm glad you made it . . ." I said, then cocked my eyebrow and lowered my voice to a whisper: ". . . *Han.*"

Then I turned to the crowd. "ALL RIGHT, EVERYONE! GRAB A CAPRI SUN AND FIND A CHAIR! BE CARE-FUL WHEN YOU PIERCE THE JUICE POUCH—THIS CARPET IS AN HEIRLOOM!" Everyone obeyed. This was it: I was in my zone.

"I'M GOING TO BE HOLDING THE AUDITIONS IN THE AUDITION ROOM. I'LL CALL YOUR NUMBER WHEN IT'S YOUR TURN." And with that I passed out a number to each kid in the room. Of course I was making this all much more difficult than it had to be: *These kids all lived in my neighborhood. I knew all their names.* But I knew the formalities of this sort of thing, and I couldn't gloss over them—I needed to show them I was SERIOUS. If I respected the protocol, they would respect my production. That was certainly how Mr. George Lucas conducted his auditions.

I looked over at Damon, and he was looking pretty serious too. He was wearing a clean white button-up shirt and a pair of black dress pants. Even his face was clean. Karen must have put him up to it. Just for playing along, though, I decided right then and there to bestow upon him the honor of being my Darth Vader. It was the least I could do. When no one was looking, I opened my binder and found the name "Darth Vader." Beside it, I wrote "Damon, obviously." Then I stood up and gazed upon the room.

"EVERYONE!" I commanded. "I'm just going to go to the bathroom before we start. One short break, and then we'll get this afternoon rolling!"

As I left the room for a pee, I stopped for a moment, then shouted out: "Please don't open my binder!!"

It was the dumbest thing I could have said to a roomful of children. Of course, I was a child and didn't understand how even I, myself, thought. When I got back, the kids were all huddled in a circle, staring into my open binder. My SISTER was staring into the binder! EVERYONE WAS LOOKING AT MY NOTES. Who were these animals?! Carrie Fisher wouldn't have looked at Mr. George Lucas's black binder. I really didn't have anything in there to hide. This was a simple matter of respect and order.

"OH MY GOD! WHAT ARE YOU DOING?!?" It's a good thing my bladder was empty or I would have peed myself right there in the audition room.

Troy looked up at me in fury, his fingers stretched and frozen in an air grip, his hands and arms shooting out. "I didn't even get to *audition* for Darth Vader!! I would have been amazing!!" He slapped his leg then made a serious face. "LUKE, I AM YOUR FATHER. See?"

I pushed my way through the crowd and grabbed my binder. My eyes took in the sight of all these horrible kids, one more horrible than the next, standing over my private notes—all but Jordan without a hint of shame.

"EVERYONE GET OUT OF MY HOUSE!!!!" I screamed, shredding my throat.

Everyone backed off except my little sister, Lauren. Idiot people always thought Lauren and I were twins because we both had dark hair and glasses. She was two inches shorter than I was and two years younger. People were idiots. Lauren whined and pleaded, "But I live h—"

"YOU ARE A TRAITOR!" I squealed as the other, non-blood-related children filed quickly out the front door. "I AM NOT SHARING A BEDROOM WITH YOU ANY-MORE!!!"

Lauren looked scared. "Why are you flipping out?" she asked. What an idiot.

"COME ON! Why am I flipping out?! I'm flipping out because you looked at the director's notes. You can get AR-RESTED for stuff like this in Hollywood. You kids are animals! I can't work with animals!!" I stormed out of the living room and into my bedroom.

The dream was over. No neighborhood penny carnival. No giving Damon the Darth Vader role. No making my dad or mom or Karen proud of me.

A little while later, my mom came into my room. She was very good at these Mom moments. I think it's what she was best at—even though I always fought the support, because to me support always felt like 100 percent failure. And I knew I was not a failure.

My mom was naturally slender, despite her addiction to Coffee Crisp chocolate bars. Her hair was thick and black and her eyes were gray, which always kind of freaked me out. When she sat down on the bed, it barely moved. "Lauren told me you flipped out."

"They ruined everything." I rolled over to face the wall so she couldn't see me crying. With all the screaming, I noticed, my voice was starting to sound a little gravelly, like Karen's. Silver lining.

"They went through MY NOTES!"

She started to rub my back. *Oh God. That's a stage three support move.* I was such a failure.

"Kids can be dumb," she said matter-of-factly. "I don't think they did it to disrespect you. I don't think they think that way."

Snot rolled down to my lip; it tasted salty. "But they DID disrespect me." I wiped my face. "Even if they didn't mean to, they did. I can't take it."

My mom sighed dramatically, playing up the drama for me. My mother was a good lady.

"I know!" she said. "Maybe you should try to do the play at school? Ask your teacher. You could do it during recess. There are so many more kids there. Ask your teacher tomorrow. It'll be way more fun! Just imagine—"

"Okay, Mom," I interrupted. If I didn't, she'd go on all afternoon. "I get it."

My school was a French immersion school. My teacher was Mme. Misbet, a French Canadian woman who looked like a cross between Celine Dion and Janet from *Three's Company.*

In her classroom, near her desk, there was an aquarium, and in that aquarium was housed a school of tadpoles—a wormy, creepy cloud of inky frog babies. If I wanted to mount my production of *Star Wars* at school, I would have to walk past that aquarium, full of giant tadpoles with their disgusting leg buds, and ask her.

The day after the audition fiasco, I sat at my desk, biding my time after completing my work early (my thing), lining up wafer cookies on my desk. Then, suddenly, a wave of courage came over me. I took a deep breath, broke one of the cookies in half, and carried it past the tadpoles right up to her desk, holding my breath the whole way. I didn't want to give her a whole cookie because I was a greedy little six-year-old and sacrificing half a wafer for my French commander was difficult enough, even if it was a bribe to get her to say *oui* to my grassroots production of *Star Wars*.

By the time I got to the front of the room, my face was purple. Mme. Misbet looked at me like I was insane. I exhaled with a gasp.

"What do you want?" she snapped. "It's almost lunch. You're supposed to be reading."

I held up my sacrificial wafer-cookie half. "I wanted to give you this cookie. And ask if it would be okay to have auditions at lunch today, for this play I wrote? Well, I guess I should say *adapted*. It's *Star Wars*."

Madame stared at the wafer half in my hand. "Why would I want that?" she sneered. "It's half-eaten already."

"Oh, no!!" I said. "I would NEVER do that! I broke it in half!" I was horrified. But how could I prove it? "Wait—I can show you. The other half matches! Just a minute—you'll see." I ran back to my desk, grabbed the other wafer half, and flew past the tadpoles back to Madame. "SEE??" I shouted, pressing the halves together. "Just like Little Orphan Annie's locket!!" With that, I put her wafer half back on her desk.

"So," I continued. "Can I hold auditions for my play at lunch today? I was going to do it at home and have a penny carnival, but the kids in my neighborhood are ANIMALS!!"

Madame reached out her hand, extended a long, contemptuous index finger, pressed her Lee Press-On nail onto the loathsome wafer, and slid it to the front edge of her desk. Then she looked at me and said, "Whatever." (Note: Mme. Misbet, if you are reading this, please know that at the time I thought you were just acting like a French Canadian, but now, as an adult with some time to reflect, I know you were also one crazy bitch.)

"EVERYONE!!"

It was midway through the lunch break, before recess, and I was standing in front of my classmates, who were all busy talking and stuffing their faces with ham sandwiches, peanut butter sandwiches, and Lunchables packed by parents who just didn't give a shit. I climbed up on a chair in front of the chalkboard and—in a move that would sacrifice everything I believed was good and true—dragged my nails across the chalkboard to get my classmates' attention.

"AHHH!!!" A wave of horror echoed through two dozen children as they all froze in place and looked at me. I'd won, but I'd also just cut two years off my life.

"Thanks. I'm holding auditions today for my production of *Star Wars*. I'm pretty sure Principal Everly will be into this idea, so we should be able to perform it for the school during an assembly. Please sign this sheet and let me know what character from *Star Wars* you'll be trying out for."

A hand shot up.

"Yes?"

It was Earl, the biggest kid in our class. He was so big that, on the first day of school, he sat down on his desk and broke it in half, sending him crashing onto the floor with a deafening thud. I'm not even kidding—and it should be entirely illegal that that incident isn't on video. Earl wasn't fat, just man-sized. I loved him because he was an instant character. He was just *more* than the other kids.

"Uh, I haven't seen *Star Wars*," said Earl the boy-man mountain. "I don't know who to audition for."

My mouth fell open. "What's wrong with your parents, Earl? You haven't seen *Star Wars*?!"

He shrugged.

I sighed. "You can audition for Chewbacca," I decided. "His character is pretty much one-dimensional. You'll get it." I looked around the class. "Anyone else?"

From a far corner of the room came a sound. It was our fifth grade lunch monitors, starting to giggle.

A bit of background: our school didn't have a cafeteria, so for lunch kids had to stay in their classroom and eat. Throughout the lunch period, three "mom volunteers" went from class to class to keep an eye on everyone. And the fifth and sixth grade students were assigned to sit with the younger kids, monitoring them, presumably because they were more responsible than we were.

And now ours were laughing at me.

I put on my game face.

"Did you have a question about auditioning?" I asked. "You guys can audition if you want to, even though you're, like, a foot taller than us. You could be extra Wookiees."

With that, the girls burst out laughing—and my tenuous hold over the rest of the class went up in flames.

As the other kids went back to talking and eating, the two older girls walked toward me. I hopped down from the chair, and they walked right up to me, so close I could see the pores on their little prepubescent faces.

"What's wrong with you?" said one of the girls—the one with the My Little Pony sweatshirt. God, I loved that sweatshirt. My mom wouldn't let me wear commercial products or logos.

Nothing came out of my mouth. She gave me the stink eye.

"Are you looking at my boobs?" she said.

"*No!*" I shouted. "I just like your shirt. My Little Ponies are great."

"Oh," she said in a mocking tone, but I wasn't really clueing in. "I like your shirt too."

"Thanks! It's not really a shirt, though. It's a fisherman's sweater. The tooth fairy left it for me."

Her friend laughed again. And I joined in and started laughing right along with them. We were all feeling pretty hilarious—until I realized they were getting mad.

I wasn't socialized enough to understand what was happening here. I was six years old. As far as I knew, everyone was my friend. Even Damon, the boy who hated girls, who'd put on a clean white shirt to come to my house. I didn't know about schoolyard bullies. I hadn't seen those movies yet.

The girls stepped into me, and I had to back up because they kept stepping into me, and finally they had me back against the far left-hand corner of the front of my class, right beside the pencil-sharpening station. I could smell the shavings because my sense of smell is very keen.

"Who do you think you are," My Little Pony girl spat in my face, "queen of the world or something?"

Queen of the world?

"No," I said, though I wasn't sure, because I had *no* idea what she was talking about.

"You think you're queen of the world with your stupid play? Well, you aren't. Your glasses make your eyes look huge."

That was it. I walked out of my classroom, down the hall, and straight to the office.

When I got there, another fifth grader was manning the secretary's desk while the secretary was at lunch. (In retrospect, either my school had NO MONEY for support staff, or my school was run by Wes Anderson.)

"I need to use the phone. Now!" I said.

"What for?" the boy asked, trying to look official and sitting up straight in the giant secretary chair, swiveling slightly back and forth.

"I need the phone, now!" I said. "Don't make me say it again."

The boy turned the phone around and pushed it toward me.

I picked up the receiver and dialed my home number.

"Mom? Remember how you thought I should try putting on *Star Wars* at school?"

"Oh my God!" she said. "Do you have a sore throat? Do you think it's strep? I'll come and get you and take you to Dr. Cotton right away."

"No. Mom. I'm fine. I'm calling about my play! You told me to do the auditions here, remember?"

"Yes."

"Well, that was a bad idea."

"Why?"

"Mme. Misbet didn't help me at all and her press-on nails are gross! I had to scrape my fingernails across the board to get attention! Some kids haven't seen *Star Wars*! Some older girls asked me if I thought I was queen of the world or something, and said I have huge eyes, and all just because I was holding auditions! I want to come home. *Nothing is perfect.*"

"Kelly, you can't come home."

"But everything is terrible! All the kids are laughing at me, and the teacher thinks I'm gross, and I'm not going to be able to do my play!" It was bad enough having to downscale from a profitable penny carnival to a pro bono school production. But getting bullied by a pair of fifth graders? "It's just not worth it. This was a dumb idea. I'm just a kid. I hate being a little kid."

"Wait—what do you mean, your teacher thinks you're gross?"

"I broke a cookie in half and gave her half, and she looked disgusted and said, 'Why would I eat that? You ate half of it.' Like I was some kind of animal."

"That isn't nice at all! Is she always like this?"

"Yeah, I guess. She's pretty harsh. But she's French Canadian. She can't help but yell and wear *ceinture fléchées* and talk about maple syrup."

"Kelly, I think this is why you got that stomach ulcer earlier this year! Your teacher is stressing you out. I'm going to come down there and talk to her. Do you want me to come down? I can. How can she call herself an educator?!"

"She doesn't. She calls herself *une professeuse*. And I'm upset about the play, not her. And my ulcer is gone as far as I know."

"You were the only diagnosed ulcer case for a six-year-old in the entire country."

"I'm not sick, Mom."

She paused. "Kelly, I don't want you to get another ulcer. But you can't just come home because things aren't going your way. You just have to ignore these people who are getting you down. Don't let them get to you. You're sweet for offering your teacher the cookie, and you're innovative for trying to turn a movie into a play for your friends to star in. You aren't doing anything wrong. Hey, remember when you went to Montessori kinder-garten when you were four?"

"Yeah, for half a day. And . . . I called Dad to pick me up!" I stomped my foot on the office floor. "I should have called him instead of you. *He* would have come here right now to pick me up."

"No. That's not my point. My point is this: when you were only four years old, on your first day of school away from home, you stood your ground. Do you remember what you did?"

I sighed. "Yeah. They wanted me to take a nap with the rest of the kids, and I told them I didn't nap, and then they said I couldn't be there if I wouldn't nap with the other kids, so I told them I needed a phone and I called Dad and he picked me up."

"Right. So you see?"

"No. You *picked me up* that time. Why not now?"

"We picked you up then because you were standing your ground. You weren't running away or buckling to pressure. If you had laid down and pretended to sleep, that wouldn't have been *you*. Telling your teachers you had to leave—that was *you*. Me coming to pick you up because of this queen-of-the-world thing is not you. You are queen of your world. Everyone is queen of their own world."

"Even Dad?"

"Even Dad."

The second I walked back into my classroom, I heard the voice I dreaded.

"Kelly, come to my desk." Mme. Misbet was back. "Where were you? The lunch supervisors told me you ran out without asking for permission."

I positioned myself so that I didn't have to look at the tadpoles next to her desk. "The supervisors were being mean to me," I said, forcing myself to make direct eye contact.

"I think you're lying," she snapped. "I think you're making excuses for your behavior."

I took a deep breath—through my mouth, so I wouldn't smell the tadpoles. "My behavior? What did I do?"

"You left the classroom without asking. And apparently you tried to get the class to participate in some sort of a play? Without permission you did this."

"I asked you to help me with the play and you wouldn't. You didn't tell me I couldn't do the play." I looked down at the wafer cookie, still on her desk.

And then, suddenly, I realized what my mom was talking about: as long as I wasn't doing something wrong, I could just be myself. Some people just weren't going to listen, weren't going to understand, and that was fine, as long as I didn't take it personally.

"Don't you have anything to say for yourself?" she asked.

"No," I said. Then, in one giant adrenaline rush, I picked the wafer cookie half off her desk, shoved it into my mouth, and said, "Your tadpoles are disgusting."

That's what the queen of the world would have done.

SHE'S A DARLING, SHE'S A DEMON, SHE'S A LAMB

A. REAL. JOB.

It was February, and I was ready to break some news to my peers—news that I was *way* more sophisticated and ready for life than they were. I stood up on the lost-and-found box and casually leaned against the ice cream machine.

"Guys, I got a job. You can add *employee* to the long list of things I am!"

My quiet but thoughtful friend Arif, who always seemed to wear proper dress pants, shook his head.

"No. Nope! You're thirteen. You can't work." His arm shot out for emphasis. "TOTALLY ILLEGAL!"

"I'm *not even* thirteen!" I eagerly corrected. "I'm twelve."

I sat down on the lost-and-found box beside Aimee. If I had a best friend, Aimee was the closest thing to it. She was a lot like me: underdeveloped, brunette, and loud. Together we looked like cloned prepubescent Winona Ryders with hyperactivity disorders. From a distance, the only way to distinguish us was the pair of giant glasses on my face.

"Kelly, are you still going to make it to my birthday party next weekend? We're going to watch *Splash* and play bingo."

Splash was my favorite movie; bingo was my favorite group game, because it involved no physical or mental challenges, making it impossible for me to totally lose my cool in a social situation from an excess of competitive fervor.

"I hope I'll make it, Aimee," I said, "but I haven't seen my schedule yet."

Arif shook his head. "It's illegal, Kelly. You can't have a job if you're twelve."

"Arif!" I threw my hand on my heart, like my gram does when she sings the national anthem. "I've had a Social Insurance Number since I was nine! The Canadian government needs my tax dollars so they can give homeless guys stitches and eye patches for free!" I tilted back, studiously, onto the heels of my purple Dr. Martens. "Okay, so, guess what job I got?"

Arif shook his head and drove his hands into his pockets. "I don't know. Delivering papers?"

I pointed at him. "THAT'S AMATEUR HOUR, ARIF!"

My peers went silent. I just shook my head. "I'm working weekends, washing dishes at a German restaurant."

The Schnitzelhaus was a steamy, sausage-y smorgasbord of all things German, a Black Forest log cabin full of scary lederhosen and employment. Like a lot of young girls with people-pleasing issues, I'd invested hours of my youth in *The Sound of Music*. I'd just finished a unit at school on World War II Germany—where I got in huge trouble for drawing swastikas on a blackboard—so I was already fully imaginatively invested in this place. If you'd told me every living Von Trapp descendant was living in the restaurant basement, making those delicious potato pancakes, I would have chosen to believe it. It looked exactly the way you might picture the witch's house in "Hansel and Gretel," only bigger, and run by a German man named Arnie and his family instead of a cannibal witch.

The Schnitzelhaus was a popular dinner destination for my family. My parents loved their schnitzel, and like any sane parents, they loved getting out of making a family dinner. I didn't particularly love the idea of people watching me eat bratwurst in public, but I loved the attention the German family lavished on the customers. Arnie would regularly tell me I was gorgeous, even though I was the only kid in the world who wore the same glasses as Sophia on *The Golden Girls*. Even if he was just trying to move some bratwurst, I didn't care.

One day, Arnie casually leaned over our table and looked straight at me. "Would you like to wash dishes here? Start next weekend. Seven dollars an hour."

OH MY GOD. Here he was, a champion of my underdog looks, and now he was basically asking me to join his family! The sideshow circus German family in the Schnitzelhaus wanted me in their fold. How could I say no?

This would be my first foray into the real world. Maturity in the making.

I went home that night, belly full of bratwurst, thinking one thing and one thing only: *seven dollars an hour*. Just think of the *Archie* comics that would buy. I was a mature dishwasher in a locally famous German restaurant!

Next stop, training bra.

I'd been dreaming of work my whole life. Not doing any, but dreaming about it. Back when I was nine, I thought I knew exactly what I wanted to do with my life. And I shared my vision with my entire fifth grade class in an oral report titled, "What My Future Holds."

I stood before my class with my French-braided hair, my giant glasses, and my splatter-painted, neon-green sweatshirt my mom made. (Along with being a nurse, my mom was also a genius at making a little cash on the side, starting this hand-painted clothing line when I was a kid. I always wore her sweatshirt creations to school to promote her and said things like, "You know who made this? Splatter Ink by Gaye. Available at Bonnie Doon Mall!") I gazed out upon my people, cleared my throat, and smiled.

Monologues were my chance to shine.

"It would be great to grow up and go to school and eventually become a lawyer," I began. "I'd like to become a criminal lawyer. I'd love to go into jails and talk to criminals about why they murder people and then try to figure out a way to argue that they're innocent. It must be very fun and satisfying work to feel like you're always right! Until then, I will get jobs and make money. I'd also like to have babies, a lot of kids. Maybe six." Then I pulled out my deadpan pause for emphasis and comedic effect. I looked out at my classmates, who were suddenly paying attention, then smiled. "Because kids are radical! Right, guys?!" Then I pulled at my sweatshirt with one hand, pointed to it with the other, and winked. "Splatter Ink by Gaye! Available at Bonnie Doon Mall!"

Flash-forward three years. I was about to become the first kid in my seventh grade class to get a job. A *real* job—not a paper route, not putting neighbors' babies to sleep and raiding pantries for treats my parents wouldn't buy, not feeding a friend's guinea pig over spring break when they got to go to Costa Rica and I got to stay home and feed somebody else's guinea pig. And I was shamelessly proud.

• • •

I woke up on my first day of work far too early and far too eager. I put on my uniform—a white blouse and black trousers—and sat down in our TV room to wait. I scanned through the channels playing Saturday-morning cartoons and scoffed. All of my friends were sitting in their living rooms in their jammies watching this dreck, and I was basically Oprah Winfrey. Making my way up in this world, paying taxes, becoming a mogul.

Two hours later, I strode into the restaurant like I was about to accept my Oscar for Best Actress in a Leading Role. I was led into the kitchen by Dirk, a tired and indifferent teenage child of Arnie's. Dirk looked like the Aryan boy from *The Sound of Music*, only far less jolly. He led me to the dishwasher.

"Take the dirty dishes. Spray them off into this sink. Fill the plastic tray. Slide into the machine. Shut it. Wait until this light turns on. Open it. Pull out the clean dishes and stack them over there with the other clean dishes."

"That's IT?!" I shouted, clapping my hands together. He rolled his eyes and walked away.

I could not believe how easy this was going to be. All my dumb friends were babysitting snotty kids, and all I had to do was stand still and move some stuff with my hands and make money? It was like magic.

But it was like *bad* magic—not the kind of voodoo or Louisiana magic you fantasize about. This was magic like when your mom hired a local magician to come to your fifth birthday party, and he accidentally killed the rabbit by asphyxiation in his top hat. I dug into the dishes with my customary vigor, but after a few minutes the novelty of standing still and moving stuff with my hands to make money wore off. I was bored. I couldn't even listen to my own music while I worked, because I'd chosen to ask my mom for purple Dr. Martens instead of a yellow Sony

Walkman for Christmas. As a result, I had to listen to German music and a symphony of guttural sounds from the bowels of the kitchen.

I looked at one plate with tiny green flowers and knew it had already come through three times that morning with different people's spit and leftovers on it.

I looked at my hands and knew I'd had different people's spit and leftovers on them.

I looked at the line of schnitzel-wanters out the front door and thought about how many more cups, forks, and plates covered in spit and chewed up gristle were already on their way back to me and my hands, and I realized: my mom would totally freak out if she knew how filthy this was.

Backstage at the Schnitzelhaus, it was quite a scene.

The oldest two kids were working the griddle with Arnie, who took frequent time-outs to flirt with the wives and pretty children. Pretty children who weren't me, that is, since I was at the dishwashing station now. He hadn't complimented me ALL MORNING, but I guess seeing me in my fancy clothes with my parents was a little different from seeing me in my now-grease-soiled white blouse and pruney hands. The youngest of Arnie's kids were setting up the cutlery and bussing tables with the mom. All of a sudden, as I gazed about, I realized: not only was I the only person working at this restaurant without common DNA, but I had the absolute worst job in the place. I began to suspect this wasn't a coincidence. There I was scraping and washing plates, cutlery, and cups—staring at bits of meat some people would spit onto the plate when they couldn't chew through the gristle. Some people licked the syrup off the plate. Some people piled all the food they didn't eat into the middle of the plate, mashed it all together, and then left a huge tongue print in the mound. My mom may have been a hypochondriac, but if there was one thing I'd learned from her, it was that any display like this should be treated as if it were an open petri dish sitting on a shelf at the Centers for Disease Control.

Here is what I knew in that moment: washing dishes wasn't glamorous, even in a locally famous German restaurant. I'd been duped into this job by a family of conspirators. Duped by Arnie, who'd been complimenting me for months just so he could sucker me into being his family's whipping girl. The family had probably been fighting for years over who had to man the dish-washing station when the patriarch realized he could solve the problem by tricking a four-eyed wannabe Maria into saying, "*Sure, I'll be your slave!*"

I stood there fuming, all seventy pounds of me, as I imagined Arnie and his family gathered around the fireside at night beside a giant stuffed grizzly bear, with a taxidermied moose head look-ing down from the mantel and an Alpine hat hanging from its antler. I could just see them laughing as they stuffed their chubby faces with apple strudel, cream puffs, and fancy German candies. "Oh! Ze little girl mit ze giant glasses and ze unibrow! She vill vash our dishes and ve vill be free!! Ha ha ha!!"

I slammed the dishwasher shut and chose revenge as my co-pilot. I would trade jobs with one of his German kids.

I set my sights on the toast job. Toast smelled better than dirty dishes, *and there were no pinkeye germs on clean toast.* I took a moment to psych myself up, then headed over to Dirk, the toast kid.

"Hey, Dirk," I said in my most convincing tone. "Let's trade. I'll handle the toast for a while and you can have some fun with this machine!" I draped myself over the machine in my best Barker's Beauties display pose.

"Uh, no, thanks," he said, turning away.

I got right up in his face. Shameless. "But I'm *really good* at toast. That's all I eat at home."

"No."

"I love toast more than you love toast."

"No."

"At home, I have an eight-toast toaster and no one ever uses it but me. I toast everything for everyone who comes through my door. Once, at Christmas, we had twenty-two family members over and I toasted everything for everyone for three mornings in a row. *And* BLTs were served at lunch, so that was a lot of toasting done by *moi*. None of them burned."

"NO."

"Toast is in my blood."

"NO."

"Speaking of blood, I'm going to eventually get pinkeye if I keep washing those dirty dishes. People touch their eyes, then touch the plates, and I will get pinkeye and my mom is going to be really mad at you. So I'm taking over the toast." I started picking up handfuls of bread and shoving them into the toaster.

Dirk grabbed my wrists and looked at me like I was totally insane. "Are you totally insane?" he shouted, pulling the bread from the toaster.

"I can't dishwash, Dirk. It's gross. You're a boy—gross is your normal. You do dishes. Look at how sloppy your buttering is! Dirk, you're doing that toast a disservice."

He looked up from the toast. "Just quit the job if you don't like it."

I couldn't quit. Quitting is not in my nature. I adapt. I'm an adapter. I find myself in a situation I don't like, and I adapt to make it tolerable. I'll play tricks on myself in order to get through an event—like the time Baba died on my birthday and I pretended it was an awesome prank she was pulling just for me.

Then again, I was also very lazy and dishwashing was too much. Trading my job for another one in the restaurant wasn't quitting, it was metamorphosis.

I stormed into the doorway of the front of the restaurant house.

"Arnie!"

He turned around, shocked to see me. *Time for a monologue*, I thought. *Time to shine.*

"Hey, Arnie." I smiled. "I'm cute, and you know it. Right? What I should really be doing is playing on my good looks to help the restaurant." I pushed my giant Harry Caray glasses up onto my face with the palm of my hand. "I should be in the front of the house. The hostess. And you can go back to the griddle!!" YES!! Remind him of what he really loves. The griddle is his passion! He doesn't want to be out there, he wants to cook! "You're the griddle *master*, Arnie! I can take over out here. I have a ton of cute outfits from Benetton I can wear." Okay, you have one Benetton sweater your mom bought for you for Valentine's Day. Don't get crazy. "Maybe you could hire my little sister to do the dishes?" HA HA HA! Lauren, payback time for everything.

Arnie dismissed me with a wave. "Go back to your station. The dishes are piling up. Go!"

Scheisse!

In the back, my good looks hidden from view, I stood at the dishwashing station and stared at a booger someone had wiped on the side of a plate. People were disgusting. My back was sore. My dishwashing lever arm was sore. Thankfully I only had another hour left of looking at the plates, these canvases of human filth.

I woke up the next day sick to my stomach after dreaming of dirty plates—stacks of them, marching toward me as I ran through a carnival naked. I didn't get up early and get dressed and sit downstairs, dying to get to work, like I'd done the day before. Instead, I sat in the claw-foot bathtub full of hot water in our family's little nook of a bathroom, and I cried. I did it quietly, of course: if my mom heard me crying before work, I'd never hear the end of the questions, "Do you have strep? Were you raped?!" But I deserved that special tub time, even if it was just five minutes' worth. If Oprah taught me nothing else, she taught me that. Bath and candles, girl. Bath and candles.

As I dried myself off, I thought about the first time I'd gone into that bathroom. My mother had hushed her voice, like it was some sort of haunted/sacred space, and told me the story of the woman who'd lived here before us. "She delivered her own BABY on this floor ALONE DURING A STORM! She tied the cord and bit it off. Like an animal!"

Standing there dripping, I tried to draw strength from our hearty predecessor. Could I ever bite off a cord? Could I even reach my belly button with my teeth? Never mind: a challenge was a challenge. I could feel my competitive spirit taking hold. I couldn't lose to the former owner of this house. If she bit the cord, I could totally bite the cord.

I mean, all I had to do was stand in the same spot, dying from boredom and avoiding pinkeye, for seven dollars an hour. I could do that, right? I was twelve, and this was my 'Nam.

I looked at my face in the mirror and wiped the tears away. I wouldn't think about how I was missing Aimee's birthday party, with everyone watching *Splash* and playing bingo and French-kissing the backs of their hands. I would never have French-kissed the back of my own hand, but I totally would have watched the girls who did.

I put on my dishwasher's uniform and looked in the mirror. I was about to spend eight hours in hell and I was going to make fifty-six dollars. No wonder adults were always miserable. A paycheck was just a bit of compensation for putting up with bullshit.

When I got to the Haus of Horrors, I tried not to think about the toast, or the food runners, or even the kid who seemed lucky for getting to bus tables and talk to customers. I just stood there, in the back of the kitchen, alone, pretending I was Paul from *The Wonder Years*. I even brought along a pair of gloves to protect myself from communicable diseases. But the Paul game got boring pretty quick because I had no one to share it with.

Using my imagination to make the best of a terrible situation is one of my favorite games, no matter who was dying, Baba or the birthday rabbit in the magician's hat. I moved on to the next thing. I pretended I was a paraplegic standing on my frozen legs, and moved only my upper body for the first half hour, bending over to grab the dirty dishes. I wondered if my dad got through his long hours at the property management company the same way. Maybe he'd pretend he was a little slow and answer the phone all crazy and say his name was Randy when someone he didn't like was calling. Or maybe he'd just start drooling when someone started telling him boring things about accounting.

I was impressed that I was able to do my job relying on just my upper body for movement. But the trouble with these little mental games is that no one else notices unless you share the love. So I decided to take action.

"Hey, Dirk!" I yelled to the toast kid, turning only my upper body around to face him. "Check it out! I've only used my upper body for the last half hour! I'm pretending to be totally paralyzed from the waist down."

He didn't even look up. "Why?"

Ugh! What was wrong with people?! Does no one have an imagination? At Baba's funeral, I told a second cousin that I was pretending Baba was pranking me for my birthday. That cousin called me insane. Then I told my sister that our cousin was secretly adopted, because I refused to believe that anyone I shared DNA with could be so boring.

"What do you mean, *why*?" I asked Dirk. "Why? Because I'm so freaking bored!! Aren't you bored? What are you thinking about over there?"

He shrugged his shoulders. God, it must be nice to be an idiot.

After Dirk the toast king dismissed my amazing feat of strength, I decided the only thing I could do next was dance. The German music was getting inside my head, and I was in danger of losing my mind to the mundane.

All at once, I let loose and started to do a little jig with my recently paralyzed bottom half. I really let myself get into it.

And someone noticed me.

"Whoa! Yes! *Vonderful!*" Arnie had wandered into the kitchen, and now he was clapping and dancing along with me. Yes! This wasn't so terrible after all. Finally, someone who was willing to feel some sort of joy.

I pulled off my gloves and started to swing and jig with Arnie. It was like when Captain von Trapp sang "Edelweiss" with the children and Maria came in and they caught each other's glance and for a moment everything was glorious, though of course for them everything eventually came up Nazis. This was like that, because of what I did next.

As Arnie twirled me around, I stomped and stomped . . . and stomped my foot down into a giant bucket of pancake batter.

Not all the way to the bottom. I stopped when I felt it—when I heard the slap.

I'll never unhear that slap.

"SCHEISSE!"

I had no idea how I'd stepped into the bucket. It seemed impossible, given how tall its sides were, but clearly this was Arnie's fault, because who puts pancake batter into a five-gallon pail on the floor when there's German jig music playing?!

I pulled my shoe out of the batter and saw a broken kitchen-floor eggshell peel off the bottom of my purple Dr. Marten and fall into the batter.

"Sorry?"

And then it happened. An adult who wasn't related to me got mad at me. I'd ruined his pancakes.

"HOW DID YOU MANAGE TO DO ZHIS?!?! VHAT IS WRONG WITH YOU?!"

I was frozen, looking at his purple face, my gaze slowly moving to his hairy ear.

My parents had been angry with me before, but never like this. My parents yelled, but my parents loved me. This guy did not love me. This guy wanted to kill me.

As he screamed on and on about the batter, his giant eyeballs popping out of his face, I started to cry a little. He either sensed the tears or saw them, and he stopped and left. I can only assume he was so angry because he realized he'd hired a small child to wash the dishes in his restaurant and thus was a monster of a human being.

I looked around at the faces of his children in the kitchen. Dirk with the smirk, one griddle boy with a look of embarrassment on his face, the other kid angry as he dumped out the pancake batter I'd stepped in. I felt like dirt, like Pollyanna must have felt when she was trying to grab her doll and fell from the roof and was TRULY paralyzed and ruined everyone's day.

Head down, I went back to the dishwashing station, no longer pretending to anyone, and spent the rest of my shift in a daze.

• • •

By three P.M. the restaurant was empty. I walked into the dining room and saw Arnie's wife, who looked like the child catcher from *Chitty Chitty Bang Bang*, only with awesome blond *Fatal Attraction* hair. She was sitting at a table reading the paper in her Garfield sweatshirt.

"I'm done," I said. "Can I go home?"

She looked at me. "You're here until five." My stomach sank. They owned me till five?

"But there's nothing to wash. If I go now, I can still make it to my best friend's birthday party."

"Vacuum," she said, the Garfield on her shirt wiggling under her giant German bosom, making it look like an actual cat taunting me. She handed me a vacuum.

That was my breaking point. No one had said a word about vacuuming. Sure, it was a better job than the dishes. But I was *done* with the dishes. I didn't believe a fair reward for finishing one job was *another* job, not at all. But I was on the Germans' watch. I had no option but to obey. I thought of the lady who had the baby on my bathroom floor and decided to bite the cord.

I hauled the giant industrial vacuum cleaner to the middle of the carpet, turned it on, and started dragging it back and forth across the wine-colored carpet. It weighed twice what I weighed, at least twenty times as much as my mom's Electrolux—and Mom had never once succeeded in persuading me to accept her five-dollar bribe and vacuum our house. Yet here I was dragging a monolith around for the grand sum of SEVEN DOLLARS AN HOUR. Vacuuming this room would take me twenty minutes, tops, and that meant TWO DOLLARS AND THIRTY-THREE CENTS. I turned the machine off.

A minute later, I stood in front of the bathroom mirror. "Sorry," I said. "This is really embarrassing, but . . . I quit!" I tried it a hundred ways: with a smile, with a frown, with a shrug.

Oh, I liked the shoulder shrug.

And then I walked back into the dining area and saw Arnie standing beside the vacuum.

"You aren't done yet," he said, all singsongy, wagging a finger at me gently and smiling. I could tell he felt super-guilty for going all mean Captain von Trapp on me earlier and making me cry.

"I know. Sorry, this is really embarrassing, but . . . I quit." I shrugged.

German Arnie made no expression. He just walked over to the cash register, opened it, and grabbed his calculator.

I picked up the phone and called my mom to get her to pick me up. When I came back to Arnie, he gave me an envelope.

"I really wanted this to work out," I said, even though Arnie was now going through the day's earnings and not paying attention to me. I really needed him to understand I wasn't a true quitter. I needed him to understand my point of view. It was my time to shine. "And I *tried*, really hard, to like dishwashing. I wanted this job more than anything. Today I thought about this woman who had a baby on our bathroom floor." I pulled out my deadpan pause for emphasis and comic effect and looked at Arnie, who was suddenly paying attention. "I thought, if this woman could have a baby on our bathroom floor, I could TO-TALLY wash dishes for a few hours on weekends. It made sense in my head. But I just can't do it. I'm a kid, you know. Maybe kids aren't cut out for real jobs." I said that last part for his kids, all of them but Dirk.

Arnie smiled. "Maybe when you get older you can try again."

"No," I said. "I'm not going to get dumber as I get older. I'm done with dishes."

I left the restaurant and sat outside against the wall in the parking lot, my armpits sweating. I admired that he hadn't begged me to stay after giving that monologue. He didn't even tsk-tsk me. I figured my monologue must have hit home.

I peeked in the envelope and counted the money. Ninety-two dollars.

I shut it and thought about that for a moment. Despite everything—the boredom, the paralysis, the jig, the yelling, the two dollars and thirty-three cents to vacuum a room—I had to admit, that was a lot of money for a twelve-year-old girl. A girl who had nothing to spend money on except products from the Body Shop. I loved soap.

My mom sped around the corner in her Volvo station wagon. She had that "You've been raped for sure" look on her face.

I opened the clunky door and made eye contact. "I'm fine. No one touched me."

"What's wrong?"

"Nothing. I quit. It was terrible."

She patted my shoulder. "I hate washing dishes too. Do you want to go to Aimee's party?"

I suddenly felt like I understood every adult complaint I'd ever heard. I understood every time my dad didn't want me to act out the entire *Full House* episode he'd missed when he got home late. I understood when my mom said, "Give me a minute," and lay down on the couch with her hand across her forehead.

I didn't feel like going to a party, and I didn't even have strep throat.

"No. I'm not in the mood."

"Wow. That's serious stuff. I'm glad you quit. You don't need the stress. You're prone to ulcers." My mom pushed the Culture Club tape into the deck, and we both started to sing along to "Do You Really Want to Hurt Me." I looked down at my pay envelope.

"Dad is going to be mad."

"Why?"

"Arnie yelled at me. When I tell Dad, he's going to be mad that he'll never be able to go back there for his schnitzel. Dad lost that schnitzel forever, all for ninety-two dollars. Not a good trade." I paused, looking off in the distance. My mom looked to see what I was looking at.

"Mom, can we stop at the mall?"

The next day, I walked up to Aimee's locker with a giant basket from the Body Shop and a neon-pink sweatshirt decorated with black paint—Splatter Ink by Gaye. She and Arif quit talking when they saw me approaching with the monolith wicker swath-filled with bottles and jars of apricot lip gloss. Arif shoved his hands into his dress pants as Aimee started squealing with excitement.

"Sorry I couldn't make it to your birthday," I said. "I got you this." I passed her the gifts. I'd spend all of my dishwashing money at the Body Shop, and I'd only bought one bottle of bubble bath for myself. (Grapefruit. Invigorating.)

"Oh my God, Kelly, I am so glad you have a job. Look at this thing. You make more money than anyone who came to my party!" Aimee squealed.

"So, how's your job?" Arif asked. I could tell he was jealous.

I shrugged my shoulders. The night before, I'd lain in bed playing out this exact conversation in my head. I wasn't going to lie or sugarcoat my failure. I was the mature one, and I would allow my peers to learn from my experience with Captain von Trapp.

"I quit. It was awful. I don't think I can ever eat German again."

Arif nodded. "Twelve is too young to have a job."

I hated being wrong, but I'd never admit that he was right.

"I'm sad you missed my party," Aimee said, digging through the basket.

"I'm sure your birthday was great and your grandma or a rabbit didn't die."

She looked up at me. "You've had some bad parties. Sorry about your job."

"Oh, don't worry about that. I'm planning on finding another one. Dishes are grosser than I expected. And I think I'm pretty lazy."

That night, I long-poured my grapefruit bubble bath into the tub and lit a thousand candles. I sank deep into the suds and thought about poor Dirk, who was bound to a life of buttering toast to a sound track of German oompah music. I wanted to want him to become the new dishwasher, but I wasn't that heartless. All he had was a locally famous restaurant to inherit, while I was going to rise up against adversity, like Oprah.

FUCK
YOU FOREVER

"If I were a tree, I'd be an oak tree. My branches would spread out over all the children who needed shade," I said as convincingly as possible to the two apathetic junior high gym teachers, Mr. Vale and Mrs. Walker, who were working their alter ego positions as guidance counselors that afternoon. Mr. Vale and Mrs. Walker were built to coach teams. They liked to clap their hands and take wide-gaited paces in the gym while they watched the thrilling competition of middle school sports. Their day jobs as counselors offered no such opportunities for handclaps or wide-gaited strides, and this stripped all life from behind their eyes.

"And who do you look up to? As a human being?" Mrs. Walker asked, with her unfocused stare, holding a pen over her clipboard.

"Mother Teresa." I nodded, bullshitting my way into this opportunity. I straightened out the homely church skirt, which I'd worn as a costume to demonstrate my pure intentions for the occasion. To underscore the depths of my bullshit earnestness, I wrinkled my brow, looked up at them, made some serious eye contact, then closed my eyes to punctuate how wholeheartedly

I was invested in my quest to dominate the school's social land-scape. "Certainly—Mother Teresa."

Mr. Vale chortled, casually covering his mouth. Excellent. He knew I was the real McCoy.

This was my interview to join Kenilworth Junior High School's Peer Support Team.

I knew that becoming a peer counselor would gain me some clout and instantly up my star ranking within middle school. As a Peer Support Team member, I'd be a modern-day messiah, a beacon of light, my student body's touchstone.

The school had just introduced the Peer Support program. The idea was to create a process where students who were having personal issues could find a member of the Peer Support Team at any time during school hours and talk to them confidentially about their problems. Boy oh boy, did I want a piece of that. How could any warm-blooded creature not want to be the school's secret keeper? Becoming part of the Peer Support Team would give me direct access to the deepest layers of Kenilworth's pre-pubescent psyche. And, because of that, kids would live in fear of me. This is what I wanted. Underneath that church skirt was me, hoping to convince these people that my intentions were purely to help my fellow students—when what I really wanted to be was the Don.

Peer Support came with so many perks. For one thing, team members could get pulled out of class at any time—and I loved getting out of class. Finding ways to get out of class was one of my greatest strengths as a student.

Another big plus was that Peer Support would play to my anthropological side, allowing me to hear about other kids' problems in a controlled, basically scientific capacity. My family was so boring and straight. I wanted to know how the bad kids lived.

• • •

Back in second grade, I'd become friends with a girl named Kyla Warren, mostly because she wore all the clothes I wasn't allowed to wear. I had penny loafers; she had jelly shoes. I had birthstone studs; she had long, dangly earrings. I had to wear blouses and sweater sets; she would wear a Garfield baseball cap over her scraggly bob and a Pound Puppies shirt *at the same time*. It was insane. I understood my mom's anxiety about branded girlswear, and on principle I agreed with her. I didn't want to be a part of a cartoon animal marketing ploy, no matter how cute Garfield was in that empty lasagna pan. But Kyla Warren looked like seven-year-old Drew Barrymore in *Firestarter*. I mean, she had a jean jacket with STUDS. I think that sums it up.

One day during recess, Mr. Armstrong, the janitor with a peg leg and cowboy hat, caught a stray dog and locked him up in the tool shed. Kyla and I were the only two kids, running from opposite ends of the field, to save the dog. It was our own private Rubicon: two children, from very different homes, brought together in a moment of canine crisis. As Mr. Armstrong went inside to call the SPCA, we sat outside, whispering through the cracks, "IT'S OKAY, DOGGIE! YOU'LL BE FINE! DON'T WORRY!"

I turned and stared at Kyla's shirt. Kermit the Frog. Oh dear God.

"Kyla, do you think I could go to your house after school sometime?"

"Yeah, sure," she said, squinting through the crack in the shed door. "Come over for dinner tomorrow."

I was shocked, suddenly in awe of her power. "Shouldn't you ask your mom first?"

She turned to me, snapping her gum. Watermelon. "Why?"

I shrugged. "I have to ask my mom if I can do *anything*."

This seemed to freak her out. "Really? Can I come over to *your* house sometime?" she asked.

"Yeah," I said. "But I'll have to ask my mom."

I was so excited. What was it like to have a mom who didn't need consulting? A home where jelly shoes were considered exactly as fancy as I believed them to be?

The next day I went home on the school bus with Kyla. Everything seemed normal until we got off the bus and started walking. ALONE.

"Where are we going?" I asked. "Where's your mom?"

"She's at home."

Panic started welling up in my throat. My hands were clammy. My mind was racing, thinking about all the kidnappers driving past us and thinking, *Maybe those two today?*

"She doesn't pick you up from the bus stop?!" I asked. I was horrified.

"No! I'm not a baby!" She was right. We *were* seven, totally capable of using toasters and stuff. Still, as we walked along that busy road, I'd never felt so small in my entire life. At any minute, I was sure a hawk would swoop down and pick me up.

"Let's stop in here!!" Kyla pointed to some kind of storefront on the corner. It had an enormous door with a large black-and-yellow awning. Overhead was a mounted oil pump jack, the old-timey kind from *The Beverly Hillbillies*, and a sign: BLACK GOLD.

This was not my neighborhood. In my neighborhood we had a fresh produce market and a tiny Italian restaurant owned by a singing fat man with a huge smile and free candy. There were no bars with pump jack awnings. "What is this place, Kyla? It looks like a bar."

"It *is* a bar," she said, and skipped up to the door and opened it.

It was a bar, or bar/pizza place, and the air was choked with cigarette smoke. I'd just walked into a scene from a movie my parents would turn off if I came into the room.

Kyla went up to the counter and waved for me to follow her. I was walking very slowly, trying not to show the fear I was feeling and that Kyla was so clearly not feeling. She looked so much like Drew Barrymore that I started to wonder if I was actually in a PG-13 movie. "C'mon!" she said, and came back to grab my hand.

In one corner of the barroom sat an old man, smoking and playing *PAC-MAN* at a table machine, his ashtray overflowing onto the video tabletop. He looked up at me and winked. *That's it!* I thought. *I'm finally going to get kidnapped. My mom is going to KILL ME!*

Kyla led me to the saloony kitchen doors and popped them open. "Hello! It's Kyla! Just wanted to say *Hi!*" A couple of people in the kitchen looked up, but no one responded. Eventually she got a wave from one of the Chinese dishwashers.

Kyla turned to me and said, "Okay! Let's go!"

That was it? All that danger just to say "Hi" to a Chinese guy? Kyla grabbed my hand and dragged me through the crowd. As we passed *PAC-MAN*, I didn't want to look over, but I couldn't help it. I glanced at him, for just a second, and he winked again. Somewhere my mom shed a tear for her daughter, whose days were numbered.

We crossed the street—it was a REALLY busy thruway, and we were less *Abbey Road* and more baby ducklings. When we landed on the other side, I followed her into a block of duplex houses. Then my heart jumped. "What's that?!"

There, in one of the bungalows, sat a monkey in the window.

Kyla stopped. "Yeah, that guy has a monkey. He won't let me touch it, though."

"You know a guy who owns a *monkey*??" I couldn't believe all this was happening ten blocks from my own house, where all we had in our windows were barking purebreds. The monkey was standing on a cat's scratching post looking at us. He was tiny and wore a diaper. He was perfect.

"I don't know him. He's mean. He told me I shouldn't be on his porch asking to touch his monkey."

"Who the heck has a monkey and doesn't want kids to touch it? It's so cute. I like his little diaper."

I'd forgotten I was seven and without a parent. I was an explorer.

"Let's get closer to it!" I said. "Let's go to the window! If the man comes we can run. We're fast runners, remember? Didn't we outrun Mr. Armstrong yesterday?"

Kyla followed me to the window. The monkey screamed in excitement.

"He's even cuter close up!" squealed Kyla.

"If I had a monkey," I said, touching the window where the monkey's hand was, "I'd put it in clothing, like a man or a woman. They have people faces. Oh my God, look at his ears!"

The monkey started pulling on his diaper and jumping around.

"It's dancing!!" I shrieked, and I started jumping around, imitating the monkey.

Then it happened.

The monkey pulled off his diaper and grabbed his penis.

Kyla laughed, but I was totally mortified. My stomach rolled over on itself. "*GROSSSSS!!*" I yelled, then covered my mouth in horror. I looked at the monkey's tiny black nails wrapped around his dink. I'd never seen a real dink before, and now I had a tiny monkey penis burned into my soul. I looked away but saw the penis everywhere, like floaters after staring at the sun.

"*Run!*" I yelled, turning around and running across the lawn back to the sidewalk, dragging Kyla behind me. We ran for blocks, blasting our way across intersections. Just as I was realizing that I'd never be able to outrun that monkey-dink image, Kyla shouted, "Up here!" and led me up the front walk of the left side of a bungalow duplex.

She threw open the front door and out tumbled two small blond shaggy dogs. "That's Tia and that's Amber," she shouted. "Look out, they're both having their periods."

I had no idea that dogs had periods, but sure enough those dogs were, all over their butts.

A creepy winking guy, a monkey penis, dogs with periods. I was learning so much about the world. All my childhood training was telling me to call my mother immediately to rescue me. But my instincts were screaming, *Dear Lord, let this never, ever end.*

"Who's playing that music?" My parents didn't listen to music in the house, unless it was Mannheim Steamroller or Vivaldi. Vivaldi is powerful, but it's not exactly, "Hey, I have stuff to say to you, listen to me" music. In Kyla's house the music was blaring as soon as she opened the front door.

"MOM!" she said, throwing her bag and shoes onto the floor. "It's Bob Marley."

The house smelled like something. Not smoke, but something like smoke. The carpet threads were really long and the walls were covered with movie posters, not paintings. And there were plants—lots and lots of potted plants. My mom had a couple of African violets and a hibiscus tree, but this was like a jungle, right there in the living room.

"MOM! WE NEED SNACKS!!" Kyla tossed her head back dramatically, as though we should already have been taken care of. Then she turned to me. "Want to see my doves?"

She pulled a chair up to the fridge and grabbed the cage that was sitting on top. Her kitchen was small, with a table in the middle and a fluorescent light box on the ceiling. On the table was a tiny nude statue. Apparently Kyla's family liked to look at the human body while they ate, which was weird, but then again not much weirder than anything else I'd seen in the last fifteen minutes. I could tell the statue was sexy from the position and size of the statue's butt, which was bigger than any human butt I'd ever thought possible. Anything even remotely sexy in my house generally arrived on the TV screen, and when it did, my father would immediately run in front of the TV and open his robe so we wouldn't see it.

I nodded at the cage of doves in Kyla's arms, trying to feign seriousness. "It looks like you had hamsters and you did a magic trick and turned them into doves." She just put the cage on the table, but I heard laughter behind me. Kyla's mom emerged from her bedroom, wrapping a large silk kimono around herself as she extinguished a tiny cigarette into a crystal bowl on a shelf in the hallway. She smelled like musk. She was beautiful, but in that really scary Catwoman kind of way.

"That's funny. You must be Kelly. Kyla said you were funny."

"Nice to meet you, Mrs. Warren."

She kissed the top of Firestarter's head. "No, please call me by my first name," she said with a husky voice. "Rowan." Rowan looked me up and down, then back up again. I felt my cable-knit sweater heat up. "Kelly, you look very smart."

"It's just my glasses," I said, adjusting my big pink frames. "Glasses make everyone look smart, but really they just have broken eyes."

Rowan opened the fridge. "See, that's what I mean. A dumb person wouldn't say that. You have an aura."

"An aura?" I looked down at my sweater. Was it stuck to my shirt?

Kyla pulled a dove out of the cage. "Mom is a Wiccan."

"Oh." I had no idea what *Wiccan* meant. I decided it was probably Rowan's last name and Kyla was bragging, like Fallon on *Dynasty* standing there declaring, "My mom is a Carrington," as she blithely pulled a dove from a cage. I must have looked confused, standing there trying to picture the Carringtons with doves on their fridge, because suddenly I realized that Kyla was laughing at me.

"You don't know what *Wicca* is?"

"Kyla, that's rude."

Then a man came out of Rowan's bedroom, pulling a shirt over his naked and tattooed chest. He looked exactly NOTH-ING like my father. He had a HAIRLESS CHEST.

"Hi, I'm Greg."

GREG?! I swallowed. Did I really have to call these grown-ups by their first names, like they were kids?

Rowan handed each of us a bowl of rolled-up salami slices smeared with cream cheese. "You're not a vegetarian, are you?"

"No. But my mom is."

"My mom is too," Kyla said.

As I sat there chewing, wondering whether the Carringtons served caviar with their salami slices, I did a mental search of the entire Wiccan house, looking for clues to what kind of family bought their daughters jean jackets with studs. Period dogs, smoky smell, Bob Marley, doves, naked boyfriends, pajamas at three in the afternoon. *Wiccan* must mean "weird."

"Oh!" Greg the boyfriend slapped the table. "I want to show you girls something I found today. It's in my van."

I looked out the window and added "dark-green windowless van" to my list of clues. *Wiccan* definitely meant weird.

When Greg returned, he was holding something smallish and dark. Was it another animal?

"I found this in the wall behind some pipes at that old guy's house today. It's an antique."

He put it down on the table. It was a gun.

This was officially the best day of my life.

I picked up two pieces of salami and shoved them in my mouth. "OUFNNDIT?"

They all looked at me. I washed the meat down with orange Tang and tried again. "You FOUND IT?"

Kyla pointed her finger at Greg. "That's stealing!"

"Kyla," Rowan said, picking up the old gun and waving it around as she spoke. "Do not call people thieves. This is a found object and Greg was meant to find it."

"Are there bullets in it?" I asked. Rowan froze. She looked at the gun, then at Greg. Greg said nothing. A long moment passed.

"Did you check it?" Rowan asked, pushing the gun back at Greg. "You didn't check it? GREG!"

Kyla and I shoved the dove back into its cage and scrambled down the basement stairs to her room. "GREG! I CAN'T BE-LIEVE YOU DIDN'T CHECK THE GUN."

"A Wiccan is a witch," Kyla said, as she shut the door to her tiny bedroom.

"YOUR MOM IS A WITCH!?!" I whispered shoutingly.

"Only when she meets with other witches. They protect us from a lot of bad stuff." She pulled out a book covered in weird forestlike drawings to show me. I was enthralled. This was like listening to a ghost story, only it was a MOM story, which made it even scarier.

"What kind of bad stuff?" Tia and Amber jumped up on the bed. I stretched out my legs and blocked them with my feet from getting too close.

"Well, there was a lot of negativity around us after my dad

left, so Mom waited for the moon to be ripe and smoked this skunky-smelling stuff."

"Like from before?" I gasped. I was totally entranced. "Do you think she and Greg were doing spells when we got here?"

Kyla pushed the dogs off her bed with her feet. "Yeah, for sure. The music and stuff was a clue. You *are* smart. Anyhow, Mom's biggest spell was the one where she got rid of the negative vibes from my biological dad."

But Kyla still looked sad to me. Maybe her mom was bad at being a witch.

"I'm not usually allowed to talk about my dad like this, but I miss him." I was glad Kyla felt able to confide in me, almost as glad as I was that she'd pushed the menstruating dogs off the bed.

Now, five years later, in the school counselor's office, Mrs. Walker, without making eye contact and with a deep nonchalance, passed me a handout about supporting my peers. She exhaled. "You made it."

I'd made the Peer Support Team.

The gods of seventh grade had smiled upon my love for oak, Mother Teresa, and church skirts.

I left the counseling office, feeling one step closer to my goal of becoming my school's Parker Lewis, and headed directly to Principal Wynychuk's office. If I was going to be the most popular kid in school, and bear the responsibility of becoming my school's peer guru, I really had to get in good with the leader of the school. I tapped on his door with my fingertips.

"Hi! I made something for you," I said, casually reaching into my army-style backpack and pulling out a mix tape.

"What's this?" Mr. Wynychuk pulled down his glasses, smiling. For an old man, he was pretty handsome. I remember hearing he played football or something in the 1970s, and my mom used to brag about dating a football player in the 1970s, so I knew this guy had a really important legacy behind him, or at least that he might have dated my mom.

I passed him the tape. "I made you a mix tape of all of my favorite classical stuff. It's a little heavy on Vivaldi, but all good work-symphony mixes are. Oh, and I put a little Sinead O'Connor on side B. 'Troy' will change you."

Mr. Wynychuk smiled. "That's very thoughtful of you, Kelly. Thank you."

I agreed. It was very thoughtful of me. "Bye!"

I left the office and walked across the hall to Aimee's locker.

"LOOK, IT'S THE ANOREXIC BITCHES!!" shouted Terry the mullet-headed ginger from his locker, surrounded by his friends, who all apparently had disdain for any girl with a body similar to their own.

"I AM NOT ANOREXIC! I EAT AT McDONALD'S ALL THE TIME!!" I shouted back at the ginger troll.

"What were you doing in the office?" Aimee asked. "And why are you wearing that weird long skirt?"

"I interviewed for the Peer Support Team," I said, then paused for dramatic effect, cleaning my glasses. "*Got it!*" I winked, putting my glasses back on.

"Kelly, what is Peer Support?" She sighed. "You're always into the weirdest stuff."

"*No, I'm not*, Aimee. It's a group of kids other kids can go to for support. You know, to listen to their problems? Help encourage them to talk to the real counselors? It's like the Baby-Sitters Club, only we listen to our peers instead of pretending we're old enough to look after little kids."

"So you work for the counselors? Like a spy?" Aimee shut her locker.

I hadn't thought of that. "I hadn't thought of that. Aimee, I really want to do something *big* with my life. I think supporting my peers is a step in the right direction—you know, like how Mother Teresa looks after orphans? I can talk to the girls with Guns N' Roses T-shirts and hear what kinds of problems they have. They have *problems*, Aims. They also have boobs—I'm pretty sure boobs are a prerequisite for liking Guns N' Roses." I pulled out the Peer Support pamphlet I'd quickly read in the counselor's office and read it to Aimee. "'*Encourage honesty. Honesty can free people of their problems.*'"

"Still sounds like mole work to me." Aimee shrugged her shoulders and pulled her lips in tight, forming the deepest and most perfect dimples I'd ever seen.

"Also, I gave Mr. Wynychuk a mix tape I made for him."

She stopped organizing her binders and looked at me with contempt. "You made the principal a mix tape?"

I twirled my index finger at my temple, making the international signal for *doy*. "Uh, yeah. He's cool."

On the way to social studies, I stopped at my locker and put on my signature Guatemalan rainbow tribal jacket to spruce up the church skirt. No need to impress the gym teachers/counselors anymore; now I needed to show my peers I was one of the people.

I sat at my desk behind a loudmouth named Craig, a dead ringer for Zack Morris from *Saved by the Bell*, season one. He was my total crush. Craig turned to me. I tried to act cool, pulling away when he leaned in, but then he whispered to me:

"Kyla Warren has had sex with *three guys*."

My mouth dropped.

"*S-E-X* sex?" I whispered back. "Like a full-on penis-in-the-vagina thing?"

He nodded, putting the end of his pen in his mouth and

making his eyes really wide. People were having SEX in the seventh grade? Like, real people?! I could barely stand close to a boy without sweating from every inch of skin on my body, including my back. This Guatemalan jacket was made of cotton, but it was the thickest thread available, and now Craig was whispering to me about sex and I was like a waterfall in there.

"Are you sure? I don't believe it!!"

I was shocked, and I couldn't fake nonchalance. Sure, Kyla's mom was a Wiccan who lived with a hairless naked gun thief. But THIS?

"It's true. She told me herself."

"Really?" I stopped a minute to think. And then it hit me.

"Oh my God, Craig! She could have AIDS!"

Craig's eyes widened again, and he whispered, "Like Magic Johnson?!"

I nodded furiously. "Exactly! Magic Johnson had sex with *at least* three people. And he's going to die any minute."

My mom, you see, had recently added AIDS to her list of disease obsessions. She told me, over and over again, that it wasn't *just* transmitted through sex. She explicitly warned me to "Stay away from all bodily fluids! Bloody tissues, bloody anything! Even bloody people. ESPECIALLY BLOODY PEOPLE!" I was ready to avoid anything bloody that crossed my path. I expected it to happen at any moment. AIDS WAS EVERYWHERE.

The moment Craig told me that Kyla had had sex, I knew there was a 95 percent chance she had AIDS. Forget pregnancy, it was all about AIDS, which could be spread by saying the word *sex*, by even *thinking* about sex. Sex and AIDS were synonymous.

I spent the entire social studies class pretending to read *Animal Farm*, but really I was thinking about how I'd be the one who would nurse Kyla in her final days. I'd be the only kid in school brave enough to be her friend. I would be her oak tree, spreading my branches out and protecting her from the storm of AIDS till it finally consumed her.

When the bell rang, I went to the girls' washroom. While the kids were tipping and rocking and robbing the ice cream machine outside, carefree, I had to shoulder the burden of knowing that a friend I'd known since second grade was about to die. As I sat in my shiny pink cinder-block stall and peed, I steeled myself for the task ahead. I took a deep breath. As soon as this pee was through, I would go find Kyla and become that open ear I'd been for her before, when she couldn't talk about her dad, when we saw the monkey penis and the loaded gun. I had to find her, I had to counsel her. I hadn't even read the Peer Support Team handouts yet, but this would be my first Peer Support success. And if Kyla didn't have AIDS already, I could totally prevent her from getting it!

The pee ended, and with that flush came the knowledge that I was about do something really, really good. I was singlehandedly going to prevent an AIDS outbreak in Kenilworth Junior High.

As I came out of the bathroom, I noticed a circle of kids staring. I looked around to see what they were looking at. Then I realized they were looking at me.

"What?" I asked everyone and no one in particular. I noticed a Peer Support poster on the bathroom door. "Yeah." I smiled. "I did totally make the team."

Then I saw her.

Kyla was in the middle of the mob. She came running at me. I lifted my arms to shield my face.

"DID YOU TELL EVERYONE I HAVE AIDS?!" she spat.

I was paralyzed. For one thing, I was in shock. For another, flecks of her spit had landed on me. Now I probably had AIDS too. My mom was going to kill me.

"No!" I said. "I didn't! I didn't say you *had* AIDS to ANYONE!!"

Kyla was momentarily deflated. She looked over at Craig. "Is that true?" I could feel the sweat start to run down my back. Damn Guatemalan cotton. *Craig?* Craig, my own personal Zack Morris, was responsible for this?

"Kelly," he said in an incriminating tone. He couldn't have been more handsome if he had actually called me Kelly Kapowski. "You *did* say it."

Kyla spun back around and melted me with her Firestarter eyes. "You and your stupid African jacket!" she yelled right in my face.

"Hey!" I said. "It's GUATEMALAN!"

We both stood there, hearts beating, breathing hard. If she was full of AIDS, I was inadvertently speeding up the death process.

I looked at Kyla straight in the eyes, adjusted my glasses, and said, "Kyla, trust me. I did NOT TELL EVERYONE YOU HAVE AIDS!"

I was shaking. This was the first almost-fight I'd ever been in with anyone besides my sister. Kyla looked like she wanted to believe me. "Fine," she said, "then what *did* you say about me?"

Oh God. She was going to make me say it? I looked over at Craig, who quickly looked away. What a pussy! Suddenly he meant less to me than Screech.

"I said . . ." *Oh God,* I thought. *I'm a* terrible *liar.* Almost inaudibly, I mumbled, "I said you *could* have AIDS."

"What?" she said, stepping closer. She may have thought I'd mumbled something else, like "you cook ham 'n' eggs," and just wanted to make sure.

I spoke up as slightly as I could. "I said you *could* have AIDS. But only becau—"

She was on me, grabbing my hair. She flew into me with her whole body and we both hit the wall. Our binders popped open as they hit the ground, and papers went flying everywhere. Then someone picked me up. It was our math teacher, Mr. Lee, a tall Chinese man who, according to junior high lore, had a drawer full of booze in his desk.

"Both of you, pick up your stuff!" he ordered. "The rest of you, GET TO CLASS!" Everyone else scrambled out of the hall. Then he smiled this really creepy "I'm going to enjoy this" smile and dragged Kyla and me into his classroom.

Mr. Lee stood us at the front of the classroom, then sat down at his desk, arms crossed, happy as a clam. My math teacher lived for misery, pure unadulterated misery. He loved it when a student failed a test, just so he could berate them with a rousing game of "What kind of job can a person who fails seventh grade math get?" ("Chicken plucker" was one of his suggestions; that made him reel with laughter. As if anyone plucked chickens outside the Sichuan Basin.)

"So, we have a couple of scrappers here," he told the class now. "I just had to pull Kyla Warren and Kelly Oxford apart out there. So, girls, what was the problem?"

Kyla and I looked at each other.

"Nothing," she volunteered. Amateur move, Kyla, amateur move.

"NOTHING?" Mr. Lee said. "Did you hear that, class? They were fighting over nothing!" Mr. Lee stood up and started pacing in front of us like a prosecutor.

"Kelly. You certainly didn't appear to be upset over 'nothing' in the hallway. Were you? Were you upset over 'nothing'?"

I felt like I could throw up. I'd never wanted so badly to sit down at my desk and do some fractals. I looked across the room at my empty desk, where my bag sat, the Peer Support pamphlet sticking out. And suddenly it hit me: the pamphlet. "Encourage honesty. Honesty can free people of their problems."

I looked Mr. Lee straight in the eye and took my shot. "I said something I shouldn't have said."

He stopped dramatically, eyes wide, mouth gaping, and then started running around the class waving his hands in the air like Phil Donahue. "Oh, so it was *your* fault, then, Kelly??"

"Yes, it was," I replied calmly. "I said something about Kyla that I shouldn't have said, but I did it out of care and concern." I looked at Kyla hoping she'd recognize me as the next Mother Teresa. "I was really worried about her."

"Oh, she was *worried* about her!" said Mr. Lee, mocking me in a baby voice. "What did Kyla do that made you worried?"

Kyla's face fell. I looked at Mr. Lee. "I can't tell you," I said.

Mr. Lee immediately cut the dramatics, stood up straight, and looked at me hard. "You can't tell me?"

"Nope," I said as casually as possible. Then I dropped the bomb. "Quite frankly, it's none of your business."

"Kyla!" His red face turned four shades darker than usual; he was approaching a true eggplant. "Kyla, go to your desk." She did. Mr. Lee came up to me, bent down until we were face-to-face. He leaned in so close that I could see the thick hairs coming out of his cheek pores. "Get your things and go directly to the office." Then, in a fit of rage, he walked over to the intercom and pulled the lever down. "HELLO?"

The secretary's voice returned a hello.

"I'M SENDING MISS KELLY OXFORD DOWN TO THE OFFICE FOR FIGHTING IN THE HALLWAY," he said, then released the lever.

I swallowed the lump in my throat, stuffed my binder and the pamphlet into my bag, and looked over at Kyla.

Did she even remember how close we once were? How the monkey masturbated to both of us? In my imagination, something beautiful and perfect could have happened in this moment. Kyla could have mouthed a simple "Thank you."

Instead, she mouthed, "Fuck you."

As I waited for my dear principal to call me in, I thought about that "Fuck you." I didn't deserve that. Everything that had happened happened because I cared. I cared enough to worry about Kyla and her AIDS. I cared enough to talk back to Mr. Lee and get yelled at by him so closely that I could smell his mouth hole.

After waiting for half an hour in the office foyer, I sat down in Mr. Wynychuk's office. "So," he said in a perky sort of way, "what happened?"

I was humiliated. I shrugged my shoulders, fighting back tears. Outside, through the window, I could see the smoking girls with the G N' R boobs. How did *I* end up in the office, when all the bad girls were clearly out there?

"Did you really start a fight?" Mr. Wynychuk said. "Honestly, I don't believe that." He sat back in his chair and put his hands behind his head, pen in hand, smiling a warm smile.

"Yeah," I said. "Because I didn't. Kyla Warren was mad at me because someone lied and told her I said something about her."

"And you didn't say something about her?" Oh God, this again.

"Okay, yes, I did. But promise me you won't tell anyone."

"I can't promise that, Kelly."

"Okay, well, I'm sure you won't tell anyone, but it'll be Craig's fault if you do, anyhow. Craig told me that Kyla had, you know . . .

S-E-X. Sex. Like full-on penis-in-one-hundred-percent-vagina sex. And I obviously flipped out because I didn't think people were doing that. But . . . also because of AIDS."

"Ahhhhh." Mr. Wynychuk sat forward, taking it all in.

"I was just worried, you know. Since she was *doing it,* she could get sick from AIDS. So I accidentally voiced my concern, rather than just thinking it. Then Craig, who is so not the leading man I'd suspected, told her I was spreading rumors that she had AIDS."

"Well, you didn't *tell* people she had AIDS, did you?"

"Of course not!" I made my eyes really wide to express how honest I was being. "I never meant to hurt her either. I was just worried."

"Well," he said, slapping his knees, "it seems like you've learned your lesson here."

"Yeah!" I rolled my eyes. "I'm just going to keep my thoughts to myself!"

"No, no. Please, don't do that. Just think before you speak. If you want to say something to someone, tell them, face-to-face. In junior high, socializing is difficult. More difficult, even, than Mr. Lee's class."

I shot him a look. "Can you imagine learning math from Mr. Lee?"

"Seriously," he said. Man, I knew this guy was cool.

Mr. Wynychuk stood up and put his hand on my shoulder. "You'll be fine. I have faith in you, Kelly. You're a good kid. I've got to go do the lunch announcements now. If you have any other problems or any issues with Kyla, come talk to me."

"Oh, I should be fine," I said. "I'm part of the Peer Support Team now."

I walked out of his office and turned down the empty hallway just as Mr. Wynychuk got on the intercom, listing all the lunch-hour club meetings and the after-school sports schedule. Then he continued:

"Our afternoon song is courtesy of Kelly Oxford, who was kind enough to provide me with a Vivaldi mix tape."

So much for being cool. So much for going incognito. I may have been small, but I just couldn't be invisible. I always wanted to, but it just wasn't me. If I was going to have friends, they were just going to have to accept me for the stupid kid I was.

The violins erupted just as the bell rang. Students were pouring into the hall as I walked back to my locker, Vivaldi's "Summer," *Allegro non molto*, filling my head, the hallways, the school. In my daze, I bumped into a kid. Unfortunately it was Terry, the redheaded nightmare.

"Hey, look who's here! IT'S THE ANOREXIC BITCH!" He stopped and laughed. I stopped and turned to face Terry and his friends.

"FUCK YOU, TERRY. FUCK YOU FOREVER." And I gave him the finger.

Face-to-face, just like Mr. Wynychuk suggested.

TWEEZERS

When I was in my early teens, lightning struck near my house.

A local modeling agency discovered Tricia Helfer in a nearby farm town; she quickly went on to become "Supermodel of the World," which is a real thing. Soon after that, two other girls were discovered and whisked away from my hometown of Edmonton, widely regarded by other Canadian cities as the armpit of the country, to Paris Fashion Week. And then all the big international modeling agencies started sending in reinforcements, who descended on the area in droves to discover the next big thing.

I was positive it was me.

At the age of fourteen, I did *not* look like a model. I did not want to be a model. Up to this point, my biggest claims to fame were my impressions of Steve Urkel and the Chicken Lady from *The Kids in the Hall.* My intentions were pure: I wanted to be famous, but I couldn't play an instrument, so I couldn't be in a band, and I couldn't memorize lines, so I couldn't be an actress. I wanted to be in Paris. I wanted to be anywhere else. I was obviously *Something* of the World.

I was five foot six and weighed eighty pounds. I had giant

pink glasses that hid most of my underdeveloped face. And—again—I had a mean Urkel impression.

To me, it seemed obvious: the next logical move was modeling.

A "cattle call" is what they call a big open audition, a model search. It's great that they call it a cattle call, because much like cows at an auction, all the lithe, ready-to-be-sexualized underage girls wear a number and strut their asses in front of potential investors (that is, agencies), who then pick the girls they want to see and write their numbers down in a book to be called on later. The only difference between the cows and the girls is weight—and the fact that people kill cows before devouring them.

My mom rarely let me buy magazines—"Waste of money! Just look at the mannequins in the Gap and dress like they do"—so I flipped through a much-cherished, seven-month-old *Seventeen* magazine to find a look to mimic. I settled on a girl who looked like Jessie Spano from *Saved by the Bell*, in stirrup pants and a blazer, and headed into my mother's closet, where the options went beyond my one Benetton sweater, overalls, and boxy jeans.

I threaded through her "fancy" section, full of outfits she'd worn to high school reunions, and picked out her Chanel knock-off blazer, which was six sizes too big for me and came down to my knees. I put on the blazer and looked in the mirror. I was *swimming* in that jacket.

Just as I was realizing what I was looking at, my mom came in. "Kelly, it's great. You look like a tiny Jackie O meets Brooke Shields!" I looked like Sally Jesse Raphael in a gold-buttoned herringbone fire blanket.

We piled into our cranberry Aerostar for the short drive downtown to the high-rise mall.

"Should I come in?" she asked.

"No," I said. "This is going to be an all-day thing. I brought my allowance for lunch. I'll call you when I'm done."

"Are you sure you don't want me to come to the audition with you?" she asked. I rolled my eyes. I would *die* if I had to walk on a catwalk with her there. Parents aren't even supposed to know what a catwalk is.

"I'm not a child," I said, putting on my backpack. "Nothing will happen to me. It's not like we live in Detroit!"

The reality was, downtown Edmonton was kind of an iffy place for a young girl to walk around alone. It wasn't a bustling hub of activity. Between the jail, the big halfway "healing" house, and the downtown drop-in psych hospital, any local hustle and bustle was 100 percent weirdos. But as a kid you might not necessarily feel wary of the guy humping the giant chess pieces in the mall, yelling, "ALWAYS! ALWAYS!" You just think it's hilarious.

I slammed the door shut and headed into the mall.

As soon as I got to the mall rotunda where the cattle call was being held, my heart rate jumped and I started to sweat. There were hundreds of girls there—girls there alone, and girls there with friends, and girls there with their moms. I told myself I had an edge on the girls with their moms and friends, who wouldn't be able to focus during their big moment on the catwalk as completely as I would during mine.

I lined up with the other new arrivals. A group of rapper boys were hanging over the level above us, catcalling. I was going to love being famous.

"Nice hair," I said to a girl with a slicked-back ponytail. Amateur. My hair was teased as big as possible. That was sexy. That was Supermodel of the World kinda stuff. My friend Mara had Cindy Crawford's workout tape. I knew my shit.

An organizer handed me a piece of paper that read "1149." I pinned it proudly to my mom's jacket, feeling like I'd already won something, like I'd just been accepted into Tisch or Juilliard.

I got into the line of girls and waited for my turn to hit the catwalk. I hadn't even practiced. I didn't need it. Instead I just studied the others as they strode down the runway, the way an actor would study a role. Swing hips, walk in a straight line. That one touches her hair too much: *don't touch hair.* That one's walking too fast: *walk slow.* As I inched my way closer to the runway, I was gaining confidence with every step. Remember how John Candy overshadowed Tom Hanks in the slapstick racquetball scene in *Splash?* That's how I felt.

At last, it was my turn to shine. I ran up the steps, hit the catwalk with a loud ★*THUD*★ from my Fluevog clogs, and started madly out-swinging everyone else's hips with my own, down the runway to the heavy dance beat. I looked out at the crowd. Everyone was busy talking or reading. Didn't they realize that greatness had just hit the catwalk? I looked over at the judges. They, at least, were looking at me. I flashed them my perfect teeth. I'd never even had braces. I smiled up at the rapper boys and waved. I'm sure some models waved on a catwalk. The boys had stopped catcalling. Now they were just staring.

This is great, I thought. *I'm already famous.*

I locked eyes with the judges as I passed, smiling the whole way. I couldn't have stopped myself if I'd tried; I was too happy. They were looking at me! How did models make that bitchy face when they had SO MUCH ATTENTION? I did a twirl. Right there, in the middle of the catwalk. You weren't ready for *that,* were you, judges? Boom! For real.

We were only supposed to make one pass down the catwalk. I did two. All the more chance of being noticed.

"Eleven forty-nine, please leave the catwalk."

Perfect! I'd graduated from Being Noticed 101.

Satisfied, I walked offstage, grabbed my backpack, pulled out a book, and waited for my number to be called. Occasionally I glanced over at the scouts. They all looked like really pretty teachers, only they were from New York, London, Berlin, Paris, and Milan. So, like, hotter, better-dressed teachers, with more intensity and worse teeth.

Finally, the first agent, the dark-haired one from New York, stood up and started calling numbers. I could hear girls squealing around me as they were called. "Woohoo!!" I cheered for the girls, hoping my support for them would pay off in furious cheers when 1149 was called. I stood up on my toes to catch a glimpse of the judges through the girls around me. GOD, did they have to be SO TALL?

The woman from New York called number after number after number. Then she sat down. She hadn't said 1149. Neither did the next agent, or the next.

The local agent, a boisterous man who looked like a sexier Chris Farley, announced that those whose numbers had been called should report to the twenty-third floor of the Manulife tower, across the street, in half an hour.

Wait? It was over?

And then everyone left. Even the rappers.

I was in complete shock. My number hadn't been called.

I looked at the number in my hand, hoping I'd read it wrong. Maybe I suffered from Tom Cruise's disease—dyslexia?

Nope. Eleven forty-nine. I had it right.

Nope. It had to be a mistake. The fashion world, Paris and New York, needed me.

And I was going to need a plan.

• • •

I walked over to the food court, past the psychiatric patients on day passes playing cards for prescription pills. Plunking myself down in front of a clock at the China Express, I pulled out the Oscar Wilde I'd been reading and inhaled a plate of lo mein.

Half an hour later, I ran across the street to the Manulife tower and into one of the elevators. It was full of tall girls and mothers whose arms were overflowing with modeling books. They all wore clothing my family couldn't afford. One of the moms was wearing an actual Chanel jacket. No one made eye contact.

"Guess it's just us!" I said, trying to break the ice. Make fast friends with my new model sisters, my future Parisienne roomies.

"I'm bilingual, so if any of you come to Paris with me for Fashion Week, I will be of major help to you. Nice jacket," I said to the pretty, gray-haired Chanel mom. "Mine's fake," I said proudly, as though I'd outsmarted her somehow. She made eye contact and smiled.

The elevators opened on the twenty-third floor. It was an entire floor with no walls—just one *huge* room, except for the washrooms in the corners. Around the periphery were desks and stations for all the different agencies. On the desks were Polaroid cameras, measuring tapes, and stacks of contracts. Behind the desks were the agents.

I headed for the Wilhelmina table, the only one with no long line of girls.

"Yes?" The agent was European and graceful as she moved, the way a spider might be if it were an old human woman.

"Hi," I said, smiling.

"Can I help you?"

"I'm here to sign up." I pointed at the sign-up sheet and wiggled my eyebrows up and down, flirting like Shirley Temple or a demented old man.

"Your number wasn't called," she said.

"I think it was."

"I chose only three girls out of four hundred. That is why there is no line here. And I know what they looked like, darling." She gave me a perfectly phony smile, like a mom praising someone else's toddler for crapping in a toilet.

But I would not be moved. I took off my Sally Jesses, put my hands on her desk, and leaned forward. "Maybe you like me better now that you can see me close up?"

The woman put her hand on mine and whispered, "I'm sorry."

I turned and walked away. Wilhelmina was a dumb name for an agency anyhow.

My next stop was the local agency that was feeding models to the Ford Modeling Agency in New York.

"Hi."

The man didn't look up. "Number?"

"Eleven forty-nine."

"Eleven forty-nine, eleven forty-nine, eleven forty-nine . . . No, I—" and then he looked up, his mouth still open, frozen in place, his tongue thrust forward a little.

"I'm sure you called my number." I wagged my eyebrows again.

"Oh, honey." His hand was already coming out to touch mine, like he was consoling someone whose dog had mange. "I'm sorry, but we didn't."

"Really? Weird!" I said, stalling for time. "I think you should take my picture with that camera," I said, pointing to the Polaroid.

He seemed uncomfortable with my confident Kimmy Gibbler act. "Is your mother with you?"

"Yeah, right. I'm fourteen, totally unescorted. You know what that means? It means I can go to go-sees in Paris and

New York. On my own. I'm very independent and would be fine living in a model's apartment. *Je parle français aussi. C'est tout parfait pour nous!*"

"Um. Well . . . we don't have you on this list, honey." He pointed at the sheet, then looked over my shoulder at a tall blonde in a skintight dress.

I moved back into his line of sight and dug in. "Look, I think you'd *really* like me. I work hard. I have since I was a small child. I can dance, I can act, but I *can't sing.*" I left out the part about not being able to memorize lines. Technically, I could act. I was acting *right that minute.*

As I tried desperately to wedge my way into his good graces, a woman from the same agency, who had been standing nearby, came over to join my new friend the agent and me.

"Can you take off those glasses?" she asked me.

I took them off.

"Can you take off the jacket?"

I did.

"Right!" I said. "You know I'm actually very, very, very photogenic. And my mother is small and has a great body, so one day very soon I will too."

Now that my glasses and Mom's jacket were off, they seemed to be staring at me differently. Not drooling, exactly. More like the way my dad stares at the BBQ while he's grilling.

The woman picked up the Polaroid and took my photo. The man looked annoyed.

"I need to see your profile," she said, pulling the camera down from her face.

"I don't think I have one. Wait—maybe in my bag!" I put my backpack on the table and started rummaging through it. For what, I had no idea.

"No," she said, making a turning motion. "Your profile. A photo of your face from the side."

I thumped my bag down on the table and stood sideways.

"Stop smiling," he said. Oh, Jesus was taking the wheel! Not the Baby Jesus, of course. You must NEVER let Baby Jesus take the wheel. But this guy—he wasn't trying to get rid of me! I made a serious face, like a soldier. "I'll do whatever it takes, you know. I don't even need to get braces. My teeth are perfect."

"What's your name?" he asked.

"Kelly."

"Well, Kelly, you are a little short. What are you, five-five?"

"Five-*six*. And I might still hit a growth spurt."

"Do you have a book?"

I picked up my backpack. "I have *The Picture of Dorian Gray*!"

"No, a *book* book. A modeling portfolio." He seemed annoyed. I couldn't let him be annoyed. I needed him to see I was serious about this.

"No. But I can get my mom to take a bunch of black-and-whites and blow them up for you at the drugstore if you need them."

The woman stopped shaking the Polaroid, looked at it, and then showed it to the man. "She is photogenic. Look at her face."

The man looked at the snapshot, then looked at my face.

I stopped smiling. *Soldier face.* He sighed.

"Here, fill this out." He slid an information sheet across the table. My heart leaped as I threw my backpack over one shoulder. I had weaseled my way into their hearts like I knew I would.

"But," he said, putting his hand on mine again—not in dog-mange condolence this time, but instead to let me know he was serious. "Promise me that you'll sign only this, and then you'll leave."

"Done."

I headed home—after signing a form with an agency. I didn't even read it. I did not care. This was it.

Two weeks later, I got a call.

"This is Jeneta, from the cattle call." I could finally stop sleeping with the phone. "We're having a class for our up-and-coming models, every Saturday for the next six weeks. Nine A.M. to five P.M. Are you in?"

"Of course I'm in! I've never been more ready to become Cindy Crawford."

"Oohhkaaaaay."

"On Saturdays I usually just reenact Lionel Richie videos, but I'll put my 'Ballerina Girl' extend-a-mix on hold. My moles are ready for stardom."

Like me, my parents didn't really seem shocked that any of this was happening. My dad had always been convinced I was headed for stardom, and my mom's chief concern was making me feel supported. All I needed from them was a ride.

I was early, as usual, and it was cold, as usual. The agency had rented a loft space on the edge of downtown: a street of original city brick buildings that weren't really even a century old; I lived in the western part of North America and it's all kind of new over there.

I was standing at the door of the building when Jeneta arrived. As she unlocked the door to the agency, I gave my mom an actual air pump, which was our signal: "I'm good, you can leave." Mom had been watching me from half a block away in our Aerostar. My parents and I cared just as much about abduction as we did about the art of looking cool and independent. Mom would never cramp my style. I watched her pull away from the curb. Independence at last.

Then, all of a sudden, I heard a noise. In the alleyway beside the agency, a trap door had flown open, crashing into the pavement. The door looked like it led to the sewers. And out of it emerged a parade of people in the most bizarre getups I'd ever seen off the TV screen.

"Where are those people coming from?!" I said, pointing as a girl with mirror pasties, blue hair, and blown-out pupils dragged herself across the sidewalk in front of us.

"Rave club."

"Rave club?"

A man in his late forties came through the door into the sunlight and let out this feral, gaspy burp sound. He looked like my father, only wearing Hanes briefs and glitter.

"After-hours club. You know, nightclubs? Dancing? They're all over the place. How long were you waiting here by yourself?"

"I don't know," I lied, pushing the story about me being ready for life as a model in New York or Paris even further. "Like, half an hour. There were some kids shooting heroin over there. I told them I didn't have a needle, but that I knew where they could get some clean ones." She called bullshit on me with her eyes. Good—now I knew my bullshit limitations with Jeneta.

I was so befuddled by the thought of my father dancing somewhere in his underpants all night that I almost forgot to soak in the moment when I walked across the studio threshold and became an internationally famous and beloved model.

The room was amazing: art deco everywhere, with a catwalk, a waterfall, makeup stations, magazines, a wall of TVs playing Linda Evangelista runway videos, mirrors, and a sound system blasting Deee-Lite. I took my coat off and tossed it into the closet, like I owned the place.

"Oh God, Kelly. Is that what you wore? Do you have anything else? The stuff I asked you to bring?"

I looked down at my overalls and Betsey Johnson T-shirt. I was in my *Blossom* best. My Betsey Johnson shirt was the ONLY TRULY fancy thing I owned, besides the Benetton sweater.

Apparently I'd been daydreaming while I was on the phone with Jeneta. While I'd been imagining bunking in NYC with a new modeling protégée named Simone from St. Louis, *manger beaucoup des pretzels,* Jeneta had told me specifically to wear form-fitting clothing and to bring a pair of heels.

"Well," I thought out loud, "I could cut the legs and the crotch off my overalls. Overall miniskirt?" I suggested, knowing full well that my mom would flip the shit out if I did any such thing.

"It's all right," she said with a sigh. "We're doing makeovers today anyhow."

This was it! The makeover scene was always my favorite scene. I was going to lose my glasses and become a woman—all to the strains of Deee-lite.

The rest of the new models made their way in and sat with me in a square of chairs facing a mirrored wall and one makeup station.

"Hey, I'm Kelly." My hand eagerly shot out to my new roomie.

"Jessica." She was at least three inches taller than me, and she wasn't wearing overalls. This girl was wearing a tube dress and spiky black heels she could walk in, and she had real boobs and perfectly lined shit-brown lips.

"Hey! I love your top," she said. "Betsey J, right?"

I nodded coolly. "Betsey J."

Then a guy named Andrew came in. He looked exactly like Matt Dillon in his football varsity jacket. It never occurred to me that BOYS would be here. I loved boys. I wanted to marry any boy who smiled at me. I was already envisioning the lovely future Andrew and I would have ahead of us. Little dark-haired kids playing with Andy in the pool while he lovingly looked over at my D-cup breasts snug in my gingham-print bikini. I ALWAYS envisioned my future self with D-cup breasts in a gingham-print bikini.

A few other models filed in—none of them very special, all of them looking at least ten years older than me.

"Wow," I said to no one in particular. "So what grade are you guys all in?"

The answers came back: eighth, eleventh, tenth, ninth, ninth.

"Cool. Me too!" I said. But my heart was sinking. Did I look too young to be considered a secure export? These kids were all my age, but they had boobs and walked in heels. It was diabolical.

I looked up at my reflection in the wall mirror looming in front of us. I was THAT KID. I was the one in the movie whom everyone wanted to make over, the dumpy kid in the nerd glasses and Chuck Taylors.

This was amazing.

I was going to win the makeover round. Hands down. This potential Canadian model export was ready to wow the group. Lionel Richie would be proud.

Jeneta sashayed down the runway in front of us and up to the makeup station. She was gorgeous. She looked like Kelly LeBrock.

"Today we're learning about makeup techniques and proper grooming," she said, flicking her hair as she glanced over at my husband, Andrew. "When you show up for go-sees and shoots, you have to have the perfect palette. Your skin has to be moist but not greasy, and then totally matte with foundation. Brows plucked. Lips unchapped."

"*Unchapped* isn't a word," I accidentally blurted out. Everyone looked at me, confused as to why I would care. "Sorry, I thought I was just thinking that. It's probably a word." I shrugged. Some people aren't interested in an education.

I smiled at Jessica and she rolled her eyes at me. I swear I could actually hear them turning in her head. What the heck was her problem?

That was it. I was totally planning on being nice to her, but now it was clear: she had become my enemy.

I'm REALLY good at picking out my enemy in a room— whether it's a grocery store, airport, or public bathroom. I generally work off a vibe (or just pick the farter). Choosing an enemy after it's clear she dislikes you was kinda cheap and lame, but in this case I hadn't been looking for an enemy. Maybe she was looking for me.

"Okay," Jeneta said, clapping her French-manicured hands together. "Who's first?"

I'm always aware of when I have to act. I feel like I must be a terrible actor, because I'm aware of when I'm doing it, but that really makes no sense. Maybe I'm a fantastic actor? I tried to muster a great "*Hmmm . . . I wonder who Jeneta will pick?*" face as I looked around, noticing one girl's posture and straightening out my own rounded shoulders. Someone once said, "If you have good posture everyone thinks you're a bitch," or something like that, but I'm pretty sure 100 percent of women with perfect posture *are* bitches.

We all knew that Jeneta was about to pick me. I was the dead tilapia in the fish tank in your grocer's seafood section, the moldy strawberry in the clamshell. I was that time in high school when you sang U2's "Pride (In the Name of Love)" into a cassette recorder and accidentally put it on a mix tape that someone played at a house party.

"KELLY! You're first!" No. Shit.

"We'll start with brows, then skin. Then I'll teach you how to do a basic natural face. With makeup. The whole thing should take each of you less than five minutes once you've perfected your grooming." Jeneta spun me around, and I stared into her eyes as she assessed the work ahead of her. I could see it there: doubt. Doubt that she'd be able to climb this mountain in under five minutes.

Then she grabbed her tweezers and went to work.

As I sat up in that chair, the most miraculous thing happened. I heard everything Jeneta said about exfoliation, moisturizer, and tweezing, but in my mind I was envisioning my future as a famous person. Being waited on hand and foot. Getting to wake up a total pig and go through a machine of people who would make me look awesome without having to do a single thing myself. I'd call them "my team," like other famous people do. As I sat there having hairs pulled out of my forehead, carving two distinct eyebrows out of my single large one, I thought, *This is what home feels like.*

Jeneta had taken my glasses off in public. This was huge. I'd been wearing glasses since I was three. Until that moment, having them off my face meant one of two things: either I was washing my face or I was going to sleep. I even swam with my glasses on, although that did cause my family to spend a day at a Hawaii LensCrafters after I forgot I couldn't bodysurf, ran into the ocean headfirst, and was pummeled by a wave and face-planted into the beach so hard I was blowing sand out my nose for days.

"Look at you!" Jeneta stood back, covered in my eyebrow hairs. Her arms looked like they belonged to Robin Williams.

She turned me around in the stool to meet my maker: the great mirror wall behind me.

There was my face. Behind the glasses and the hair, there was a face.

I had two eyebrows, eyes, cheekbones that weren't being used to prop up my fake eyes.

I squinted at the mirror.

"You have contact lenses," Jeneta stated. Like, if I didn't, I would have to.

"Tooooootally," I lied. I was so enchanted with myself. I felt like the Prince from *Beauty and the Beast* after he was stabbed and then came back to life as a hot, hot prince after Belle cried, "I love you."

Sitting there at the makeup station, I was stunned. As I sat there staring at myself, Jeneta straightened my hair with an archaic contraption that was basically two clothing irons taped together. She gave me blush, eyeliner, lipstick. By the time I stepped down, I was transformed. Brace yourself, Andy. Kelly, as I knew her, was gone. I was like one of those pretty Barbie paper dolls wearing a shitty farmer doll's outfit. My head no longer fit the overalls I came in with.

I kept my glasses off.

That meant I couldn't see a thing that was happening at the makeup station, but judging from what I heard, the girls weren't getting nearly as much attention as I did.

Jessica sat down beside me after she got out of the makeup chair.

"She didn't need to pluck my eyebrows," she said, smirking. "Guess they were perfect." *Fuck you.*

"God," I said, slumping forward exaggeratedly, preparing for the setup. "You were up there for, like, a second."

"I know!" she said, all smirky smirk smirkerson.

Fly, meet web. "Whoa," I said, sitting back as I prepared to detonate my personal TNT. "Must be kinda sad to know that no one can make you look any prettier," I said, giving her the side eye. "You've peaked at fourteen."

Her face dropped. Boom. YOU DON'T WANT TO BE MY CHOSEN ENEMY!

I was riding so high off my Jessica blaster that I forgot all about my makeover. When I climbed into the Aerostar and saw the looks on my mom's and sister's faces, I was confused.

"What?!"

For a moment, they just stared at me. Expressionless. Not a word.

Silently, my sister passed me a McDonald's bag containing my mainstay, McChicken and fries. I *always* got the McChicken. Never gave a shit about the McChicken Tumor Rumor.

Then I looked back at my shocked mom and my shocked sister, and I was suddenly kinda shamed. Here I was, the only girl in the car who was a top model. I'd been saved and they hadn't. I wondered if this was how Jewish girls in the Hamptons felt when they got nose jobs and then hung out with their original-nosed Bubbies on Yom Kippur.

I reached into my backpack for my glasses and put them back on. Now all three of us were wearing glasses, and sitting in our Aerostar, and all was right with the world.

"What are you waiting for, Mom?" I said. "Let's go!"

"Whoa, Kel. You look . . . *old*." My little sister's mouth hung open. She was generally a mouth breather (tiny nostrils), but this time her open mouth was a sign that her brain was trying to make sense of my face.

"Let me look at you," my mom said, looking at me over the top of her glasses. "Come on, come on, take them off so I can see you!" She was smiling and giddy.

I tried to fight off my smile, but I couldn't. I took the glasses off.

"HOLY DYNA! Why do you look so different?"

I took a bite of my McChicken.

"I got my eyebrows shaped," I said, my mouth full of breaded bird and bun. "Tweezed."

As my sister and mom leaned in to get a better look, I looked back at *their* eyebrows—big, bushy replicas of what mine had been a few hours ago—and started feeling guilty again, as if I'd betrayed my family somehow.

Then my mom turned around and sat back in her seat. "Guess we're buying tweezers," she said contentedly. She started up the Aerostar and we drove over the tracks, back to the wholesome side of town, where dads didn't wear glitter and kept their Hanes-clad asses indoors.

I PEED MY
PANTS
AND THREW UP
ON A CHINESE MAN

Once, I peed my pants in a gas station while standing in line to buy cigarettes.

At the age of fourteen, I guess this was a sign that I wasn't cut out for the smoker's lifestyle. But I didn't listen.

It was 8:30 A.M., the line at the Gas Bar was long, and I was at the end of it. I'd walked across the street from my high school alone to pick up a pack of Benson & Hedges. Back then, no one ID'd for cigarettes. Back then, you'd see helmetless babies in buckets on the backs of bicycles holding packs of cigarettes for their parents as their parents rode and smoked. I'd started smoking because I hated the smell of cigarettes. My new friends all smoked. And if I smoked too, I realized, the way they smelled wouldn't annoy me so much. I guess I'm lucky they didn't smoke meth.

At the end of junior high, I'd decided I wanted high school

to be a fresh start. I didn't want to go to the same school as my childhood friends; I needed a new cast of characters.

I lived downtown, but when I entered my district high school I discovered it was filled with a bunch of suburban kids who were bused into the city. These suburban kids were *way* worse than the kids from my neighborhood—my neighborhood being the inner city. And by worse, I mean *bad*. Like they'd been having sex, smoking, drinking, doing drugs, and wearing kohl Wet n Wild eyeliner since they were twelve. At twelve, I was going to Disneyland with my sister in matching hot-pink-and-gray fleece jackets. At twelve, I found a lump under my nipple and thought it was cancer until the doctor convinced me it was just my boob developing. That's the kind of kid I was.

But now I was convinced I could be one of these kids. I could drink and smoke and party with them.

Whatever that meant.

"One pack of Benson & Hedges Special King Size, please. One pack of Benson & Hedges Special King Size, please," I repeated in my head as I stood there in line. I was the only one of my new smoker clique of friends who smoked B&H. I chose it because the little black-and-gold pack matched all my clothes.

It was a one-pump gas station, a refuge for drivers who needed cigarettes or Mountain Dew. Of course, it also catered to kids from the school across the street, who presumably smoked for the same reason I did, because they hated the smell of cigarettes. This mid-September morning I'd finally decided it was time to grow up, to stop bumming cigarettes off my new friends. There was a party that weekend, and I wanted to look prepared. Having your own pack of cigarettes, when your parents don't smoke and you can't steal a pack from them, is a traditional symbol of rebellion. Time to step out. Kelly the Rebel.

Suddenly, I started getting nervous. The line wasn't moving

fast enough. What if they didn't have my brand? What if they asked how old I was? *Oh my God, I have to pee.* Maybe I could leave the line and go pee? Then my mind kinda went into a spin—like in old TV shows?—with my head floating in the middle of the screen and a bunch of little items flying around it. Items like cigarettes, your mom's floating head, six-year-old me in a nightgown with bronchitis. When you're buying your first step into the dark side, your subconscious can be a motherfucker.

And then it happened: I was peeing my pants.

As the warm piss soaked into my eighty-dollar Guess jeans and trickled slowly down to my ankle, I just stood there, dumbstruck by my own body. Was I dying? How had this happened? Why did I have to have a FULL bladder before I got in line? And this was no tiny spritz of pee gently wetting the inside of my underwear either. It was a bucket of fresh pee. I looked down, praying there wasn't a puddle, but there in the middle of the tile was a tiny pool of my pee.

I looked around for faces of horror, pointing fingers, gaping mouths, but no one in the line seemed to notice the dark blue, lightning-like stain zigzagging its way down the legs of the jeans I'd begged my parents to buy me. They were all just waiting in line, like a bunch of breathing mannequins at some horrible laborer-clothing outlet. I took tiny footsteps toward the counter as the line got shorter, trying to keep my legs together to prevent the pee marks from showing and the pee smell from spreading.

I looked up at the clock. I was almost late for French class. If my French teacher knew I was here, in a gas station covered in my own bodily fluids, she would laugh and laugh and say, "*Mon Dieu! Mon Dieu!*" and spritz more Chanel No. 5 around herself, forming an even larger cloudlike barrier of vanilla and musk to protect her from the mortals.

"Hi," said the woman behind the counter. She was short and

heavy, with a crazy, thick, short, red haircut, and I was about to blow her mind.

I knew I couldn't bullshit my way out of being drenched in urine. I certainly recognized that I couldn't go back to my school with wet pants. But it was 100 percent BEYOND QUESTION that, after all this early-morning bodily function trauma, I wasn't leaving this gas station without the black-and-gold pack I came in for.

"Um, I just peed my pants. Can I use your phone?" I said. "Also, one pack of Benson & Hedges Special King Size, please." I slid my five-dollar bill across the counter to her.

"Did you say you peed your pants?"

"Yeah. Do you mind if I come behind the counter to use your phone?"

The look on her face said "I mind, sweet Baby Jesus, I mind," but I stepped behind the counter anyway and stood there beside her as she passed me the cigarettes. Then she stood back, about ten feet from me. AS IF she'd never seen someone pee her pants in line before.

"Can I use your phone?" I repeated, a bit annoyed that it was taking her this long to make sense of my urine-soaked pants.

She passed me the phone, but I could see she was still staring at my jeans. "Yeah, I have a condition. My kidneys, my bladder—something!" I laughed, feigning complete exasperation as I dialed my house. I'd watched enough women complain about medical conditions on *Sally Jesse* to know how to pull this kind of shit off. "My doctor's been bugging me to get an operation for months, and I keep putting it off. But this? This has never happened to me before. I hope I don't have full kidney failure or something. Maybe I should just get the operation. What do you think?"

The ginger gelfin lady didn't move.

My mom answered the phone.

"Mom? Can you please come and pick me up from the Husky gas station by my school?" *pause* "Yeah, I'll tell you when you get here."

I hung up and turned back to the leprechaun. "Thanks for letting me hang out. I guess I'll have to go under the knife after all. Hey, if I pass out or something, call nine-one-one. Maybe my insides are all leaking. I'm not really sure how this body stuff works, but apparently my doctor was right! Can you believe that?! I needed the operation."

And I just kept talking for the four minutes it took my mom to pull into the parking lot.

"What happened?" my mom said as I sat down in the passenger seat of her gold 1978 Volvo station wagon. Lucky for me, her shiny, well-worn leather seats wouldn't soak up the pee from my pants.

Mom looked a little frantic—though maybe that was just her housewife clothes talking. In her best bleach-out-a-tub leggings and a giant T-shirt, she looked like a hobo. I knew I wouldn't be able to sell her the lie about my bladder/kidney failure, so I bit the cord.

"I peed my pants."

"OH THANK GOD!" She clutched her chest and looked over at me. "I THOUGHT YOU'D BEEN BEATEN UP!"

I made a "Huh?" face. (I'm a big body language person. I'm the Helen Keller of body language. If Woody Allen and I had dinner, we wouldn't even have to open our mouths.) "What do you mean, 'beaten up'?! Why would you think I'd get beaten up?" said the fourteen-year-old freshman with pee in her pants.

"Your kid calls you from a gas station and tells you to pick her up," she said, shrugging her shoulders, "your brain says RUMBLE."

"*Rumble,* Mom? No one says *rumble* anymore! No one!"

I was waiting for my mom to ask me why I was at the gas station. That would have been my VERY FIRST QUESTION. I was already a better mom than she was. My parents always knew where I was. Didn't they assume I stayed at school when they dropped me off there? Mom probably figured I was too ashamed to go into my high school's office with piss in my pants. And, oh God, she was right: What if this *had* happened at school? What if I had to go through high school as the piss-in-the-pants girl?

"Kelly?"

"WHAT?!" I snapped, thinking she was about to tell me the cigarette jig was up.

"I was just going to ask if you were okay. I forgot to ask that. I probably should have asked that first."

"I'm fine," I said. I quickly added, "I ran to the gas station when it happened." I had beat her to her own possible game and ended my misery, all with one little lie.

She nodded. "Smart thinking."

With a mother named Gaye, back on the elementary school circuit I'd flip out once a day at kids who were making fun of "fags." "MY MOM IS GAYE, OKAY?!" I'd shout. "SO JUST LAY OFF THE FAG JOKES, YOU GUYS!"

Mom had graduated from nursing school in '74 at the height of her hot little disco queen days. She admits to trying cocaine once, "but it didn't do anything. Drugs didn't work for me. But don't ever do them—you'll get schizophrenia or something." She'd worked the nursing night shift on a psych ward when I was little, and she'd tell me stories about it over breakfast. "One patient said he wouldn't listen to anyone but God, so I got on the speaker and yelled, 'GERRY? THIS IS GOD. YOU HAVE

TO TAKE YOUR MEDS NOW. AND, YEAH, THAT'S RIGHT—I'M A WOMAN.' Oh! And one patient said she was going to kill herself. She asked me, 'Should I take pills or jump off the roof?' I told her to take the pills and *then* jump."

Now she was in the car with her piss-panted teenage daughter. All I had wanted was a pack of smokes. All I had wanted was to be a normal teenager. Why couldn't my body just cooperate?

"Well, Kelly, I thought you'd been beaten up, okay? When your fourteen-year-old kid calls *you* from a gas station and needs to be picked up, give me a call and tell me what your initial thoughts were."

"That's not fair. I'd know she just peed her pants."

As we pulled up to the curb, my dad was just leaving the house on his way to work.

"Hey, honey, what happened?" he said.

As I got out of the car and stood there with my own acidic piss burning my inner thighs, I recalled a deep-seated sense memory from infancy: it itches when you piss yourself. But of course I couldn't tell my DAD what happened. This was a guy who rarely even talked to me about anything other than pancakes and *Melrose Place*. If he thought I couldn't control my bodily functions, he'd totally drive me to the hospital to see if I was dying, because (a) I wasn't a toddler, and (b) I wasn't over ninety.

"Nothing," I said, and snuck past him as briskly as possible.

"*She had an accident,*" Mom whispered, and he looked over at me standing on the front porch, keeping his eyes above waist level. I waved at him weakly. I could tell Dad heard the phrase *had an accident* and thought *period period period*, so I knew we'd never, ever speak of this moment again. When a dad thinks of his daughter's period, it's like that moment in a terrible futuristic action movie where your memory is erased with some sort of technological magic wand. POOF! GONE!

"Can someone unlock the door for me? I need a shower."

"Mom, tonight I'm sleeping over at Mara's house."

I got out of the shower, dropped my piss pants and underwear into the washer, and scrunched my wet hair into a towel. For years, my mom had blown my hair dry every day with some kind of Russian high-output blow dryer—until she stopped in 1991, saying that fourteen-year-olds were too old to have their mothers blow-dry their hair. I was too lazy to do it on my own, so I let my hair air-dry for the first time in my life. Without the blow dryer, I discovered, my hair was actually curly. Ever since fourth grade, I'd gone to bed every night with stick-straight hair and wished I'd wake up looking like Tiffany. Now I realized that all I had to do was scrunch it dry and it was as springy as Glenn Close's perm.

And that wasn't all. Ever since I was three, I'd been forced to wear these glasses, which seemed to get smaller in photos as my head grew larger every year. Then, just a few months before all this, I'd gone in for a regular eye appointment—and suddenly my vision was 20/20. After years of embarrassment, by some Zoltar-the-wish-granter miracle, my eyes were working on their own. Of course by this point I no longer liked Tiffany, but now I looked like her, curly hair, no glasses, and all. Maybe it takes five years for wishes to come true, I thought. The same way that the best time to start something was five years ago. My glasses-less face and wavy hair did not land me on the Paris runways, but they were famous beyond belief in the West Edmonton Mall catalogs.

This glorious long, curly hair and glasses-free face may explain why I'd just landed my first boyfriend: Alex Brown. Alex was in the same grade as me, but he might as well have been twenty years old, because he came from the suburbs and had experience with girls who drove their own 1970s sports cars. It was such a cliché to get my first boyfriend the same day I stopped wearing my glasses, but that just made my life feel more real, you know? It was like I'd emotionally gone from living a Dickensian life of charcoal and dust to living like Cher in *Clueless*. But I didn't give a shit about living the cliché, because my new boyfriend was a blond hockey player AND A TWIN. Tonight was my first high school party, and I was so ready to *just do this*.

I'd had a crush on Alex since before my eyes were 20/20 and I looked like dogmeat. I was friends with Ken, a guy on Alex's hockey team, and I spent most of my time failing Math 10 while talking to Ken about how I wanted to date Alex. Somehow Alex was interested, even with the glasses. He met me in a stairwell one day at 2:10 P.M. so I could pass him a note, which pretty much laid out our lives together—from first date through our third baby. I don't think he talked to me again until I came to school sans glasses. This party would be our first event together as a couple.

Not only was I in a new school with new people, but I'd naturally developed a new face and new hair. And now I was going to this party with the guy of my fourteen-year-old dreams who suddenly liked me. I basically convinced myself that I'd wished my way into this dream scenario. I'm pretty sure this fucked up my sense of reality forever and is directly responsible for many of my fearless decisions.

And I knew exactly how to prepare for the party—thanks to a million ABC Afterschool Specials and that season two episode of *Roseanne* when Becky mixed all of her parents' liquor and called it a Tornado. I told my parents I was having a sleepover at my friend Mara's house, and Mara told her mom she was sleeping over at my house. Meanwhile, we were both planning on sleeping over at the party. CLASSIC AFTER SCHOOL SPE-CIAL LIES WE LEARNED IN OUR PARENTS' LIVING ROOMS.

I got out my little army surplus backpack and filled it with my toothbrush, pajamas, and a Perrier bottle full of straight gin, vodka, and rum: the makings of a top-notch Tornado. I also grabbed a beer out of the fridge, in case the sixteen ounces of pure liquor didn't take or something. Of course there was enough alcohol in that Perrier bottle to kill a person my size, but I had no clue, because my parents never really drank around me. (Thanks a lot, you sober jerks.) I'd never been drunk before, and I had no idea how much alcohol it actually took to get drunk; I just wanted to make sure I had enough, because if I was going to take the risk of stealing my parents' alcohol, I'd better take enough to make sure I got good and drunk. At five foot six and ninety pounds, I figured it would take at *least* a Perrier bottle full of Tornado to do the trick.

My dad was always up for driving me anywhere. In my mind, except for sleeping and eating, he spent his life driving around the city nonstop; wherever I was, I'd just call him and he'd show up. On the way to the party, I asked him to stop at McDonald's. I am an absolute product of McDonald's cradle-to-grave market-ing. When I'm upset, I eat a burger. When I'm excited, I like to add fries to that. Thankfully I don't get too upset about anything in life, so I'll never be obese.

My first true best high-school friend was Mara. She was bubbly, social, pretty, and funny, and those were my only re-quirements for friendship. My dad dropped me off at her house, and I sat down in a park across the street with my bag of McDon-ald's and my bottle of Tornado mix. I wasn't going to bring the alcohol into her mother's house. Sure, I stole the alcohol from my parents, but that was for a good cause. I respected parents on the whole, and I didn't want to be the Bad New Friend who snuck booze into her house. I'd seen that special too. Her boyfriend, Korbin, was going to drive us to the party later on, but it was his dad's birthday, so he couldn't stay.

I'd set Mara up with Korbin after he fitted me with skis at a local ski hill. He was cute, but he had a really small head, and I already had a boyfriend I was obsessed with. To me, the important thing was that I really needed a friend to be going through all the same stuff I was going through. I mean, what good was a BFF if I couldn't ask her sex stuff because she wasn't having sex? Giving her a boyfriend was really my way of enabling her to have sex talks with me. It was a selfless gift to myself.

"What is that?" Korbin asked.

"It's a Tornado. A bunch of alcohol mixed together."

Korbin shook his tiny head. "That's not a good idea. You shouldn't mix different types of alcohol."

"It's the *only* idea," I said, taking a long, burning swig of straight gin, vodka, and rum, then chasing it down with a bite of McChicken. "I couldn't take just one kind of alcohol—it would be too obvious that some was missing. So I just took a little from each."

"You're a smarty, Kelly Oxford!" Mara said. She took a swig from the bottle and made a great whiskey face. Mara had blue eyes, dark hair, and bigger boobs than me—and to make things worse, she was the youngest of three. I envied all of those things, as a flat-chested eldest child who was "so full of shit her eyes are brown," as my dad charmingly put it.

I took the bottle from her and started to drink—and really fucking fast, because I was DETERMINED to get drunker than her. I drank three-quarters of that bottle and chased it with a bottle of 7 percent beer (Canadian), washing it down with my McChicken and fries. Mara drank the other quarter bottle. It took me only ten minutes or so, and I must say I was impressed with my time, like a Tornado marathoner.

As I was choking down the last of my fries, Korbin stood up. "I have to get home for my dad's birthday party," he said. Mara clung on to him and giggled as they headed toward his parked car. I tried to follow them—only to discover that I was thoroughly fucked up. I staggered along behind, trying to keep my eyes focused on the ground, which was moving a lot.

And then the first bad thing happened. I saw a Chinese man on a bicycle coming toward me, fast. I tried to jump out of the way, but my body wasn't having it.

Vomit just started flying. It flew out of my mouth and nose.

I vomited all over the Chinese man's bike wheel.

"Stommm-ach fluuuuuuu," I slurred, looking up at the man.

He just shook his Chinese head and yelled at me in Chinese, with a fist in the air and chunks of McChicken on his tires. Then he pedaled off into the darkness.

This whole thing was instant and unexpected. My brain was telling me, *This is bad*, but my body was no longer mine to control. I was beyond the kind of drunk you can hide. I was the zombie with the fucked-up face and walk, staggering sideways across the street with my backpack on. This was as close to palsied as I ever hoped to get. But somehow I was also the fastest drunk in the West, scrambling to make it across the field and catch up with Korbin and Mara, who had managed to miss all this. Which was a shame for a couple of reasons:

1. Who wouldn't want to see a Chinese man riding a bike get barfed on and then just keep pedaling and yelling in Chinese?
2. They could have suggested I *not* get in the car for a little while.

• • •

The drive to get to the party was only ten minutes long. But in the backseat I was going through a metamorphosis, transforming from girl to monster. I spent most of the ride with my head against the car's blue interior, realizing I'd overdone it. Then my stomach, very quickly and violently, churned onto itself.

"Oh God! I'm gonna barf!!"

Mara and Korbin turned around simultaneously, she laughing in anticipation and he in complete horror.

"HOLD ON!" Korbin said. "I'M PULLING OVER! Hold on for TWO minutes! ONE minute!!" But we were on the freeway; there was no place to pull over. So I did the only logical thing: I pulled my shirt out, tipped up the sides to form a container, and then vomited an ocean of McChicken and fries and booze into my shirt. With force.

It was quite a spectacle. "Guys, I don't chew enough," I said distractedly. "Look! There's a whole fry in there, Mara. And it still smells like McDonald's."

And then the second bad thing happened.

I opened the window. Then I grasped the hem of my shirt tightly and gave the pool of vomit a good flick in the general direction of the window. But the window wasn't open quite far enough and my aim was drunken and everything I'd caught in my shirt hit the ceiling of the car. And it stuck there until, slowly, pieces peeled away and fell at my feet. It was raining vomit.

"FUCK, NO! KELLY, THIS IS MY DAD'S CAR!!"

By now we were just a block away from the party. Korbin pulled the car over near a ravine.

"GET! OUT!"

I didn't feel like Korbin was even yelling at me. I knew he was really angry at the alcohol.

As I sat there patiently, scooping vomit fries off the floor mat and throwing them onto the road, Korbin was totally freaking out. "Here I am, doing you a favor driving you to this party, and you just throw up all over his car? On my dad's birthday?!"

I was having kind of a hard time registering any of this, really. So I just sighed, looked up at the forty Korbins who stood before me, wiped my vomit hands off on my jeans, and said, "Your head is *so, so small*, Korbin! Mara, how do you even look at it?"

This whole time, Mara had maintained her composure. She was just drunk enough not to be upset about the vomit. Now she came over and sat down next to me. I rested my head on her shoulder and fell into a slump.

"Kelly, do you have a change of clothes in your bag?" she asked.

I pulled open my bag. Inside was the set of pajamas I'd brought to the party. *What a loser.* Who the fuck brings *PJs* to a high school party? I mean, at what point during this party did I expect everyone to put on their pajamas and go to sleep, like normal people, instead of just drinking and playing loud music until they passed out under the kitchen table like animals?

But Mara saw we had a job to do. She helped me get up and stagger over into the woods along the ravine, then helped me take off my wet, vomit party outfit and put on my pajamas: a cotton top-and-bottom set in a multicolored star print. "Thank you, thank you," I slurred. "We aren't gay just because you saw me naked, right?" And I vomited again.

I pulled out my toothbrush and dry brushed the vomit out of my mouth. Like a real lady would. Like Princess Diana would. Then I crawled into the backseat of Korbin's dad's smelly car—the clean side this time. The other side still looked like the Hamburglar had exploded all over it.

Korbin opened my window. "Kelly, put your head out the window." I did as I was told. Korbin started to drive, and I lifted my chin and face up toward the sun, and thought, *You know, being a collie wouldn't be so bad.*

Two minutes later, I arrived at my first high school party like a queen: in pajamas, with my head out the window of a vomit-filled car.

Korbin pulled up to the garage door and turned his micro-cephalic skull around. "I'm going to get Alex. Get out of the car."

I stumbled out of the car with my backpack on, into the crowd of kids on the lawn. Everyone stared. Then one of the girls looked me up and down in my jammers, then spit.

This girl was known as Shar. She was the toughest girl in this group from the 'burbs. She was short and Greek, with dark hair except for two white blond streaks that framed her face. She looked like a lightweight boxer. She was basically the head bad girl of this crew. Like if *Mean Girls* wasn't about prissy bitches, but instead about blue-collar suburban kids, Shar would be the Rachel McAdams.

At this point I was really, really drunk. All the remaining al-cohol had hit my system; I was a green-light go. A few minutes later my boyfriend, who had a great, regular-sized head, and pinhead Korbin came out of the house with a bunch of garbage bags, paper towels, and a bucket of water. I wasn't humiliated at all, mostly because the day before I'd peed my pants in public, but also because I wasn't sober. I could have taken off all my clothes and curled up in the fetal position on the front lawn and crapped at this point and it wouldn't have fazed me.

From that point on, I have only flashes. I remember put-ting my face under the kitchen faucet and rubbing it viciously. I remember lying down in the master suite, on the ugliest frilly gray bed set in the entire world, and yelling at someone to turn off the ceiling fan. I remember Alex's friend Matt coming in the room and standing on the bed and singing me a song about Kentucky Fried Chicken. I remember looking out the window and seeing my boyfriend washing out the car, Korbin's dad's car, on Korbin's dad's birthday. I remember thinking I was going to die. And hours later, when the room stopped spinning and I could sit up and open my eyes, I thought,

Wow, my parents were right.

I am clueless.

I am an idiot, a complete fuckup child with no idea how to navigate this world.

That lasted about five seconds, until my boyfriend came in the room to check on me. When he saw I wasn't Janis Joplin dead, he whispered, "Do you feel better? Do you want to come outside for a cigarette?"

I checked the clock. It was three A.M. and I still felt like shit. Not "I could die" shit, but "You almost died, you fucking moron" shit. Sudden panic set in. *My parents.* I'd told them I was at Mara's house. I'd never lied and I'd never spent the night away from my parents in an unreachable location. What if they needed me?

And then Alex started kissing me and reason flew out the window. We were in a master bedroom in the middle of the night alone, and we hadn't had sex, and—I wasn't about to do it now! I mean, *he'd just cleaned up my vomit.* Did this guy have no fucking compass for vileness? Of course, with age I would learn that the Force is strong in the male libido, especially in a teenage boy. And he was a really sweet guy, athletic, and a blond twin. I realize I've mentioned this twice now, that he was a blond twin, but that's because I loved it. He was basically the male version of Jessica Wakefield from *Sweet Valley High.*

Most of all, though, I really didn't want to fuck on that ugly bed. I stopped kissing him. "Let's go outside for that cigarette."

Out on the deck, twenty or more kids were hanging out smoking and listening to Jane's Addiction. We headed over to a picnic table. As we were walking, Alex put a cigarette in my mouth, like I imagined people in *Grease* might have done. (I was the only white girl in my school who had never actually seen *Grease*.) This guy we knew named Zane Morley passed me a lighter. Zane was a funny guy; he looked like my farmer uncle: taller than everyone, thin, wearing a trucker hat—but not a brand-name trucker hat, like a real dirty hat. He was one of a few of Alex's non-hockey-league friends who I liked a lot. He was smart and jaded and a full-on antagonist, so I related to him.

"Thank you, Zane Boon Morley." I never missed an opportunity to say his full name. It was such a good name.

"Feeling better?" he asked. I nodded and lit my smoke.

He gave me a funny look. "I saw you get picked up by your mom at the gas station yesterday."

My eyes darted up and back down. I nodded in acknowledgment, praying he'd go no further.

"Why did your mom pick you up from the gas station?"

As soon as he said it—and he was smiling when he did—I realized there were, like, six other kids listening. I stared at him and just kept nodding, which meant nothing. I was an idiot.

"I KNEW IT!" he shouted. "You totally got caught stealing!!"

I am not a big fan of lying. In fact, I'm the most pathetic liar on earth. But in that moment I knew I had a decision to make. For the next three years, I realized, I could be known by one of two monikers: Gas Station Thief or Pissed Her Pants Pussy. It was up to me to choose.

Between those two, I would take Gas Station Thief all day long. But since I couldn't lie, I kept nodding and smoking, thinking about all the bullshit that being a teenager was going to mean. I had to make friends, but be myself? It seemed impossible. I had to not die from drinking, and stay out all night, and smoke? This was a lot of stuff for a kid who just two years ago was getting Peter Pan's signature in her California vacation autograph book.

Then, just when I needed to change topics, I remembered something. "Where's Mara?" I hadn't seen her since we got there.

"After we got through cleaning out the car, she went with Korbin to his dad's birthday party."

"Ugh. I feel so terrible that you guys had to clean that up." I really *didn't* feel terrible, and I know that just makes *me* terrible. But I was more embarrassed about the McDonald's vomit than anything, and frankly I was just glad someone else dealt with cleaning it up. Plus, I wasn't mature enough yet to realize I could just laugh and tell Alex, "Ha ha! You cleaned up the barf because you love me, or you want to have sex with me—and we didn't have sex, you fucking sucker!" like I can now with my husband. I was a fourteen-year-old little liar who still thought I had to appease people's sensibilities to keep them loving me. I wasn't old enough to realize that I could be my terrible self and have people love me for that.

I went in the house to pee, walked into the bathroom, and ran right into Shar.

"I like your makeup," said the goddess of Goth, nodding at me.

I looked in the mirror. DEAR GOD. My eyeliner and mascara were all around my eyes, up to my eyebrows and down to my cheekbones. My hair looked like a beehive that got knocked down as I was getting screwed on a piece of plywood in an alley behind McDonald's. You know how Bugs Bunny used to get in drag and be all sexy? I looked like the Tasmanian Devil version of that.

How did this happen? Oh, right, washing my face in the kitchen sink after I got to the party. Stupid makeup.

"Thanks. I didn't really do this on purpose. I got— I mean, I think I have alcohol poisoning. I barfed all over my friend's boyfriend's dad's car . . . on his birthday."

"The boyfriend's birthday?"

"The dad's birthday."

"Ouch."

"I know."

Shar had other things on her mind, though. "I heard you got caught stealing at the Gas Bar. It's cool that your mom picked you up like that. My mom would have told the cops to pick me up. She doesn't give a shit." She sat up on the counter and started picking at her cuticles. "You have a good body. What'd you steal?"

Wait, what? Was Shar hitting on me, or was this how tough girls and teenagers made friends? I was tired, and my patience was wearing thin. "I didn't steal a fucking thing. Okay?"

"Then why'd your mom pick you up?"

I looked at her and suddenly her rank and the Greek hair didn't mean a thing. I didn't owe anyone answers. "That's none of your business." There. I'd done it. I'd done the one thing I'd been suddenly afraid of since becoming a teenager. I'd been honest to myself and mouthed off to someone who hadn't decided if she liked me or not. I could have kept my mouth shut and let her roll with this wave of Kelly compliments, but I wanted to shut this operation down.

Shar stopped picking her cuticles. "Oh. Sorry." She hopped off the counter and walked out of the bathroom. I shut the door behind her, lifted the fuzzy pink toilet seat, pulled my pants down, and peed . . . into a proper toilet.

I spent the next few hours on a couch in the yard, surrounded by people, talking to no one. As the sun came up, I realized I was watching my innocence fading with the night sky. I'd always been led by this invisible hand of optimism: "Friendships are all about fun!" I'd always expected that self-discovery would be great, you know? *Who am I going to be when I grow up?*—the very thought gave me tingles. But as I sat there that morning, I realized I already *was* who I was, and all of this social garbage was going to make growing up, and feeling optimistic, pretty difficult. Did I want to smoke and drink before I met these kids? It hadn't even occurred to me. I was the kid who peed her pants, with black makeup all over her eyes and cotton candy for hair.

Shar came and sat with me.

"Do you want to come to the mall later?"

So what now? After all of this, somehow I still seemed cool? I felt like such an asshole and yet I'd won. Now the bitchiest girl wanted to befriend me because ★I★ looked like a hard-ass thief who gave zero fucks.

"We could meet at the mall and have dinner in the food court," she said. "I want to take you shopping." This was the part where the loser girl goes shopping with the Goth queen and turns into a Goth. The next step would be me becoming cooler than her, and her turning on me because "she made me." I'd watched enough coming-of-age films to figure all this shit out.

"No," I said. "I'm going to be sleeping. Then I'm going to make cookies and eat them and drink tea while I watch *60 Minutes* with my mom and dad. That's my Sunday thing. But I'll see you at school on Monday?" I gave zero fucks.

I got up and went into the house, leaving Shar with her cuticles.

I called my dad. "Can you come and pick me up?"

Exactly thirteen minutes later, I saw my dad turn around the corner in his Mustang, puffing on his morning cigar. I sat there on the sidewalk for a second, wiping my hands in the dewy grass, hoping to get rid of any smoke smell I'd missed in the bathroom. Then I climbed into the passenger seat. My dad is built like an ox, and he has a big mustache, so everyone always thinks he's a cop. This morning, he'd put on his dark gray intimidation suit and his get-shit-done *Sopranos* attitude. "Do you need me to go inside? To do something?"

"No," I said, pulling on my seat belt. "Let's just go." It suddenly occurred to me that he wasn't angry. And then another fear washed over me: *My parents have let me go. They aren't freaked out that they didn't know where I was.* I was the only one upset about it. Another little bit of innocence lost.

"I'm such an idiot."

He paused and puffed on his cigar. "Don't you have any stuff?"

My bag was somewhere in the house, but all it had inside were empty bottles. I'd left my cigarettes on the couch, and my clothes and my toothbrush full of vomit were in the ravine.

"No," I said, my eyes filled with tears. "Why am I so stupid?"

He revved the engine and laughed. "Shit," he said. "You're a teenager."

We pulled away from the sidewalk and drove home.

WORK
EXPERIENCE
101

ADVISER: MRS. MOLIN, SCHOOL COUNSELOR

MARCH 22, 1994

I'd like to start this report by admitting that I only took this course to get the final ten credits I need to graduate high school. As you know, I dropped out of chemistry class earlier in the semester, but I had a really great reason: ketones were driving me crazy. The truth is, I know I don't want to be a doctor or engineer, so I decided not to put myself through it. I could have totally finished chemistry—I want you to know that. I'm smart. But I'm also lazy, and that combination just makes me very efficient in everything I do. Bottom line: I want to graduate from high school efficiently and move into the workforce as soon as possible.

My Work Experience course is teaching me some really great things about the real workforce and what kinds of moral situations you can find yourself in as an employee. I applied for a job at a local video store, and I've almost completed my one hundred hours of work.

I've felt really lucky to get the job at the video store. Everyone

I know wants to work in a video store, especially since discovering that Quentin Tarantino worked in one. I get to wear whatever I want. I get to watch movies for my entire shift. I get VHS movies before they even come out for anyone else to rent, which is something I did NOT know happened in real life. I love recommending movies to people, and I love getting free posters. I think they'll come in handy when I need to decorate my first apartment. Since I've decided against becoming a doctor or an engineer, I pretty much know I won't be able to afford real art anyhow.

My boss's name is Chad. He looks a lot like Tony Danza in *Who's the Boss*, season one. I'm telling you this so you aren't bored out of your mind as you read my report. I can't imagine anything worse than reading student reports on jobs all day, but I assure you this one will be the best. If there is one thing I'm good at, it's trying to make things easier on other people. That's one of the lessons I've learned on the job.

The owner of the video store lives across the street, which has definitely come in handy. On my first day he gave me his phone number, and I was a little worried I'd have to file a sexual assault report with you, but it turned out to be just an emergency number, so I was relieved. Chad is friendly, but right off the bat I didn't agree with how he organizes his store. I like having videotapes behind the empty cases, on the floor in the shelves. He likes having them behind the counter. That means people have to bring the empty video box to me; then I have to look for it behind the counter and give it to them. I do not understand this extra step. I think it causes a lot of wasted time, and I've brought this to his attention, as I do not believe that people are really going to steal his movies. But Chad seemed upset when I told him it was stupid. So I guess one of my lessons has been: don't argue with a guy who looks like Tony Danza.

Another part of the job I find wasteful is rewinding the tapes. I believe that renters can do this themselves, even if they've just rented the movie and the previous renter hadn't rewound. I particularly don't like rewinding the pornographic videos that come in, because I know they are dirty. I hope you aren't upset or shocked that pornography was a part of this Work Experience course. I'm perfectly able to stay professional when a man hands me *Ultra Kinky #79: Bowlin' in Her Colon.* It comes with the job. Even people who aren't doctors can pride themselves on professionalism when it comes to seeing penises while at work.

There is a small section in the middle of the store that contains a lot of pornographic movies. I've seen these sectioned-off rooms in video stores all my life, but this job has given me an opportunity to be the actual boss of a porno room. It never even occurred to me when I applied for the job that I would be the porno room boss. It's really cool, but there have been two issues surrounding this heavy responsibility. The first is that rewinding returned porno tapes is gross. I'm always expecting one will be wet or tacky to touch. And trust me . . . no one finishes an entire porno tape. No one. I have to rewind every single one of them. But I do it without complaining because that's my job. The second thing involves the porn and my morals and my ability to be a good employee. I will be very specific about these events, because I want you to understand the important lesson I learned from this course.

One night, it's snowing. I'm by myself, manning the store. And here, rolling down the street toward the store, comes a guy in a wheelchair (not a motorized wheelchair, just a do-it-yourselfer) making his way through the parking lot. I run to open the doors for him and he propels himself in.

"Thanks!" he says.

"No worries! I do that for every customer, not just the ones in wheelchairs," I lie, because I'm a really friendly employee who doesn't want to make this guy in a wheelchair feel *less than capable* just because this store doesn't have automatic doors.

He tells me his name is Dwayne and I immediately start calling him "Dwayne the Wheelchair Guy" in my head. This is because everyone loves a nickname. Then I go back to dusting the shelves and watching *What's Eating Gilbert Grape* (huge Leo fan).

A short time later, out of the corner of my ear, I hear a weird squeaking sound. It takes me a minute to realize it's the sound of Dwayne attempting to push the swinging doors to the porno room open. He keeps pushing, and they keep shutting in his face before he can get in. I am the boss of the porno room, so I go over to let him in. He really seems like a nice enough guy. Big doughy face. Casio wristwatch. A bit of drool, but that only makes him more lovable.

I hold the saloon doors open. I don't do this for everyone, but he's the only customer in a do-it-yourself wheelchair who I've met.

Dwayne rolls inside the room and I go back to watching *Gilbert Grape*. As soon as they finish the scene where Arnie's mom is telling Arnie he should be able to bathe himself, I suddenly realize I'm ignoring my customer. *But he's in the porno room,* I think. *Do I really need to bother him?* I let ten minutes pass, and then I start to get worried. I hesitate, then walk over to the saloon doors. Keeping my back to the wall, I slowly peek around the corner and through one of the tiny slats in the door.

His back is to me; he's facing the back wall of the room. We call that the Ass Wall. Then I notice it. The shaking. His whole body's moving up and down.

He's jerking off. *He's jerking off in my porno room.*

My whole body gets hot and I get a head rush so brutal I almost fall over. I slam my back up against the wall and cover my mouth. I creep back to the counter, not sure what I should do to address the situation.

I look at Leo DiCaprio on the screen. WWLD??

This is real life, Kelly, I think. *This is the workforce. This is what happens when you drop out of chemistry class, can't be a doctor, and have to work as the boss of a porno room in a video store. Sometimes a customer's just going to jerk off and you have to roll up your sleeves and deal with it.*

THEN IT HITS ME. Dwayne has no idea, but this jerk-off chauffeur is onto him. *He isn't going to rent a thing.* He isn't even a REAL CUSTOMER, for crying out loud!

Mrs. Molin? Here's the part of my Work Experience course where you'll be really proud of giving me ten credits to graduate, but then also be really sad about what I learned about myself in the role of dutiful employee: Dwayne, I realize, is stealing! Every other person who goes in that room has to take the movie home to watch it, and they have to pay five dollars a movie to do it. My boss, the one who's always worried about people stealing his tapes, is getting ripped off by a jerk-off con artist, right under his nose. Even his movie-behind-the-counter strategy isn't working. Meanwhile, this guy is working off the VHS covers alone.

I call Chad.

"Hey, it's Kelly." I look out the window toward his apartment. "You have to come over right now. We've got a theft in progress."

I see Chad fly out the front door of his building and run across the street to the store. I stand in the doorway of the store and put my finger to my lips. He's in a panic. "Calm down," I whisper. "It's okay." Making a "follow me" gesture, I lead Chad to the porno room, put my finger to my lips again to make sure he stays quiet. We both bend our knees, lean forward, and look into the porno room together. There's Dwayne in his chair jerking off.

Chad covers his mouth with his hand and walks over to the counter. He motions for me to come over to him.

"He's stealing porn!" I whisper.

"Should I call the police? I can't call the police on him." He runs his fingers through his Danza hair.

"No." I shake my head. "He's paralyzed and everything."

"I should call the police." Chad grabs the phone and I stop him, my hand on his. I suddenly realize I'm sexually harassing him. It's a very charged situation. "Well," I say, pulling my hand off his *really* hairy arm. "What you should do is tell him to *rent* your goddamn movies like everyone else!"

"Hello?"

We both look toward the porno room.

"Can I get some help with the door?" It's Dwayne. I can see his wheels under the saloon doors.

"I'm coming!" I shout back, regretting my word choice immediately. I turn to Chad. "He needs me to open the doors for him."

But Chad passes me and gets to the doors first. He swings them open to see Dwayne, his ruddy post-jerk-off face looking horrified.

"Hi!" Chad shouts. "IS EVERYTHING IN THERE TO YOUR LIKING?!"

And here's when I *really* got the "experience" part of the Work Experience course. I was suddenly overcome with guilt for calling Chad and outing Dwayne's jerk-off session. I knew it was my duty, but I felt horrible. I recognized it for the petty theft that it was—but now I could see the big picture, and I realized that I would never want to get called out for masturbating in public. And I'd just done that to Dwayne. It wasn't really worth it.

I look at Dwayne over Chad's shoulder.

Dwayne's eyes and mine lock.

I'm clinging to my African medallion, holding it in front of my mouth so he can see what a sensitive person I am. Then I lower my hands a little so Dwayne can read my lips.

"I'm so sorry," I mouth to him.

"IF YOU AREN'T RENTING ANYTHING," Chad bellows, "I SUGGEST YOU LEAVE." He's not goofing around.

Dwayne rolls himself to the door. I open it for him.

"Take care," I offer weakly, my whole entire being feeling so terrible for shaming Dwayne the Wheelchair Guy.

And, Mrs. Molin, I haven't seen Dwayne since.

Chad has offered to hire me, after my hundred hours are over next week, because I'm an exemplary employee—you'll find his letter attached—but I can't take the job because I can no longer enter the video store without worrying about Dwayne. I can't get through a shift without thinking about him wheeling up to the store. Where is he getting his porno now? Does he have to wheel himself through the snow to the next video store, eight city blocks away?! I can't take the pressure.

Of the many lessons I've learned in my hundred hours of work, the biggest was this: that being a good employee can very possibly mean having to bend your own code of values. I was so engrossed in my position at the store that I didn't even consider the feelings of the customer. From now on, I will always consider the feelings of the customer, even if I am being paid as an employee. Work Experience has taught me this. I would be a terrible soldier. I would be a terrible police officer. I would be a terrible teacher. But the good news is, I do NOT need ketones to not be any of those things.

Mrs. Molin, thank you for giving me the opportunity to work for school credit. I have no idea what I want to do with my life, but now I know what I don't want to do with my life. And thank you for the opportunity to write this report for you. It was my favorite part of the Work Experience course.

FINDING
LEO

"Leo's going to be in a BLOCKBUSTER!!!"

Behind the Sugarbowl café, in an alley along a ravine on the university campus, I showed Aimee the tattered coffee-shop copy of *Us* magazine. We weren't students; we just liked to hang out in the alley and smoke pot.

"Look!" I shouted, thrusting the magazine in her face, feeling that prickly, about-to-sweat sensation in my armpits. My hands were trembling. I shouted the article out to her: " 'Leonardo DiCaprio is currently filming the movie *Titanic* with director James Cameron, due in theaters next Christmas.' CHRIST-MAS, Aimee! Movies that are released at Christmas are BIG. The *Titanic* was big, and this is going to be BIG!"

Realizing the seriousness of the situation, Aimee pulled her Natty Gann hat down over her red dreadlocks, put out her joint, tucked the corners of her lips up to deepen those dimples, and exhaled dramatically.

"You're fucked. He's going to be the next Johnny Depp. I'll never get Johnny, and now you'll never get Leo."

I stroked the photo of Leo's face—his almond-shaped eyes, his chiseled Ted Danson jawline—and tried to lower my heart rate. "You're right. He'll never date me once this movie comes out."

Unless I could make him my boyfriend first.

Leo DiCaprio was my Lionel Richie love song. I'd been projecting all the qualities of my ideal man onto him ever since *Gilbert Grape*. Yes, I found that little handicapped kid hot. Judge me, I don't care. I loved Leo, and I was TERRORIZED at the thought that he'd soon be a household name. Within months he'd have millions of girls throwing themselves at him, offering him blow jobs in elevators. This was war. This was my Normandy.

There was only one solution: I had to get to Los Angeles and stalk Leo before it was too late. To me, this wasn't an outlandish idea. It was perfectly normal. And it was my only option.

I dragged Aimee across the street to the travel agency and stormed in. The quiet room was suddenly under my control. I pointed at a rotund woman behind the desk and commanded: "I NEED TWO ROUND-TRIP TICKETS TO LA, ASAP!"

The woman gave me a look like she was up against Andre the Giant in *WrestleMania 2*'s "Battle Royale." She quickly tapped out a few words on her computer.

"I-is tomorrow okay?" she stammered.

"Tomorrow might be too late, but we'll take it!" My life had suddenly become a male teen road movie: I was running on 100 percent gut-lust.

Aimee called the coffee shop where she worked and told her boss she'd be gone for a few days because of a family emergency in Quebec. I called my boss, who was also my dad, and told him I wasn't coming to work, or coming home, for the next three days. I'd been doing basic office jobs for my dad for over a year. Making coffee, organizing files—I was basically the reception-ist's assistant who had great lunchtime office stories for the girls who worked there. Aimee and I were horrible employees who lived at home and had less than a thousand dollars to our names. And now we were sinking almost all of that money into two tickets to LA.

When I got home later and explained to my dad what we were doing, he sat back in his chair. "What do you *mean* you're going to LA?"

"I'm going to find Leonardo DiCaprio and become his girl-friend. He's going to be in this huge movie soon, and if that happens I'll never get my chance."

"Who is Leonardo DiCaprio?"

"Exactly." I pointed at him. "You won't be asking that after Christmas."

"Do you need some money?"

Dad gave me a hundred dollars, which doubled my available spending money. As far as I knew, that was plenty; I'd never paid for anything in my life. I had no idea that flying to LA with two hundred dollars to my name was basically deciding to become a hobo. But let's face it: I shopped at Goodwill, I smoked weed in alleys, and I believed I could circumvent the future if I headed to California. In essence, I *was* a hobo.

The next morning, Mom gave us cookies for the flight and drove us to the airport. As soon as we got our boarding passes, we were picked out by security, probably for smelling like pot-smoking hobos. My search went quickly; all I had was my one little orange suitcase I'd picked up at Goodwill. Aimee's took longer. As I sat on a gray plastic chair watching two agents comb through her dreadlocks one by one, I ate every single one of Mom's cookies.

"WHAT DO THEY THINK THEY'RE GOING TO FIND IN THERE?" she shouted to me.

"PROBABLY WEED," I yelled back.

Of course, they found nothing. We knew enough not to travel with weed—and we knew we didn't need to. Weed always found us.

We got on the plane safe and sound.

"I can't believe you ate every cookie," Aimee said.

The flight attendant asked if we wanted drinks. "Sure, a Coke," I said. "The regular kind. With sugar. Can I go to the cockpit?" I leaned forward and touched her arm to show her I was being sincere and also to make sure she was listening to me. "I usually visit the pilot on my flights. I don't really like flying. Hanging out with the pilot lowers my heart rate." (Note: This was my first flight without my parents, and it was back in the days when armrests had ashtrays and children were allowed to stand three inches from an airplane's control panel. I loved being in the cockpit; it was like hanging out in the front of your grandparents' RV as they drove down the highway. Only instead of a highway, you were in a tube in the sky.)

For reasons unknown to me, the flight attendant took my teenage request very seriously. After bringing me my Coke, she escorted us into the cockpit.

"Do you want to know what these buttons do?" said the younger pilot. He looked like Woody Harrelson. *Natural Born Killers* Woody.

"No," I said. I suddenly realized I was leaning against the wall like I was James Dean or something. I'm the Isaac Newton of embarrassing myself with body language.

"Do you want to sit in my seat?" Woody asked. His copilot, a Tom Selleck look-alike, shot Woody a WTF look.

"I DO!!!" shrieked Aimee, and she jumped onto his lap. Can you imagine the fucking animal sounds that would have come from the passengers if they knew a white girl with dreadlocks was behind the buttons and levers that were keeping them from becoming a pile of shitty pants and flaming metal?

"I'm, like, basically only in here to prevent myself from freaking out," I said, trying to talk through my anxiety. "I hate flying. It really scares me." I stared straight ahead and had a vision of a slower plane's ass popping out from the clouds ahead of us, just in time for us to plow into it. I saw Big Bird up there too, with his striped tie and tiny suitcase, getting sucked into the engine as he was giving us the Queen's wave. Only a bit of tie was left behind, and the cabin filled with the smell of KFC.

Tom Selleck spoke up, licking his mustache like a pervert. "You know, flying is safer than driving. You don't have to be scared of it."

"I don't drive either," I said. "My dad told me that if I got my license he'd buy a sedan limo and make me drive him around like a chauffeur. I'm not going to get my license until I move out."

"But you're in cars all the time," he said condescendingly.

"Yes, well, please forgive me for having an opinion on this, sir, but crashing a car doesn't scare me as much as falling from the sky strapped to a small chair."

"Look, there's Vegas!" said Woody, pointing out the right window.

And there it was: Las Vegas, looking like a computer chip someone dropped in the sand.

We landed, said good-bye to Tom and Woody, and disembarked from our flight, bags in hand.

When we got to baggage claim, I spotted a guy holding a sign reading CHICKEN CATCHATORI.

"There he is!" I shouted.

The guy with the sign was Johnny, a guy I'd met the night before on the Internet. It was 1996, the Internet was a BABY, and I was invincible. It didn't occur to me until years later, while I was watching *Dateline*, that this was one of many events on this LA trip that could have landed me on *Dateline*. "Chicken CatchaTORI" was my chat room handle, one of my famous plays on the name Tori. (After Amos, that is. It was 1996 and I had a vagina.) My other Internet names included NoTORIous (which Tori Spelling would totally steal from me in the future) and RheTORIcal SarTORIal (way over Tori's head).

I'd started talking up this guy in the chat room because his name was Johnny. Only I'd been envisioning a Depp, and this guy was more of a Johnny LaRue. I peppered him with questions about Leo, but he didn't know anything about him, which I found irritating considering he was in a HOLLYWOOD chat room.

Aimee and I walked up to him. "Johnny?"

He put the sign down and looked at both of us. "Hey! Uh, whoa. It's *crazy* that you guys came. Like, you're actually here!"

He was soft-spoken and sweet, and a 100 percent bona fide computer nerd. Heavy, with an all-gray wardrobe and the complexion of the bottom of a white sock. He wasn't ugly, though, and that made the free ride okay in my mind. I couldn't get into a car with an ugly stranger.

Johnny was supposed to drive us to the Banana Bungalows on Cahuenga, but when we got in his rusted-out Datsun, he asked if we could stop by his mom's place first. I knew this wouldn't get me closer to Leo, but since it was a free ride and his vibe wasn't too creepy, I said sure. Aimee and I sat in his backseat (neither of us wanted the front; it was a *Driving Miss Daisy* situation in there), smoking cigarettes and asking Johnny questions.

"Where do you live?"

"With my mom."

"No, *where* do you live?"

"Compton."

We laughed. Johnny the Internet nerd had a sense of humor. "Are you a Crip?" I asked, throwing my head back and hitting my knee with my hand, like a seventeen-year-old girl who thought she was fucking hilarious.

"No," he said, then paused. "But neither of you are wearing head-to-toe blue, right?"

Wait. Johnny was serious! I sat straight up in my seat.

"No blue. Johnny, take us to your house immediately. You live in COMPTON?! I gotta see Compton." As a sheltered white girl I was obsessed with my gang films, especially *Menace II Society* and *Boyz n the Hood*.

"Yep, my mom's lived there since the sixties. She isn't really my mom—I mean, she is, but only because my real mom gave me to her. Dad's black, Mom's white."

I suddenly felt really shitty for Johnny, not only because he was half black but looked 100 percent white and lived in Compton, but also because he was an abandoned baby who was willing to drive strangers around LA. I guess I was also terrified for myself. I mean, we were little white girls. Oh, and Aimee had those fucking white-girl dreadlocks, which I'm sure would mean immediate social acceptance in Compton.

I tried to look on the bright side:

1. I was about to see my favorite movie genre, up close and personal.
2. It was dusk, so maybe our whiteness wouldn't be as apparent.

"Whoa—so have you ever been, like, gangbanged? Or shot?" Aimee said as she threw her cigarette out the window.

"Well"—Johnny sighed—"last month I was walking up to my house, along the hedges, and I knew someone was behind me. And then he grabbed my arm and swung me around and shoved a gun into my stomach, hard, and said, 'MOTHA-FUCKA, MONEY AND DRUGS OR YOUR GUT ON THA GROUND!'"

I sat up and put my hand behind his headrest. I was EN-THRALLED.

"What did you do?"

"I kinda pissed my pants. And shit myself, like at the same time. And I gave him my wallet. He left."

Aimee sat back. "Good for you," she said. "I would have to-tally shit myself too. That's always been my plan if anyone ever tries to rape me. I'm going to have instant diarrhea, then rub it all over. No one will want to rape that."

I shook my head. "Girl, the rapist would go haywire with all that diarrhea and totally just kill you." I was already saying "girl" like I was Tyra Banks when she's talking black to make it obvi-ous she's having fun. (Tyra only talks white when she wants you to know she's serious.)

His house was a seven-hundred-square-foot kind of place with bars on all the windows and doors. The yard was covered in spiderwebs. I felt very privileged to be there: I knew this was the kind of neighborhood I wouldn't normally get to visit unless I was an actor traveling with a police officer while researching a role. This was my version of the Universal Studios tour. And, from the looks of it in the dark, it was actually a very nice-looking community.

"Johnny, thank you so much for bringing us here."

I looked around for any lowriders bouncing on hydraulics,

then got out of the car. The entire walk up to the front door, I was braced to hear gunshots and feel stings in my body. I imagined getting shot, like, twenty times.

The house was dark, and it smelled of weed and incense. It looked like the home of a clean hoarder: lots of stuff, but no garbage, mummified animal carcasses, or rotting meat. The place was full of gold-plated statues and artwork. This family truly gave a shit about their house. I saw a hookah pipe in the corner, and there was a cat sleeping on the keyboard of a computer on the far wall. I imagined Johnny sitting there the night before, chatting with me, a far cry from the Johnny Depp in a pristine Victorian that I'd imagined.

Then, all of a sudden, a large black woman in a belly-dancing costume rounded the corner and swept into the gilded living room, her electric-green outfit bedecked with hundreds of clanking silver disks. Her top and bottoms were separated by at least four rolls of body, but I tried not to stare; I had perfect teeth and I didn't want them to get knocked out. I assumed this was Johnny's mom, but I'd just learned about a thousand lessons in assumptions in a short period of time, so I tried not to get too far ahead of myself.

"Mam, these are the girls I told you about. Aimee and Kelly, this is my mam. She's a belly-dance instructor."

The way Johnny said, "these are the girls I told you about" made me feel like I'd just walked into a slave ring. Girls go missing all the time. Maybe we were about to be herded into an underground tunnel feeding into a warehouse two blocks away, where hundreds of girls all shared cigarettes and mattresses and made the neighborhood gangs' new XXL jeans and puffy coats. All I wanted was to find Leo.

"Hi!" I stepped forward and shook her hand. "I'm Kelly. We're here to find Leonardo DiCaprio."

"Gurrrl, shit. Leo, that kid always yellin' outside? He ain't here." She giggled and took a hit off a joint I hadn't noticed she was holding.

"Mam!" Johnny said, motioning for her to put the joint away. "Mam!"

"No, he's an actor," I said.

Aimee stepped up from the brown velour recliner where she'd already made herself at home. "Can I have a hit of that?" Weed always found us.

Mam took a long hit off the joint and passed it to Aimee. Then she seemed to look her up and down for the first time. "Gurl!" she said. "You have a ras on yo' head?" in that weird voice people make when they're holding the smoke in their lungs. "You have a ras on yo' head?"

Aimee nodded. "Ja, man."

Oh, sweet Jesus, I was not going to smoke the weed. I knew where this was headed: we'd get stoned, forget all about Leo, and end up on the couch for two days wrapped up in a Raiders blanket eating Cheetos, drinking Fanta, and watching *Moesha* on UPN while Leo was twenty minutes away waiting for me to find him and change his world.

"Sorry to sound like a total bummer, but we really have to get going to our hostel and check in. We've got major jet lag." Of course we'd flown into the Pacific standard time zone from the nonfictional mountain standard time zone, so we'd only lost one hour. What a liar.

I let Aimee finish bonding with Mam (one or two more tokes to form lifelong affection) and told Johnny it was time to hit the road. We were out the door before *Moesha* came on.

To get our Hostelling International cards, we'd needed photo ID stating that we were over twenty-one, since that was the legal drinking age in Los Angeles. To get our fraudulent IDs, we had asked around at the coffee shop until we found two girls who were willing to lend us their Social Insurance and health care cards, which had their birth dates printed on them. Elizabeth and Veronica were both twenty-two, and now we were Elizabeth and Veronica.

When Johnny pulled the car up to the hostel, we said our good-byes and got his phone number, in case we needed another ride. I didn't feel guilty about not inviting Johnny out with us. I mean, I'd made it very clear that we were here for one reason, and having Johnny with us wasn't going to help, because:

1. Johnny didn't know Leo.
2. Two underage girls trying to get into clubs to find a guy was much more functional than two underage girls and a guy trying to get into clubs to find a guy.

Then we got our keys from the front desk of the hostel and let ourselves into the room.

The hostel was a converted one-level parking lot motel, and our room was a standard motel room, with a dresser, a TV, and a wooden chair. There was only one difference: it had three sets of bunk beds.

Aimee threw her suitcase up on the top bunk. "Mind if I take the top?"

I sat on the bottom bunk. "Nope, take it. Ladders are kinda blue collar."

We lay out on our beds and discussed the plan for that night.

"I think we should spend the night at the Viper Room and then go to Damiano's Mr. Pizza."

Aimee rolled over and looked down at me. "How do you know he goes there?"

I just shook my head. "The Internet! Those are Leo's hangouts. And this girl Brit who I met in a Hollywood chat room told us to meet her at Damiano's at one A.M. She said she knows Leo."

Suddenly, the doorknob to the room turned, then started jiggling violently. Someone pounded on the door. "WHAT THE FUCK IS GOING ON?!?!" a woman's voice roared from the other side.

Neither of us moved.

"What do we do?" Aimee said, peeking out the window. "Should I open it?"

"No." I shook my head. "We have a key. Whoever that is, if they belong in here, they'll have a key. Do you see anything?"

The banging stopped. "She stormed off," Aimee said. She dropped the curtain.

From the bed I had a clear view into the bathroom. A second later, I saw movement at the bathroom window. The window looked out on a retaining wall—there was probably no more than a foot of space between the wall and the window—but standing out there was someone who looked exactly like Gary Coleman, only she was six feet tall and a girl.

"Aimee . . ." I whispered. "She's coming in through the window."

I stretched out stiff on the mattress, pulled the top sheet up to my chin. I couldn't die yet. Not before I'd kissed Leo.

The girl's legs came through the open bathroom window, like a spider's.

"MO-THA-FUCKAHS!!" she screamed as she stormed into the room.

I lay there with my eyes shut, pretending to sleep. Aimee sat up in bed, dangling her feet, staring right at this girl, who stared right back at her.

"DON'T LOCK THAT FUCKING DOOR!" Gary Coleman puffed.

I opened my left eye and took a peek. The girl's nostrils were flaring. That was it for me. I faked waking up. I'm always the worst at fake waking up.

"What's going on?"

"DON'T LOCK THAT MOTHAFUCKING DOOR, BITCH. THAT'S WHAT'S GOING ON!"

"Okay, can we just calm down here and not yell so loudly, please?" I said, remembering to rub my eyes like someone waking up in a cartoon. "Why can't we lock the door?"

She put her hand on her hip. "I LIVE HERE. THIS IS MY ROOM." Then she grabbed the chair and sat down in front of the TV, her back to us.

I took a photo of her with my disposable camera. Suddenly, I felt like instigating.

"Then why don't you have a key?" I instigated.

She turned her head around to face me, slow and deliberate, giving me the "Oh no you di'int" body language I was so hoping to receive.

"If this is your room, you must have a key," I continued.

She stood up and stomped to a drawer, opened it, and pulled out a key.

"Here's my key."

"Great." I smiled charmingly. "You should bring it with you, because I'm not leaving this door unlocked so that anyone can just walk in here and murder me. Okay? Hey, do you know Leonardo DiCaprio?"

Gary Coleman laughed. "*Pffft.* White girl." She sat back down in her chair.

I looked up at Aimee. "We're leaving in ten minutes."

• • •

Aimee and I took a cab down to the Viper Room on Sunset Boulevard. I hopped out of the cab wearing blue velvet pants, black platform boots, and a velvet tiger-striped crop top that tied up in the back. Aimee was wearing a short skirt, boots, and a tank top. (It was the '90s, people.) The line to get into the bar wrapped around the corner, so we followed it to the front of the line at the door, looking for Leo in the line along the way. (I knew he wouldn't be in the line, but I had to dot my *i*'s.) We got to the front of the line and pulled out our IDs.

The night before, I'd gone online and done some reconnaissance. For some reason the Viper Room website had a "special VIP reservation" page, so I put my fake ID name and a plus-one on the form, hit submit, and hoped they'd receive it.

The bouncer looked up at me with his giant bouncer head.

"Hi, I'm Veronica Miller. I'm on the list," I cooed saccharinely.

I was on the top of the list.

He checked both our IDs. "What's this?" he asked, tilting the ID and looking at the hologram.

"We're from Canada," I said. "It's travel ID."

He passed them both back to us, pulled aside the velvet rope, and let us in.

We were stopped immediately by a small, skinny Mexican man. The maître d'.

"Ten-dollar cover," he said curtly.

"We're VIP," I said, smiling and shaking my head like I'd been there a thousand times before. "Is Leo here tonight?"

The man looked confused. I repeated myself. "DiCaprio? Is he here?"

"I don't know, but you're each going to have to give me ten dollars."

What a useless asshole. I gave him a twenty.

We walked into the club. "Let's just walk around and look for him," Aimee suggested. We took the main room first, but it was busy, and we didn't see him. Then Aimee pointed out a sheet of one-way glass on the back wall.

"That's where Leo is. The VIP room."

"No, Aimee, he wouldn't be hanging out in there. Leo is a dude of the people. I know him." God, I hoped I knew him; I'd just spent 10 percent of our budget getting into this bar.

We headed into a smaller room, which had a much quieter vibe. I took a table against the wall. I handed Aimee a few two-for-one drink vouchers I'd printed out from the Viper Room website. "Get me a vodka, 7UP, and lime." I knew what I was doing; I'd been sneaking into bars since I was fifteen. I thought the only advantage of being a girl was getting into bars underage.

I watched Aimee go to the bar with the online voucher. I'm sure they were shocked that anyone had bothered to go online and print them.

Then a girl slid up beside me. "Can I sit here?" she asked.

I squinted at her. "Are you Rudy Huxtable?!"

She laughed. It was totally Rudy Huxtable.

"No, honey, you can't drink beside me," I said apologetically. "I can't have Rudy Huxtable drinking beside me. It will ruin my night. Cliff wouldn't like it."

Four drinks later, I started feeling less disappointed that Leo hadn't shown up yet. We were now upstairs in a booth with a guy who was in Joan Jett and the Blackhearts. He'd been hitting on Aimee for twenty straight minutes when I got up.

"I'm going to go hang out around the pool tables for a while."

I crossed the dance floor, passing Bill Maher, who was dancing with an Amazonian black woman in a neon-pink dress. When I got to the bar, I leaned up against it, sipping my drink. A little ways away, I spotted a tall twentysomething guy wearing a great face and a suit. I loved that he was wearing a suit. My dad wore suits.

I walked up to him. He wasn't Leo, but my drunk instinct told me to talk to him.

"Hi."

He smiled. "Hello."

"I like your suit." I turned away from him and looked at the dance floor. I initiated the conversation, but then turned: casual, detached, cold. This is how I flirt.

"Thanks," he said.

I peeked back and caught a bit of self-satisfaction crossing his face. He was no fool. That suit was a calculated woman magnet.

"I'm Steven." He extended his hand.

"I'm Kelly." I shook it.

"Are you an actress?" he asked.

"God, no."

"Then you must be on vacation, because if you lived here, you'd be an actress."

"Yeah. I'm on a vacation."

"Where are you from?" He took a good sip of his whiskey. Zero whiskey-face reaction. Impressive.

"I'm from Canada."

"Kelly from Canada. I've been to Toronto," he offered. "I was in a musical when I was a kid; we went there on tour."

"What, like *Cats* or something? Were you Mr. Mistoffelees? Rum Tum Tugger?"

"No, I was in *The King and I*."

"You were the kid in *The King and I*?"

"Yep."

"Fuck, that's cool, Steven. No wonder you wear suits to dive bars."

That was a much more obvious flirt from me.

"How long are you in town for, Kelly from Canada?"

"I'm only here for another forty-eight hours." As soon as I said that, I wanted to take it back. Saying "forty-eight hours" was a MAJOR jinx, as in, *Did you ever see the episode of 48 Hours where two girls like me and Aimee get murdered on a trip to LA?*

"Well, if you'd like to go sightseeing or anything, I grew up here and I like taking people around."

He was either a genuinely nice guy or a total murderer, but not both. Time would tell.

"Cool. Thanks. New topic: Do you know Leonardo DiCaprio?"

He laughed. "No." I put on an ironic face, hoping he'd assume I was being sarcastic.

"Do you have the time?"

Steven checked his wristwatch. "Almost one."

"Oh," I said. "I have to go and meet someone. But give me your number." I grabbed a pen and paper from my bag. Then, as I was writing down his number, LL Cool J's "Mama Said Knock You Out" came on.

"I'll call you," I said, running onto the dance floor. I couldn't help myself—it was my jam.

My dancing was so intense and hard-core that people formed a dance circle around me. I'd started a dance circle at the Viper Room. This really was the "fuck it" time in my life. I was doing what I wanted to do.

Then some guy in the dance circle started doing Russian dance kicks at me. This was some kind of weird flirt dancing, and I wasn't into it. I hadn't trusted Russians since the '82 Tylenol murders in Chicago, when a story about Russian crime overlapped in the paper with a story about Tylenol and I somehow concluded that Russians were poisoning our painkillers.

I stumbled out of the dance circle, gave Bill Maher a high-five, and headed back to Aimee, who was laughing at the Blackheart.

"I can't have sex with you!!" she was saying as I sat down. "I was roller-skating to your music when I was in third grade!!"

"Let's go to the pizza place," I yelled across the table to her. "I'm starving."

Aimee slid out of the booth and Blackheart was already on to the next girl.

"Hold on!" Aimee said. Then she walked up to the one-way glass, banged her palms against it, and yelled, "JOHNNY? JOHNNY!!!!" Then she licked the glass.

We opened the door onto the street. It was strangely bright out there, despite the fact that it was almost one A.M. There was a large doorman standing guard nearby.

"Hey," I said, tripping over nothing, then leaning against the wall with one arm. "Which way is Fairfax?"

The doorman pointed with his left hand. "You need a cab?" he said, cocking his bowling ball of a head to the side.

"No way. We're walking. See? I have my walking shoes on!" I pointed drunkenly at my platform boots.

As we headed down Sunset, we found ourselves walking beside a preppy guy in a button-down shirt.

"Hey, which way down Fairfax is Damiano's Mr. Pizza?"

He pointed to the right.

"How long will it take us to walk? It isn't that far, right?"

He crinkled his brow. "You're walking?"

We didn't know that walking in LA was as common as flying somewhere for breakfast.

"Yeah. Is it far?"

He nodded. "It'll probably take you about half an hour?" And preppy guy turned right and left us walking down Sunset.

Half an hour? Perfect. We'd sober up a bit, then be ready to sit and enjoy pizza.

But the walk got scary when I walked through a massive cobweb beside a very empty lot. All of a sudden I realized that *no one* was out walking, not even homeless people. At least there were crazy people out all the time on Hollywood Boulevard. There was no one on the street at one A.M. I didn't even see a hooker! And that worried me, because if anyone wanted a hooker, they'd probably come to us.

Then, just as I was worrying about being mistaken for a street prostitute, a Jeep YJ pulled up beside us. It was the preppy guy in the button-down shirt, and thankfully he wasn't there to be the Richard Gere to our Julia Roberts.

"Hey, get in the back. I'll drive you to Damiano's."

We climbed into the back of the Jeep, stepping over the large dog on the floor.

"THANKS!" I shouted at the front of the Jeep from the back-seat, but either he was ignoring us or he couldn't hear us over the wind and music. I looked at Aimee, pointing to my ear and rolling my eyes—the international sign for "He can't hear me."

Preppy dude just kept driving. I leaned over and whispered to Aimee, "This is kind of embarrassing." The dog was looking at me with his WTF face.

"Why would this be embarrassing?" But she yelled it too loud, and the guy turned around.

"Thanks for picking us up," I said. "We didn't realize it was this far."

He nodded. "It's on the next block."

"He totally doesn't want to drive us," I whispered to Aimee. "We're just stupid girls. We're going to be the *stupid girls he had to help out* when he tells this story!"

She spit her gum out the window. "So?"

Sometimes I wished Aimee was a little more like me. I couldn't explain everything to her—like why it bothered me that this guy probably considered us stupid losers—but at the same time I think we were best friends because our reactions were usually so different.

We hopped out of the Jeep in front of the pizza place. Before I could thank prepster again, he was gone.

Damiano's was stage two in my plan. Along with arranging to meet Johnny at the airport, I'd arranged to meet this girl Brit for pizza. She said she'd be wearing a plaid dress and moto boots, and lo and behold, there she was in the promised outfit, sitting on the bench outside Damiano's.

I was finally getting my lead. My Leo hookup.

Brit was a thin, pretty girl with long and mousy-brown hair. I was hoping maybe she was an ex-girlfriend of his who could coach me on his weaknesses.

"Brit?" She looked up and smiled. She looked frail.

"Hi," she said, and stood up. She was almost six feet tall. "You girls are way cuter than I imagined."

I'll admit it, we were pretty cute. Seventeen-year-old girls, great taste in clothes.

Out of the corner of my eye, I saw Aimee bumming a Marlboro off a hobo. Then I looked back at Brit and caught her picking at a pimple. *God, that's gross.* "Uh—what do you know about Leo?"

Brit sighed. "Are you crazy? Are you serious about this?"

I lifted my eyebrows. "I'm here, aren't I?"

Brit shivered and rubbed her arm. "He's a punk. You don't want to date him. Him and his friends are total punks."

Oh my God, this information made me so happy. I was an asshole too! Leo and I *really were* soul mates.

"Where do they hang out?" I gasped, trying not to show my overwhelming joy.

She sighed again. "You're serious?"

Why this girl chose to show up and meet me was a mystery. She was starting to totally freak me out. "Well, here and the Hollywood Athletic Club," she said, still fingering her zit.

"I'M STARVING!" Aimee yelled, throwing her arm around my shoulders.

"Are you guys going inside?" Brit said.

I nodded, opening my eyes really wide, in that "Yes, we're here to eat" look.

She reached into her bag, and as she was fumbling around a small box of chocolate Ex-Lax fell out. "I don't really eat," she said. "That's why my skin is bad right now." Was this girl for real? She arranges to meet us at a pizza joint, then drops the Ex-Lax and says, "I don't really eat"?

"Brit, did you really come all the way here to meet us for a minute, just to see if I was serious about meeting Leonardo DiCaprio?"

She shook her head. "No, I was across the street. My boyfriend is at Canter's, so I knew I'd be here anyway. Anyhow, good luck."

We left Brit outside on the street with the hobos and her anorexia. I imagine her to this day still chatting online, sighing, thinking she's better than Leo DiCaprio while nibbling on her cocoa laxatives.

I knew Leo wouldn't be in the pizza place—Brit would have told me—but I still scanned the room like the Terminator. It was shoulder-to-shoulder crowded. Aimee snagged a booth from a couple on their way out, and I headed for the restroom. On the way, I passed Andy Dick in a back booth with three beautiful large women. I gave him a knowing wink for absolutely no reason except that I was drunk.

In the bathroom I looked in the mirror and was instantly reminded that I was drunk.

"Niiiiiice," I said, giving myself a thumbs-up, solidifying the feeling of emptiness in my soul. I hadn't found Leo.

"This is stupid," I whispered. "I'll check the Hollywood Athletic Club and then I'm done. Done. Just enjoy your trip, Kelly."

I was squatting over the toilet, spraying pee all over the floor. A cockroach skittered past. "Oh my God!" I whispered, trying to pee on it.

When I got back to the booth, I found Andy Dick sitting with Aimee. He was writing on a napkin: "Oh, you're from Canada? You must know *D-A-V-E F-O-L-E-Y.*" I sat down beside Aimee, trying to figure out which one of us looked worse. "I just tried to pee on a cockroach on the floor in the bathroom," I said. "Total accident. But I washed my hands *so good.*"

Aimee slid me my pizza. I folded the large slice in half and inhaled it.

"Do you guys like weed?" Andy said, sitting back and crossing his arms.

"Yeah." Aimee nodded before Andy finished the word *weed.*

"Look at her, Andy," I said like we were old friends. "She's a white girl with dreadlocks. What do you think?"

Andy pulled out a bag with a fist-sized clump of weed in it and put it in the middle of the table. "Voilà! For you, ladies." Then he got up and walked away.

Aimee grabbed the weed and put it in her bag. Weed always finds us.

"What the fuck was that?" I asked, wiping the grease from my cheek.

"He just came over here while you were in the bathroom."

"What, he just came over and gave us a big bag of weed? That's normal for him?"

"It's a lot of weed!" Aimee whispered loudly through a goofy smile.

I scanned the room again for Leo. How was I going to find him in a day and a half?

"I'm going outside for a cigarette," I said, and stood up. Aimee was right behind me. Aimee bummed another two cigarettes off bums. Nearby, a guy was leaning against the wall, pulling Saran Wrap off his dick to show everyone his new tattoo.

"I think we should just enjoy ourselves tomorrow, go to the Hollywood Athletic Club to look for Leo, and then give up if he isn't there," I said, passing the cigarette back to Aimee. She nodded in agreement.

Just then, Andy Dick came out the door with his women and started walking toward us.

"Hey," I said. "You want to have some of this . . . *stuff* with us? The *stuff* you gave us?"

He threw his head back and laughed. "Honey? I've got a couple of ladies here who want to do a little more with me than smoke weed tonight. IF YOU GET WHAT I'M SAYIN!!!"

I got it all right, Andy. The whole sidewalk got it, thanks.

"Aimee, how are we going to get back to the hostel?" I said. "A cab? I don't have any money left."

A man I assumed was the manager or owner of Damiano's had just come outside.

"You okay?" he said with a European accent and a look of actual concern. "Don't worry for him. You need something?"

"Yeah," I said, putting out my cigarette. "A ride home."

"No problem. Wait here. I'll come round and get you. I need to make delivery." Oh my God. I'd always wanted to deliver pizza.

A minute later, he pulled up in a Volkswagen. Electronic dance music was blasting from the speakers. "WHOA! SORRY!!!" he said, turning it down.

His name was Vlad, he was Czech, and he had a pizza to deliver before he could drop us off at the hostel. I got in the passenger seat; Aimee climbed in back with the pizza.

The delivery wasn't for Leo, which bummed me out. Instead we watched as Vlad drove into Hollywood and pulled up to an apartment building. Then, a minute later, a woman on a balcony sent down two rapper-looking guys to get the pizza.

"It's probably Mariah Carey," I said to Aimee, who was rolling a joint.

Vlad got back in the car.

"Hey, Vlad, do you want some pot?" she offered.

"Noooooooo," he said. "I need to stay up and deliver. I have second job after this one." He flashed his gold teeth at me. I gave him a soft "Putting up with this for the free ride" smile.

"I need to stay up all night, I do this!" He pulled out a bag of white crystals.

"Is that crank?!" I blurted out. I wasn't even sure what the fuck crank was.

"Yeah, it keeps me strong. Keeps me alive!!!"

He turned up the music really loud. Then he opened the bag, took out a crystal, and crushed the rock in a spoon. Just as he was about to snort it, he looked up at me, wide-eyed in the passenger seat.

"VANT SOME?!"

"Uh, no, thank you," I gasped. "I don't have a second job

tonight." I put my hand up, as if to block him from throwing the meth at me.

He snorted the powder, put the bag back, and blasted away from the curb.

For the next few minutes, I felt like I was being driven by a five-year-old in a game of Super Mario Kart. We were speeding and hitting curbs to a techno backdrop, my hands sweating so much I couldn't hang on to anything in the car.

Then, as we spun around one corner, we saw trouble ahead: flashing police lights, a bunch of cops holding two guys up against a car.

With a look of seriousness, Vlad reached out and turned up the music. "Detour time," he announced, pulling a quick right down a side road.

"Why? Because you're high on meth?"

Vlad laughed. "You're funny woman! We detour from LAPD. No point in get into cross fire."

We pulled up to the hostel in the vibrating Volkswagen. Aimee and I got out as fast as we could, and Vlad zipped off into the night.

We sat down on a bench outside and smoked our joint.

Maybe we'd find Leo tomorrow.

The next day we woke up to find we were the only people left in our hostel room, because it was noon and we were assholes. I changed clothes and told Aimee we should go to the beach. Our only true mission that day was to go to the Hollywood Athletic Club to look for Leo, but we couldn't do that till it got dark. Things were looking grim for Leo and me, but I wasn't going to let that get in my way. My chances of finding him had always been slim, but I took comfort in the fact that I was totally still his soul mate. As the trip went on, I'd come to see it almost as a

Peace Corps mission. I was saving Leo. I was going to make his life so much better.

After grabbing muffins at the hostel, we got a ride to the beach with another guest, a boring Australian girl. It was a very normal ride: no drugs, no stopovers in Compton, no dog on the floor. For a moment I felt like everything was ordinary again. She dropped us off at the end of the Santa Monica Freeway. The beach was cold. It was empty. It was March.

"Wow." I nodded, looking out to sea. "This is terrible." I wrapped my arms around myself. After a few minutes, we decided to go back to Hollywood.

By bus.

What we didn't know: the city bus to Hollywood seats all unstable patients, poor seniors, and young black girls who sing like TLC.

At the back of the bus, we met a crazy guy from Venice Beach who thought he was Jean-Michel Basquiat.

"I'm Basquiat!" he said out loud to no one in particular.

No one else answered him, so I did. "Basquiat died in the eighties," I said, looking at him skeptically. "After he dated Madonna."

He looked pleasantly surprised that I responded. He leaned his head back into a patch of sunlight and shut his eyes.

"I'm glad you believed that lie," he said. "It's given me so much peace and freedom to live."

"What do you do now?" He was actually better looking than Basquiat, but I could see why he'd chosen him. There were similarities. They were both black, for one.

He sat up and looked at me. "I live in Venice. I draw people on the beach."

"Oh," I said. "You gave up being a lucrative artist in New York to be a street sketcher in Venice Beach? Makes total sense."

I noticed an old woman a few seats ahead of us moving her hand in her purse.

Basquiat nodded. "It was the smartest thing I did."

"Hey! Hey! BUGS AND BOYS, BOYS AND BUGS!!" It was the woman with the purse. She pulled a sharp pencil out of her bag, then raised it over her head. She didn't plunge it down into the kid in the seat beside her; she sort of just brought her arm down and slashed him a little with it. Like she was using a butter knife to spread butter on toast, only with the sharp tip of a pencil on his throat.

The driver stopped and kicked the woman off the bus. The boy was fine, with the exception of probably having nightmares about old ladies for the rest of his life.

"This is why I take the bus," Basquiat said. "Inspiration."

We got off the bus in East Hollywood, without a case of crabs or stabs. After walking for a few blocks, I spotted the Bourgeois Pig, a restaurant I'd heard was a Leo hangout, so we went inside.

"Are you an actress?" The guy working behind the counter looked, as a lot of guys in LA did, like Adam Goldberg. I was more sick of the actual answer to this question—"No, I'm a Canadian stalking Leo"—than the question itself, so I lied.

"No, I'm in a band."

He passed me my cappuccino. "So am I. I play lead. You?"

Shit. "I'm the singer." I'm a terrible liar. "But I have nodules right now. So I can't sing for you or anything. It's tough not being able to use my instrument." I sipped my drink.

Aimee made a tour of the café and came back shaking her head.

"He isn't here, but I met a guy back there who wants to play pool."

I looked past her and saw five Asian guys with one white

guy—who, again, looked like Adam Goldberg. I shrugged, and Aimee went back to them.

"I'm Dave," the guy behind the counter said to me, holding out his hand.

"I'm Veronica. So that castle over there—is that the Scientology Celebrity Centre?"

Across the street was a giant and beautiful building and garden with a huge yellow neon sign on the roof: CHURCH OF SCIENTOLOGY CELEBRITY CENTRE.

He nodded. "Yep. That's where Tom Cruise and John Travolta like to play. It used to be a hotel, like the Chateau Marmont. It was going to be demolished in the seventies, but the church bought it." So it was a church full of bedrooms? I appreciated the convenience.

"Well," I said, "I'd consider becoming famous just so I could apply to the church and get into that place."

"Don't even joke about it." Dave looked around and leaned in. I returned the lean. "I had a friend, and he met this actress who brought him there and he didn't get out for days."

"Why?" I whispered. "Because they were fucking in one of the suites?"

He shook his head, still serious. "They were trying to brainwash him."

Oh. "Leonardo DiCaprio isn't a Scientologist, is he?"

Dave stood up straight. "No. Why do you bring him up?"

"I don't know. I just like him. Does he hang out here?"

Dave yelled over the coffee grinder. "Yeah, he plays pool here sometimes. But he isn't a Scientologist. They don't really come in here. Everything they need is in there."

Aimee walked back over. I pointed out the front window. "Aimee, wouldn't you join a cult if it meant you got to hang out in that exclusive club every day?"

She nodded. "Sure. Hey, Kelly, let's go hang out with this guy Trent. He has a suite at a Beverly Hills hotel."

"Kelly?" Dave stopped. "I thought your name was Veronica."

"I'm a terrible liar," I said apologetically. I turned back to Aimee. "Why do we have to go to this guy's hotel? That's creepy."

Aimee shook her head. "He's cool. They just want to smoke weed at the hotel."

"You're sure about this guy?" I looked over her shoulder at him. He seemed harmless, but he was hanging out with a group of Asian guys, which I did not think was normal. That's not racist, that's observational.

"Yes. And just think: Leo might be in Beverly Hills. We haven't been there yet."

Okay, I was fine with leaving. Leo wasn't there, and Dave was getting me nowhere.

Two of the Asian guys, Aimee and I, and the white guy piled into a Mercedes-Benz. The men all started chatting in Chinese.

"Aimee," I whispered. "What are we doing?"

We sat in the backseat and the white guy, who was also speaking Chinese, was really freaking me out. I'd been in Havana once and I'd met a bunch of Japanese students who spoke Spanish and no English, so we'd communicated with each other in Spanish and that freaked me out the same way.

"That's Trent. He said he's Jackie Chan's interpreter. This is Chan's entourage. He invited us to hang out with him after I told him we had weed."

I gave Aimee an "I don't trust these guys" face, which she interpreted correctly. "My intuition says it's fine," she said.

My Jessica Fletcher glasses were definitely on: Trent's hotel turned out to be a Marriott on Olympic Boulevard. "Aimee," I shout-whispered, "you said he was staying at THE BEVERLY HILLS HOTEL."

Aimee shook her head. "I said *a* Beverly Hills hotel."

His room was the cheapest standard room in the place, with stucco walls and multistained carpets and even though I was from Canada, I knew this was *not quite* Beverly Hills. A black light would have revealed too much.

I didn't believe Trent's story, but otherwise he wasn't giving off too many bad vibes. He was polite and not creepy, except when he spoke Chinese.

Trent, Aimee, and I sat in his room smoking and watching bad TV. Then, inevitably, I got a hankering for pizza. "LET'S GO TO DAMIANO'S!!"

"I'm tired," Trent whined. "Let's get room service."

I was not eating Marriott room service, I knew that much. And we weren't going to bump into Leo anywhere in that hotel.

"Can we borrow your car for half an hour?" I said.

Trent looked at me like I was crazy.

"Look, I'll leave my passport here so you know we'll be back."

I have no idea why—maybe because we were girls (totally because we were girls)—but he let us take his Mercedes.

I didn't have my license, as I've mentioned, so Aimee drove. We pulled up to Damiano's and I saw the owner/manager through the window. He looked surprised.

A minute later, he came out to see us. "Yesterday you girls didn't have any money. Today you have a Mercedes?"

I lit my cigarette. "That's how we roll." It wasn't how we rolled at all.

I ordered a large pizza and two calzones to go right there on the sidewalk. Then I stuck my nose in the restaurant's front door and looked around. No Leo.

"Aimee?" I exhaled, feeling low. I had no reason to feel low.

I'd managed to get by for two days in Los Angeles spending only fifty dollars, and now we had a Mercedes to show for it. But still. "I'm so bummed we haven't found Leo. It's like this whole trip is solidifying the fact that I'm a rash, irrational asshole."

"You are. It's great," she said, plucking the cigarette from my fingers. "God, I'm still stoned. That Andy Dick weed was good."

She was right, the Dickweed was really good. And I was glad she wasn't falling into my pity party.

"Did you leave the weed with Trent?" I took the cigarette back.

"No way." Aimee exhaled. "He would have totally smoked it all. I just left him a tiny bit. The rest is in my bag." She stroked her bag like it was a precious white cat from the cat-food commercials.

We got our food and headed back to the swanky Beverly Hills (Century City) hotel (shithole motel).

Five minutes into the drive, an LAPD car pulled into the lane beside us.

"Oh God, Aimee." I froze. "I'm so scared of the LAPD. Usually I'm not scared of police, but the cops back home are like kittens compared to these guys. These guys are like the meth of cops."

The light ahead turned red.

"Aimee, don't pull up beside him! Don't! We have weed on us! This isn't our car!!"

She started to panic. "I can't get behind him! There's no room!"

The cop car was at the stop line. We pulled up beside him. "Don't line up with him!" I whispered. "I don't want to be beside him." Aimee hit the brakes a little too hard, then rolled forward . . . right past the stop line.

My heart stopped. I looked over my right shoulder. There, a little bit behind us, was the LAPD officer in his car.

"Aimee," I said, talking through my teeth like a ventriloquist so the cop wouldn't see me. "YOU-CROSSED-THE-STOP-LINE-WE'RE-FUCKING-DEAD!!!"

She shook her head subtly. "No flashing lights," she said. "We're cool. We're cool. The light will change in a minute. We're cool." She may have been ventriloquist-talking back to me, but I wasn't sure because I refused to turn my head and look.

Then. *Bwoop! Bwoop!* The lights flashed twice. I felt a bead of sweat squeeze out of my armpit and roll down my side. An engine roar, then another siren blast: *Bwwwooooop!* This was my fate: I was a rash, irrational asshole; weed always found me; and I was going to end up in some *Brokedown Palace* jail cell spooning with a woman named MizMAY because I was following my heart. Typical bullshit.

I turned around, ready to surrender. But the cops just tore through the red light and went off after someone much more dangerous than two stoner white girls in a Mercedes.

Back to the shitbox motel with our food.

Ten minutes later we'd devoured the cheese and carbs and were getting stereotypically tired from the weed/pizza combo. Before we went out that night, I suggested, maybe we should take a nap. It was our Hollywood Athletic Club night and I wanted to look as fresh as a stoner full of pizza could look.

Trent offered up half his bed to one of us. Aimee took it. I called the front desk and asked for a wake-up call in two hours.

Trent pulled the blackout curtains and hopped into bed. For a moment I listened anxiously, worrying that he might molest Aimee, but I figured he was too lazy to rape anyone, and maybe I was being paranoid. I curled up on the stinky couch, with a blanket I'd never want black lit from the closet, and began to pass out. And that's when I heard it.

Trent picked up the phone very quietly, dialed a number, and started speaking in Chinese.

I felt an adrenaline rush, which to me is the last primordial instinct we have in this civilized world. I bolted upright off the couch and looked at the front door. It was unlocked. As far as I was concerned (and I'd watched so many *Datelines*—I knew my shit), I'd put the pieces together: Trent had just called his Asian buddies, who were also in the hotel, to come over and gangbang us or maybe even take us away to that underground slavery ring to make those puffy jackets and XXL pants.

I ran to the door and locked it.

Trent stopped talking his sneaky Chinese talk. "Wait! What are you doing?"

I picked up the floor lamp.

I was standing in a tank top and my underwear with a lamp over my head.

Aimee swung her legs over the bed. Both of them stared at me, waiting for something to happen.

I thought, *THIS IS YOUR MOMENT. MAKE STONE PHILLIPS PROUD.*

"Trent, if anyone comes through that door *I will kill them.* Who were you on the phone with?"

"My girlfriend," he mumbled. Total mumbly liar!

"C'mon, Aimee," I said. "Get your stuff. Let's go."

I wasn't sure if I was overreacting, but I wasn't going to risk it if the outcome meant having a bunch of old Asian dudes run a train on me.

All of a sudden Trent changed. His face got all hostile. "Do not go into the lobby. You'll go down the back stairs."

What the fuck?! As if I was going to go down the back stairs! That was clearly where all his Jackie Chan karate buddies were hiding.

Aimee grabbed our things. I sped down the hall to the elevator in my panties and a tank top, and we headed down to the lobby.

"Can I use your phone?" I gasped when I got there. "The guy in room three-fourteen is a freak and I need a phone." The front desk clerk passed me a phone without question. He probably thought we were hookers, like Vivian Ward. But I didn't give a shit—I was not going to get raped by those guys! I pulled on my pants and cardigan, dug Steven's phone number out of my bag, and prayed he was home.

"Hello?"

"Steven? It's Kelly. From the Viper Room last night?"

"Oh, right. Hello!"

"Hey, do you think we could do that sightseeing thing right now? Or maybe go hang out?"

"Sure. I'm just watching *The Thin Man* and eating deviled eggs right now, but I'm headed to the Good Luck Club in half an hour. Do you want to meet me there? I'll give you the address."

I dug for my pen—and that's when I realized my passport wasn't in my bag.

I'd left it upstairs with Trent the rapist.

"Oh, fuck."

"What's wrong?"

"I left my passport with a rapist."

"A rapist? Get it back."

"I'm scared."

I told Steven I'd call him back and passed the phone to the clerk.

"Can you come upstairs with us?" I asked him. "I left something in the room and I'm scared to go back alone. You don't have to come in—just stand outside the door."

As Aimee, the front desk guy, and I walked to the bank of elevators, the door of the elevator opened. Trent was standing there.

We froze. The desk guy walked right in and stood beside Trent, who wasn't moving. He looked like he was going to kill us.

Aimee and I got in the elevator with the desk clerk and the rapist, and the door closed behind us.

I broke the silence. "I need my passport."

Trent cleared his throat. "You didn't take the back stairs."

This was horseshit. "Trent, I brought your car back. My passport isn't yours. I think I can call the LAPD on you for keeping it from me."

Aimee piped up. "This is the manager of the hotel!"

The little front desk clerk looked like he really didn't want to get involved. "Oh, no, I'm just the desk clerk."

"Yeah, but he knows *everything*, Trent," I added.

The elevator doors opened, but I stood my ground. "The three of us will wait here," I said. "Please bring me my passport."

Trent went back into his room. For a moment I was horrified that he might walk out the door, hold the passport in the air, and then light it on fire with my lighter, which I'd also left in the room. (Although I didn't ask to have that returned. No need to push it.) But he came out a minute later, slapping the passport against his hand, and slapped it into my hand.

"You're crazy," he said.

I agreed with him. "Yeah, maybe I'm crazy. Or maybe you were going to gang-rape us with a bunch of Chinese men. I don't know. The lesson here is, you can trust a stranger with your car, but don't nap with them. Or something like that."

And then Aimee put on some pants in the lobby restroom, and we walked out onto Olympic (me with passport in hand) and hailed a cab up to the Good Luck Club.

"So what are you doing in LA?"

Aimee and I were sitting across from Steven and some woman friend he'd run into at the bar. She was a studio executive of some sort.

The bar, like the entire day, was a dive with an Asian theme.

We'd been there only half an hour, but already I was two shots and half a martini in, which was excessive for me. Then again, I'd just run through a lobby half-naked, convinced I was being chased by a hundred Chinese men.

"Well, long story short," Aimee said, "we came here from Canada to find Leonardo DiCaprio. We haven't been able to find him, but we've been taken home by a stranger from the Internet, driven around by a Czech meth head, and attacked by a hostile hostel roommate. We've also borrowed a Mercedes and smoked weed in Compton."

I pointed at Aimee. "Well, *she* smoked weed in Compton. What else? Well . . . we saw a stabbing on a bus. We got pot from Andy Dick. We saw Bill Maher dancing with a black woman. Oh, and we were almost gang-raped by a bunch of Asians." I sipped my drink.

"No!" Steven's friend said. "Really?!"

I stirred my drink with a tiny plastic samurai sword. "Why would I make that up?"

"Have you been offered your own sitcom yet? Because that would really round off your trip." She and Steven shared a Hollywood laugh. I was totally ready for this trip to be over.

"Well," I said, downing my drink, "I think we're off."

Steven asked, "Where to? We were thinking of heading

over to the Derby. I know a guy who can get us in. It's been jammed since October when *Swingers* came out. Have you been there?"

In my head, I was already packing up my stuff. I was ready to find no Leo at the Athletic Club and leave and go back to Canada and go back to smoking weed behind the coffee shop every afternoon.

Aimee could sense that I was wandering into drunken "fuck this shit" territory and took over. "No, we haven't been there," she told Steven. "I think we might just head over to the pool place, though. It was nice meeting you," she told the movie exec, then shook her hand, because that's what you do with a woman who's wearing a business suit in an Asian-themed purposefully divey bar.

Steven walked us outside to catch a cab. "Are you sure you're all right?" he asked.

I shook my head. "No, not really, but I really appreciate you letting us come and have a drink with you. You're a nice guy." And I meant it. He wasn't creepy or gross and didn't smell like cologne.

Then I had a thought. "Do you have the Internet?"

"No."

"Well, do you like to write to people?" I asked. "Because you seem to like nostalgic things, and I wouldn't mind a pen pal. I hate the phone."

"Really?" he said. "That's surprising. I mean, I'm just basing this on the entertainment value of your one phone call to me. It was highly entertaining."

Steven and I exchanged addresses while Aimee bummed cigarettes off people and put them in her empty cigarette box.

This is the part of the story where I always say we got to the Hollywood Athletic Club and didn't find Leo, but it's okay because I did play a game of pool with Tobey Maguire. I apologize to all of my friends, because this is a lie. I didn't meet Tobey. But I hate it that I didn't find Leo there. It always seemed like a terrible end to the story. I don't think finding Tobey Maguire makes it a better story, but it at least makes my detective work sound like it was half-decent. Like I was legit Jessica Fletcher *Part Deux* material.

What really happened was this:

Our cab pulled up to the club just as a BMW full of guys pulled a U-turn and drove off.

"*Shit!*" I snapped my head back, looking at the BMW. "That was totally them!"

I was already preparing myself for the obvious no-Leo letdown—which was 100 percent confirmed a few minutes later when we stepped into the virtually empty club.

"Kelly, why do you even care about finding him anymore?" Aimee asked, exasperated. "It was fun in the beginning, but now it's annoying me. Can't you try to forget about him and have some fun?"

Aimee was right. I wasn't super-obsessed with him, but I did hate being wrong.

And I hated the thought that I couldn't even manage being a good stalker.

I wandered up the stairs alone, following the hall to the bathroom to Ace of Base's "All That She Wants," while Aimee set up a table for us to play on.

"Good evening, ma'am."

I was startled. There, on a chair in the bathroom, sat an old black woman.

I was confused. I'd never seen a bathroom attendant before. So I stopped to talk to her.

"Hi there. Are you okay?" I asked.

She wasn't wearing a name tag or anything that would make it obvious to me that she was working there. Except maybe the bow tie, but that didn't occur to me until later.

"I'm fine," she said. "How are you?"

"You really want to know?" I asked, completely ready to divulge everything.

"Sure," she said, rolling her hips back, getting comfortable.

"I'm not good." I leaned on the counter. "I'm seventeen years old and I'm not going to university. I work for my dad. I don't drive. I never got a year abroad."

She snorted. "Neither did I!"

I shook my head. "I don't think that I'm *owed* these things. I mean, a European vacation would have been great. My friend Aimee got to go to Europe. You hear this song?" I pointed to the ceiling, where Ace of Base's "All That She Wants" was streaming from the speaker. "I lost my virginity to THAT SONG! To a twin named Alex, when his twin brother was in the kitchen making a tuna sandwich." I lifted my eyebrows for emphasis.

"Look, girl. Now you're annoying me."

"Oh." I wasn't expecting that.

She sighed. "I'm probably going to lose my job for saying that."

"Why would you lose your job?"

"Because you're a guest. But you deserved it."

Then I noticed a plate full of one-dollar bills sitting next to her. "You *work* here?"

"No, I just pass women hand towels because I like it." She could see I was confused. "I'm a bathroom attendant."

"A bathroom attendant? What the hell is that??" This woman sat in the fucking bathroom all night giving people paper towels? What kind of hell was this?

"Where you from, girl?"

"Canada."

"Oh," she said, as if that explained everything. "I been to Toronto."

What, she was in *Cats* too?

She looked me up and down. "You seem like a nice girl," she said. "But look at you. You got it together. You need to stop complaining about bullshit. Look at me, sitting in some dark bathroom passing people towels for dollar bills. I don't want to hear your shit!!"

It suddenly occurred to me: this lady was my Magical Negro.

There she was, sitting in the toilet. My Magical Negro!! Helping the white girl come to grips with her reality. This, dare I say, was better than Oprah. And the reality was, she was right. I had absolutely nothing to complain about. I had my friends. I had the freedom to go to another country to find Leonardo DiCaprio. I had fifty dollars left and a plane ticket home.

I went into the stall, took a piss, and gave her five dollars when I was through washing my hands. She smiled a halfhearted, detached kind of smile, and I returned it with a big, warm grin and a thank-you.

When I got back, Aimee was playing pool with two guys.

"Aimee! I found my Magical Negro in the bathroom!!"

Everyone stopped talking and stared at me.

"You know?" I continued. "The Magical Negro who helps the white person? Like Bubba in *Forrest Gump*? Or Oda Mae in *Ghost*? Only I guess this was a smaller role."

Aimee looked at me in mild horror, then tried to brush it off. "Great! Happy for you, Kel! So this is Carlos and Jonathan. Guys, this is Kelly, who I swear is not racist."

The guys looked uncomfortable, so I worked my ice-breaking magic.

"Right, right. Rule number one, don't mention another race EVER, OR YOU ARE A RACIST. Jeez, Aimee. So, Carlos, you Mexican? Ha! I'm kidding. Let's break these balls!"

With just a few words, the Magical Negro had totally altered my mind-set. She had managed to make me feel so grateful for what I had. I really hadn't been living in the moment.

Now I would.

Carlos and Jonathan ended up being great, absolving Aimee of her bad intuition about Trent. They were both twenty-seven, from Long Island, and they were in Hollywood trying to make it as actors. Four more drinks, and I had an epiphany.

"Oh, man! You guys!! We should go to Vegas!! Just for the day. We'll come back tomorrow night for our flight home!"

Carlos looked at Jonathan, then back at me. "Like, just go to Vegas? Like in *Swingers*?"

"I haven't seen *Swingers*. Oh, but we *were* invited to the Derby tonight. So that's a sign we should go!" I could feel the blood pumping in my veins. "Vegas!!"

"Let's go!" Aimee said.

Jonathan nodded to Carlos. "We haven't been there yet. Let's do this!"

The four of us ran out of the club and hopped into Jonathan's convertible Toyota. This was exactly what I'd wanted adulthood to be like: ideas only kids would have, but with the means of actually accomplishing those ideas. You know how kids all want to grow up so they can do what they want, and adults all wish they were kids again so *they* could do what they want? I had just found the middle ground.

We went back to the hostel to pick up our stuff. It was one A.M. and the lights in the room were off.

"Gary Coleman is going to kill us when we go in there!" I said to Aimee.

"Gary Coleman is in your room?" Carlos asked.

I ignored him. "Carlos, come in with me to get the stuff. I don't think she'll kill me if you're there."

"Who?" he asked.

"Our roommate looks like a tall version of Gary Coleman, but she's a girl," I said, getting out of the car and getting down to business. "Jonathan, keep the car running. Aimee, Carlos, and I are going to grab our bags and pull a runner."

I stopped right outside our door. I paused a moment, deep in thought.

"What?" Carlos said.

"Okay, I'm just trying to plan this. So our bunk bed is on your immediate right once we get in the door. Aimee's stuff is in a little suitcase on the top left-hand side of the bed. I'll grab my stuff below. Got it?" I nodded, gave him a thumbs-up, then patted him on the shoulder. I was like James Bond and Fred Rogers rolled into one.

The door creaked open. We both shot to the bunk bed and started fumbling around in the dark. Then, *wham*, I cracked my knee on the ladder.

A light flew on. It was Gary Coleman.

"YOU FUCKING STUPID-ASS BITCHES!"

She jumped out of her bunk on the far side of the room, eyes wild.

I grabbed my suitcase and looked at Carlos, who'd found Aimee's suitcase. Then we *ran*.

I don't think I've ever run that fast in my life. I was outrunning a six-foot-tall black girl, and I was *just* out of her reach when I dove into the car. Jonathan hit the gas before I could swing my door shut.

"We did it! WE DID IT!!!" I shouted to no one in particular.

Carlos turned around from the passenger seat. "Oh my God!" he said. "She did look like Gary Coleman!!!"

"I KNOW!" I shouted back in a frenzy of adrenaline. "SEE? I'M NOT A RACIST!!"

On the road to Vegas, our excitement dwindled—from a 1:30 A.M. chant of "VEGAS!! VEGAS!!" to a bleary "Are we in Vegas?" to finally, a few miles out, a hearty "JONATHAN, ARE YOU ASLEEP AT THE WHEEL??"

Now it was 5:30 A.M. and the sun was up, and we were driving down the Strip. None of us had ever seen it in person before.

Aimee suggested that we use the convertible like a convertible. Jonathan hit a button and the top came down, revealing four exhausted people in a Celica.

Carlos turned on the radio.

The drums. That opening drum line. I knew those drums.

"Carlos!" I sat forward. "Turn it up!"

It was Stevie Wonder's "Superstition." I knew it! *This* was the reason I'd taken this trip. For that moment. Driving down the Strip in Vegas with my best friend and two strangers from Long Island in a convertible with Stevie Wonder playing. That was why I was there.

"Guys? I need something."

Aimee wanted a toothbrush. We'd forgotten ours in the hostel bathroom. (Thankfully, they were our only casualties.) We pulled into the CVS parking lot and opened the doors to stretch our legs. Aimee and Carlos went inside the CVS.

"GET *AGUA*!!" I shouted.

Jonathan lay down on the pavement of the CVS parking lot, propping his legs up on his driver's seat, and sighed. I sat down on the pavement beside his head, avoiding a fresh piece of gum.

"Tired?" I said stupidly. "You have a case of the LA sighs. They're very contagious."

"Yeah, I just—I'm trying to decide whether I should give up and go back to Long Island or not. I've been thinking about it for pretty much the entire drive. Except for the part where I fell asleep."

I lit a cigarette. It burned my throat.

"Jonathan, you should do whatever your gut tells you to do. Do whatever your senior citizen self would want you to do."

He sat up and looked at me, shielding the sun from his eyes. "What do you mean?"

"Look." I tapped my ash. "Life is so random. It's a fucking miracle that you're even alive and your body works minute to minute. You just have to do what makes you happy and try not to fuck with a lot of other people along the way. You know, so that when you're an old man you can look back and feel good about things."

"That's what *you* do?"

"Yeah, that's what I do. I might not have a lot to show for myself."

He laughed. "You're seventeen."

"Yeah, I'm seventeen, and I barely graduated high school because I thought it was so boring that I basically stopped going. I'm not in college, and I don't have a trust fund, so I can't intern. I write—I love writing—but I haven't figured out a way to make money at it. But I *always* follow my gut and say yes to everything I can. Anything that doesn't fuck with someone else's existence. I just try to live, because as far as I know my whole life is a blip. This whole thing about DiCaprio was just a diversion. I still think he needs me, but more important, I needed some excitement. I need to survive and be thrilled and be happy."

"LA does that for me," he said.

"There you go."

Aimee and Carlos came back, brushing their teeth as they walked through the parking lot, foaming at the lips like rabid beasts.

"Here," Carlos said with the toothbrush in his mouth. He passed Jonathan and me a bag holding two bottles of water, two toothbrushes (pink and blue), and the toothpaste. Jonathan reached in and took the pink toothbrush. We all stood in the lot at six A.M. and brushed our teeth.

A looked up and saw a plane flying overhead. I wondered how many people up there were looking down at us, thinking how much we looked like a computer chip.

The four of us got a hotel room with two queen-sized beds and slept for five hours. No raping, no Chinese whispering. Later that afternoon we turned twenty dollars into quarters, fed them all into losing machines, called Johnny to ask for a ride, and drove back to LA.

Aimee and I waved good-bye to Carlos and Jonathan from a street corner in Hollywood, my orange suitcase in hand.

"Crazy," I heard behind me. "I can't believe you're here."

I turned around and saw Johnny.

"I'm parked up the hill."

"So did you find him?" he asked as we sped down the 405.

I sighed. "No, but I tried."

"It went beyond Leo." Aimee exhaled a mouthful of smoke. "It was a magical trip."

"It was," I agreed. "Thanks, Johnny. You've been really cool."

Johnny blushed. "You gave me something weird to do and say I've done. So thank you."

• • •

I didn't even need to see the cockpit on the flight home—I was exhausted. The cab stopped at my house first.

"What was your favorite thing?" I asked Aimee before shutting the door.

"I love that we never found Leo."

Hours later, I woke up in my own bed, my house still empty. I opened my window and smoked a little pot, noticing how much quieter my city was, my life was.

I looked at my bag at the end of my bed, reached over, and pulled out my phone.

"Hello?"

"Steven? It's me, Kelly."

"You're calling?"

"I know, don't worry. I'm not about to get raped or anything. I just felt like I had to call you and tell you I'm really glad we met and I think we're going to be bona fide friends."

"When are you coming back?"

"I know I will, but I don't know when. Probably when I have a life. Write me a letter, promise?"

"Promise."

THE TERRIBLE
HORRIBLE

Have you ever done something so terrible, so horrible, that you were simultaneously transfixed by your ability to come up with the plan and totally appalled by what you were capable of? Something so terrible horrible that just the thought of it makes your armpits tingle and sweat, and in the middle of the night you wake up just to Google charities to throw money at? This is one of those fantastic and terrible, horrible somethings.

It starts like a Seth Rogen movie. (I'm Seth in this story, because I'm the leader and I love weird voices.) We have a camper van, a crapload of weed, and a Canadian journey. Sounds sweet? Innocent, right? Maybe even ends with a high-five. WRONG. It ends with my actual terrible horrible. Usually when people tell you their terrible horrible, they are lying. Maybe it's their *second-*worst terrible horrible. Maybe they're confusing their terrible horrible with their worst terrible humiliation, like the time they peed their pants in a gas station.

Nope. Not me. This is it: I'm telling you my truest terrible horrible.

Imagine this: There we were, Aimee and me, standing in the middle of an Eastern European woman's oniony kitchen during a lightning storm. We were nineteen. We were stoned. We were looking to buy a camper van. The steam was bubbling from silver cauldrons on the woman's electric stovetop as she secured her bandana on top of her seemingly hairless head. The smell of the soup reminded me of my Ukrainian Baba—only Baba was a cute little lady in 1960s brocade shift dresses and had candy dishes full of those chocolate-like pastel mints in the corners of her rooms. This woman was wearing dirty chinos and had two sweaty middle-aged sons in the corner of her room.

Aimee and I locked bloodshot eyes, and she nodded. I reached out to pass the woman the largest wad of cash I'd ever held.

"Is nine hundred?" She wiped her downy mustache with the back of her left hand and snatched the money with her right. She counted it quickly, then stuffed the cash into her deep cleavage, the kind of cleavage you want to swipe with a debit card. With our exchange complete, we now owned a white Dodge van, complete with a kitchen, a bed, and tiny blacked-out diamond windows in the back—100 percent rapey.

"I hope you enjoy it the way my sons did!" I barely managed to contain a shudder. "My sons are mechanic. They keep in tip-top shape," she continued, tucking her single coil of pubic-thick gray hair back under the bandana.

Thunder rolled through the greasy wallpapered kitchen, leaving vibration rings hanging atop the soup. I should have seen it as an omen warning of the terrible horrible, but I was too mesmerized by her cleavage. She wiped her sweaty red face and began to cut cabbage with a giant cleaver, her long tits swaying back and forth over the yellow-and-brown linoleum. I worried the money would fall out, but then realized it would have a long way to travel in that crevasse.

I glanced over at her sons. They looked like really poor, greasy Guy Ritchies. We'd found the van in an ad in the paper, so based on that alone, I had already decided they were trouble. Aimee thought I was overreacting, but I laid out the math for her: greasy Guy Ritchies + white van with a bed + tinted windows = probably rapists.

"Can we get the keys?"

Her boobs stopped swaying and she looked up at me. I could actually see one of my hundred-dollar bills peeking out, like it was gasping for a final breath before drowning in tits. "Keys are in the van. I had boys clean their stuff out."

I made a mental note to burn some sage in that van to get all of their terrible horribles out.

Aimee and I were two blocks away, still reeking of onions, when we heard a *pop* and steam shot out from under the hood.

"This is unbelievable," I deadpanned. "We just drove away from their house. We had it inspected. This kind of thing doesn't really happen."

Aimee pulled into a gas station. We parked, hopped out of the van, and ran through the downpour into the station to call Baba Knockers back.

"Uh, yeah. I'm, like, two blocks away from your house and the van just broke down . . . Yes . . . Steam from the hood . . . Yes . . . Send one of your sons over, or bring us our money back."

I imagined her arriving and reaching deep between those long tits to fish out our nine sweaty hundreds. Maybe she'd pull out a kitten or a curling iron before she got to the money, like Mary Poppins with her carpetbag. But deep down I knew that money would never escape her magic-carpetbag boobs, that she'd send her creepy old sons over to "help."

• • •

"Just a hose. This will do it. No problem." Erno, the creepiest son, reached under the hood, pulled out a short black hose with a hole in it, and replaced it with a new, holeless hose. Aimee and I stood under the gas station awning, watching him from a safe distance, as the rain poured onto the ground like a rich person's powerful showerhead.

"There, she'll run as good as new." Erno shook his black rain slicker, shut the hood, and turned to us. Then, laughing, he stuck his cigarette in his mouth, grabbed the broken hose, and waved it in front of his crotch at us.

"You were right," Aimee whispered. "Total rapist."

Aimee and I had decided to buy the van on a stoned whim. We'd spent a week drinking mushroom tea and mall walking with psychedelic eyes. We ended the week inside the mouth of a whale statue that sat in the middle of West Edmonton Mall, scaring the children who dared looked inside.

"THE WHALE ATE ME! GET OUT WHILE YOU CAN!" I shouted at one six-year-old who ran away screaming. I turned to Aimee in the echoey darkness of the whale's mouth. Her face was half-Aimee, half-Colonel Sanders. "What are we doing with our lives? I need a sign!"

"Hey!" It was the child's mother. She leaned into the mouth of the metal whale. "What is WRONG with you two?"

"That's what I want to know, lady!"

And then it happened. She threw her newspaper at me—and it opened to a photo of our van. FOR SALE. It was actually glowing, actually surrounded by a halo—maybe just because of the mushrooms—and I knew. That was my sign.

"This is IT," I said to Aimee. "We're supposed to buy. This. Van." I poked at the paper to punctuate every word, rainbow ripples bouncing off the paper and around my new friend, 100 percent full Colonel Sanders face.

We chose Hornby Island as our destination because it sounded like "Horny Island." We pictured ourselves living among artists and other stoner teens, going to an endless string of van parties and beach parties. As it turned out, Hornby was really small, and only a hundred or so people lived there off-season. It wasn't *just* an island either. It was an island off an island off a larger island. All this remoteness helped explain why most of the residents were Vietnam War draft dodgers, convicts-turned-painters, or loggers. Some were all three. There was only one bar/restaurant at the ferry dock, one grocery store, one liquor store, one "corner" store, one outdoor restaurant/café.

We drove the van to the island and spent an entire month sitting on a beach, doing nothing but smoking weed and talking, alone. At this point in our lives, we smoked a joint every few hours. I guess some people would have considered it more of a lifestyle than a habit at that point. I felt stranger being not-stoned than stoned.

I looked around the beach. We were alone again, us and the van. "What are we going to do now?" I asked, as we sat on a blanket in our bikini tops and shorts smoking and eating a bag of baby carrots. "This is more boring than I thought. I wish we were back in the whale's mouth, scaring the crap out of kids." Other than the boredom, we didn't have much to complain about. But we were broke. We'd started with only $250. (Clearly we'd (a) learned nothing from the trip to LA, and (b) still had shitty jobs.) When you're a stoner living at home, $250 is a lot of money—as long as you already have your drugs. By this point, though, we were down to $100 between us.

"Why is this a problem?" Aimee said, putting out a joint.

"Oh, I don't know, maybe because we spent a hundred and fifty bucks in gas to get here, and even if we spent all one hundred dollars we have left on gas we wouldn't make it home?" I rolled onto my stomach to give my back moles a good dose of UV. Free health care is fantastic.

"You're making a decent point." Aimee picked a carrot from the bag. "We *could* get jobs."

I was angry. "Maybe there *was* no sign? Maybe the glowing van in the paper was just me on mushrooms?"

She shook her head. "Whatever. This place is great."

"What do you mean it's great? It's *boring*. There's nobody here." I watched Aimee stare far too intensely at her tiny carrot. "I thought this place was going to be like a Canadian hippie Bali, but instead it's just . . . Canada."

She tossed the carrot into her mouth. And then she grabbed her throat. "EEEEEGGGHHRRR."

I didn't want to move—my left cheek was comfortably ensconced in the warm sand—but Aimee looked like she might be choking to death. "Aimee?"

Her face was turning purple and a tiny bit of white froth had crept from the corner of her mouth. Then again, maybe I was overreacting.

"EEEEEEEEEGGGHHHRRR!"

"OH MY GOD!!" The Heimlich had always seemed violent, so I jumped up and started hitting her in the back.

"DON'T WORRY, AIMEE, YOU'RE MAKING SOUNDS! SOUNDS ARE GOOD—SILENCE IS BAD. TRUST ME. I OVERHEARD SOME NURSING STUDENTS TALKING ABOUT THIS ONCE AT THE SUGAR BOWL. JUST KEEP TRYING TO GET IT UP!!"

The baby carrot shot from her mouth onto the blanket. I got

up and looked at her face. Her skin was still mottled red and purple and her eyes were full of tears.

"Holy shit," she croaked, and rubbed her throat. "I almost died."

I pulled my notebook and Sharpie out of my bag and wrote something. I turned the notebook around and showed her. "RIP AIMEE. Found in a pool of her own urine. Death by baby carrot."

"This is totally what I would have written for your obituary."

She laughed. I pointed at the carrot, covered in bubbly mucus on my side of the blanket.

"That's your side now," I said. "Shove over."

The showerhead stopped spitting lukewarm water onto my head.

"QUARTER!"

Aimee's hand shot into the public shower stall where I stood shivering, trying to warm myself with my wet arms. I grabbed the quarter from her fingers, put it in the slot, and cold water shot down from the showerhead, rinsing the ninety-nine-cent shampoo/conditioner combo out of my hair. There was only one good thing about coin-operated showers: 50 percent of the time, the water was so cold you never spent more money than you should. This is an important concept for people who have found themselves in a life position where they have to use a coin-operated shower.

When my quarter's worth of water stopped, I toweled off in the stall and then got dressed. Aimee hopped in the shower and it was my turn for quarter duty.

"YOU GIRLS USE UP ALL THE HOT WATER?"

In the distance I saw Jake, wearing a backpack and holding a six-pack of Lucky Lager. Jake was a single male logger, but he wasn't a threat to Aimee or me. We'd met him on our first day on the island, and in the month we'd been there he'd never hit on us. Obviously he was gay. A very manly, closeted gay logger.

"QUARTER!" Aimee yelled. I shoved my quarter-clenched fist through the curtain.

"AIMEE? IS IT STILL COLD? JAKE IS HERE AND WANTS TO KNOW IF WE USED ALL THE HOT WATER?"

"WITCH'S TIT!" she replied.

"IT'S COLDER THAN A WITCH'S TIT!" I yelled down the road to Jake.

"Well, sheeeeit," Jake said. He dropped his cigarette and started walking up the hill toward us.

"You girls give me a lift across the island?" he said when he got there. "I want a hot shower, but I want to go to my boy's place over there to get it."

"No," I said, shoulders slumped to let him know I was telling the truth. "We don't have much gas or money left. Only driving up here for showers every three days." We were totally cool with showering every three days; that's how stoned on the reg we were.

Jake stopped and nodded. "I just can't shower in that thing when it's cold."

The shower turned off. "TOWEL!" I passed Aimee her orange-and-yellow towel as Jake pulled a Lucky Lager from the six-pack ring and cracked it open. It was nine A.M. He took a long swig from the can, then stopped.

"What if I give you girls a big bag of weed for a ride over there to my boy's house?"

I didn't need to check with Aimee. "Sure."

Two huge, barking dogs charged the van as we made our way up the road to Jake's boy Kurt's house. They were so close we couldn't see them through the windows. Aimee stopped and turned to Jake.

"Are they going to run under the van?" Aimee asked. "I don't want to hit them."

Jake cleared his throat. "Open your window." He got up on his knees on the van floor between Aimee and me and crushed his empty beer can. "Open the window and sit back." Aimee did as she was told, and Jake whipped the can out the window. "GET IT!" he yelled to the dogs, who were already chasing it into the bush. Jake turned to Aimee and said, "Go!"

Up ahead was a dirty white house surrounded by a makeshift fence made of what looked like ancient monolithic satellite dishes and firewood.

"Here." Jake reached into his backpack and gave us a brown paper bag. Inside was one giant bud of weed, almost as big as my forearm. "It's still a little wet. Just put it on the dash to dry out."

The inside of the house was just as filthy as the outside: the open main floor had stained white walls, a DIY-disaster kitchen, and a muddy dog smell. Jake left us in search of hot water, and I decided I would never need to see the condition of the toilet in this house.

"So dirty," Aimee muttered.

"You want a beer?" some hairy guy offered.

"No thanks," I said, not even knowing which one of the three guys on the couch was Kurt. These loggers were totally socially retarded; even the gay one hadn't made introductions.

"So this is how men live without women," I tried to joke. No response from any of the men, who were watching three different football games on three different TVs.

The dogs came over and started violently sniffing our crotches.

One of the guys turned around and passed me a joint. "Hailey! Stop it!" he snapped at the smelly German shepherd, whose nose I tried to crush with my thighs to fend her off. The dog slunk away.

"Thanks. I think she just committed a felony." I took a long haul off the joint and passed it back to him.

"Kelly, look at that TV!" Aimee pointed. It was Steven, the guy we'd met at the Viper Room six months before. Steven, in a beer commercial. Steven, selling popcorn at a baseball game.

"Holy shit!" I exhaled. "Aimee, this is a sign." I smiled and tapped the back of the La-Z-Boy couch in some weird rhythm, the nerd's official Morse code for happiness. "We're on track."

Aimee nodded and returned my smile. "You're right. What are the odds?"

"Of Steven being in this room with us via television? I don't know. But I do know it's a sign!" And then, like any stoned person encountering an odd event, I started to feel a creeping sense of paranoia. If it was a sign, what did it mean? That we were actually *supposed* to be in some filthy house with a bunch of dogs and loggers? What the hell was that about? The house instantly seemed grosser, the dogs meaner. One of the loggers spit into a beer bottle.

"Let's get out of here," I said.

We drove down to the one café in the middle of the island and sat at a picnic table next to one of the local hippie kids. "A van?" he said. "That's cool. We live in a yurt my dad made in the seventies. I was born in it." This skinny kid looked exactly like Jesus. Not on-the-cross, all-bony-and-bloody Jesus, but young, hot Jesus. I mean, just like seventeen-year-old Jesus, only on this island he had no bros and no whores. Instead, he had the next best thing: Aimee and me.

I sipped my coffee, looking at Young Jesus's sandaled feet. "Do girls ever want to wash your feet because you look like Jesus?"

He shook his head and laughed. "You think you know what Jesus looked like?"

"Jesus was hot," Aimee muttered. "Really hot."

"So you've been here your whole life? On this island?" I asked.

Young Jesus nodded. "I've never left this island."

"You've NEVER LEFT THE ISLAND?!" I shook my head. "That's crazy talk. What's your name, anyhow?"

"I'm Gryphon." Of course he was. "So how long are you here?" he continued. "You guys want to go fishing sometime?"

"Maybe. But we're probably going to leave soon. We're almost out of money and we need to figure something out." I finished off my coffee, ready to go back to the van, plan our next move, and sleep.

Young Jesus Gryphon sat back, stroked his whiskers, and smiled. "You only *think* you need money. You could live here and never need money again. We grow our own food, we trade. My family makes wine."

Aimee's radar went off. "*Red* wine?" She looked at him very seriously. "*Vino tinto?*"

"Yes. It's very good. I actually . . ." He paused and started digging around in his burlap Jesus sack. "I have some right here. You can have it. On the house."

"Oh my God, you know exactly what you're doing," I said. "You sit there, looking like Jesus, and now you're giving us wine? Gryphon. Come on. Where are the loaves?" I wasn't kidding: it had been a while since I smoked that joint, and my munchies alarm was going off. I was *praying* he had some delicious home-made bread in that bag.

Gryphon feigned innocence. "I've never even been inside a church!"

"You invited us *fishing*!" I pressed on accusingly.

"Did Jesus even fish?" he asked, shrugging his shoulders.

"I have no idea. I'm sure he did. They were all living by the river. Seems like he'd be a fisherman."

"Isn't Jesus's symbol a fish?" Aimee muttered again.

Gryphon finally passed Aimee the wine. "Coincidence."

"Niiice!!" She held the bottle up to the sun, examining it like some old Italian vintner. "*Vino tinto!*"

"AIMEE! KELLY!!" It was Jake: wet hair, bag slung over his shoulder, yelling down the street again. "AIMEE! KELLY!! DON'T GO ANYWHERE."

"We have nowhere to go, Jake!" I yelled back. "We live in a van on a tiny island!"

"WELL, YOU LEFT ME, GODDAMIT!!!"

Shit. I looked at Aimee. "Were we supposed to wait for him?"

She shrugged her shoulders. "He didn't say anything about waiting. Were we just supposed to wait for him to shower?"

I hate being an accidental asshole. I don't mind being an outright asshole, but doing it by accident is terrible. Accidentally being an asshole can lead to a snowball effect that cascades into something terrible horrible.

Jake marched up to the table, threw his bag to the ground, and dropped a newspaper on the table. "You didn't tell us to wait," I said meekly. Aimee just ignored him. She spun his paper around on the table and started to read.

"I traded you girls some weed for a ride," he said. "*A ride* means to *and* from."

I tried to make my face look interested. Ninety percent of the time I'm listening to someone is spent wondering if my face looks interested enough.

"HELL, girls, my Lucky Lager is in your van. You drove off

with my beer like a couple of goddamn Jezebel thieves," Jake complained.

"Oh, shit. Sorry." I guess I was an accidental asshole.

"Gryphon, these mainland girls don't know shit about rides." Jake spit and sat down beside me, in the same dirty clothes he was wearing before his shower.

Gryphon patted Jake's hand. "But they do seem to know a lot about Jesus."

"Don't mock me!" I said. "I don't go to church either! This is common knowledge, observational stuff! You look and act like Jesus. THE END. Aimee, let's go. Thanks for the wine, Jesus. Jake, come on, I'll get your beer."

That night, Aimee and I entertained ourselves with an *Archie* comic routine. With no TV and nowhere to go, that had become our one source of fun. I'd brought a Discman with me, and the new Radiohead album, but the batteries were almost dead. So for entertainment, we popped open the roof of our van and used it as a makeshift stage. I'm sure the Eastern European brothers did the same thing.

"I'll meet you at the food court around noon, Ronnie! I have to pick up a gift for my cousin Marty at the electronics store."

"Sure, Betty! See you later. I heard there's an unadvertised sale at Darcy's Department Store!"

"My cousin Marty sure likes video ga— Oh my *God*, Aimee, what are we doing?"

I jumped off the perch and opened the fridge, looking for something to do. "We have water, potato chips, and ketchup."

She climbed down and grabbed the chips. "I totally forgot we had these."

We lay down on the bed and I started squeezing ketchup onto the chips.

"We're, like, really poor. This is weird. I can't live here like Gryphon or the loggers. We need to do something."

Aimee nodded. "We need to get jobs."

I licked the ketchup off a chip. "I didn't even *like* ketchup before I lived in a van. Let's go to Victoria. We'll get off this island and go to the big island and get jobs so we can drive home."

"I don't know," Aimee said, popping a greasy, ketchupy chip in her mouth. "You really want to go home?"

I spread my arms and gestured at the world around us. "Right, and leave all this?"

"I guess." She licked her fingers.

"HEY!"

It was a man's voice, but not Gryphon's and not Jake's. Aimee and I sat straight up, dropping ketchup all over ourselves. It was two A.M.

"OH, LAAAADIES!"

Our van was in a parking lot beside the beach. There was no one around for miles. I suddenly felt that surge of panic, like I was a nineteen-year-old girl stuck in a box in a parking lot on an island off an island off an island off the mainland. We were living the best *Dateline* ever.

"HEY! You girls in there?"

"WHO IS THAT?!" I shouted, almost passing out from the adrenaline rush. And then, like a cartoon character going all flat and sliding down the stairs, Aimee slowly melted off the bed and onto the floor.

"IT'S DANNY AND JOE!"

"Who the fuck are Danny and Joe?" I asked Aimee. They didn't sound friendly.

Aimee lay flat on her back and cried. "You were right. You were right. We *are* going to die. I choked on that carrot and almost died, but I didn't, and now death is chasing after me. Jesus Gryphon *was* a sign!"

"Aimee! Do not do this to me now. Stop it." Aimee never, ever lost her shit. This was bad.

I backed up against the wood-paneled van wall and put my face inside the black diamond window. It was a perfect fit—a tiny bit of magic that momentarily distracted me from my SVU fears. I could barely make out the silhouettes of two men outside, but they were definitely walking away.

I slid down the wall and Aimee hunkered beside me. We listened to the gravel crunching under heavy boots and the sound of the men mumbling in the dark. When it was quiet, Aimee turned to me. "Tomorrow we leave."

As I crouched there on the ground, I spotted Aimee's bag and remembered the wine. "Tomorrow we leave," I said. "But tonight we drink the blood of Jesus until we fall asleep."

I opened her bag. Inside I saw the bottle of wine—and Jake's newspaper. "You STOLE Jake's newspaper?" No wonder death was chasing her.

"There's no way he reads. There's something in there I had to show you."

While she flipped through the paper, I opened the wine and took a swig directly from the bottle, like a hobo.

"They have a program here," Aimee said. "A program for homeless street kids. The Salvation Army sends them home for free."

"Cool. Maybe we should do that. Get flown home for free." And even though I was joking, and even though I could never possibly lie to a charity to get a free flight, I stopped and my eyes locked with Aimee's. Then I laughed. "Oh my God, that would be terrible!" I took another swig of wine.

Then Aimee said, "It would be awful. Truly."

Then we stopped laughing, and after a pathetic beat of silence she said quietly, "Maybe we could do it."

I shook my head. "Aimee, we aren't homeless. We have families!"

"Homeless kids aren't orphans, Kelly. They have families."

"Yeah, but we have families that could buy us tickets home."

"Are you going to ask them to do that?" she asked.

"And disempower myself to them even more than I already have? No. But we can't ask the Salvation Army either."

"Then we need jobs," she said.

I agreed. "Let's leave the island, go to Victoria, and get jobs before Stone Phillips starts narrating the tragic end of our lives."

Gryphon was on the dock as our ferry pushed off. He held his fishing pole with one hand and waved good-bye to us with the other.

"Are you disappointed in us for not staying and living off the land?" I yelled to him.

"NO!" he shouted back. "But I think you are capable of more than you know."

"So are you. We escaped certain death on that island, Jesus. You'll have to get us another time."

"Until next time!" Gryphon said, then looked away thoughtfully and went back to fishing.

I turned to Aimee and passed her a joint. "Did you hear that? *Until next time.* He's talking about Heaven, Aimee."

At the first gas station into Victoria, we sat down on a curb and checked the classified ads for jobs.

"We should be waitresses at a bar. That's the easiest way

for girls like us to make quick money without taking off our clothes."

A clean-cut guy walked across the parking lot toward us. He looked like a grad student. Those could be dangerous.

"Hey, is this a Dodge camper van?" he asked, all jocular, pointing with his fingers in the shape of a gun.

"Yeah," Aimee responded.

"Some people are only into Volkswagens, but I've always been more meat and potatoes."

"Yeah, Dodge is the meat and potatoes of vehicles."

He stood back and put his hands in his pockets. "You even have the tinted diamond windows? Do you want to sell it? I'll give you eight hundred dollars for it."

Aimee and I both stood up. I hadn't realized it from the curb, but he was really tiny. Like a less-lovable Alex P. Keaton.

"Are you kidding?" I asked.

"I'm dead serious."

I shot a look at Aimee. "Hold on. I need to talk to my friend for a second."

Aimee and I walked around the back of the van to be alone.

"When did we decide to sell the van, Kelly?"

"We didn't," I said. "But this is a sure sign we should. This guy came out of nowhere and wants to buy it. Don't you see, Aimee? We won't have to be waitresses!"

Aimee took a deep breath. "I guess if we're going to end it anyhow, it's kind of the perfect way to do it."

I was so relieved.

"Yes! It is kinda sad. I mean, this was our home. It was, like, the first thing I ever bought myself that I couldn't smoke."

Napoleon came around the back of the van. "Okay, fine. I'll give you a thousand bucks. But that's the most I can offer."

I grabbed his miniaturized hand in my miniaturized hand. "Deal."

I had a thousand dollars, a duffel bag of clothes, my Discman, and an *Archie* comic as I watched our van drive away.

"I pray to God we didn't just enable a date rapist."

Aimee turned to me. "That isn't funny."

"It wasn't supposed to be funny, I was being earnest. I left the weed with him too."

"Kelly! You IDIOT!"

"Aimee, weed always finds us, remember? That's our rule. Besides, we can't exactly take it with us to the airport."

"Kelly." Aimee grabbed my shoulders and looked me in the eye like she was a hockey coach. "We should totally tell the Salvation Army we're street kids and get a free flight home!"

Diabolical.

"NO!" I looked up at the storm clouds that were rolling in and realized that we were all alone. We had nowhere to go, and no way to get there without the van.

"However," I said, breaking the silence. "We ARE homeless without the van."

Aimee nodded. "Good. Good! This is good!"

"I mean," I continued, lowering my voice in case some Salvation Army employee with superior hearing was lurking nearby, "we did just lose our home."

"We didn't lose it. We sold the van, Kel. We have money."

I nodded. "I have almost as much money now as I did before the trip."

We sat in silence for a moment again, and then it was punctuated by a single clap of thunder. My thoughts were racing, and I could not believe what I was about to say, but I was fascinated with my own mind at that moment. Terrible.

"However," I said, leaning in again, "if we didn't have the money, we'd be homeless *and* broke—and we'd actually fit the profile for needing a free flight home." Horrible.

Aimee returned my lean. Our foreheads were almost touching, right there on Douglas Street. "What do you mean, 'if we didn't have the money'?"

I can't speak for Aimee, but as I passed the Club Monaco cashier $489 for a dress and a coat, I knew this was my terrible horrible. And yet I couldn't stop myself. It was the perfect plan. I was now penniless and homeless and ready to take my free flight home.

"Your blouses are gorgeous," I said to Aimee as we left the mall. We walked in and out of Value Village with our haul of mismatched clothing, all of it baggy. Our mission was "hobo," not "hobo chic": we needed to look homeless.

A block away from the Salvation Army, Aimee and I stopped inside a bus shelter and started layering the Value Village clothing on top of our own. I pulled on two sweaters and a pair of filthy training sneakers, and put my white Chuck Taylors in the Value Village bag. Aimee pulled on a pair of ugly old-man brown pants.

"Hold up," I said, and reached for her pocket. "There's something in there." I grabbed the white thing sticking out of her pocket and pulled it out to reveal its true nature: little girl's panties.

"*AHHHHHH!!!*" I screamed at the top of my lungs, dancing around in disgust. I did three hours' worth of voguing in less than twenty seconds. "LITTLE GIRL'S PANTIES IN YOUR OLD-MAN PANTS!"

"Throw them in the garbage," Aimee ordered, so coolly and matter-of-factly, like she was James Bond all of a sudden. "Let's just do this."

And then I caught him out of the corner of my eye, walking down the street.

It was Jesus.

"Aimee," I hissed. "Aiiiiiimeeee!"

She dropped her swagger for just a second, looked around, and saw what I was looking at.

"It's Gryphon!" she said. "He left the island."

My blood ran cold. "I told him he'd have to get us another time. Has he come for our souls? Oh GOD, Aimee. We can't go through with this!"

"If he's Jesus, then he already knows and he's forgiven us."

"He did like to hang out with beggars and thieves, right?"

"Yes."

"You're right. I'm actually kinda proud of him for leaving the island."

I collected myself and pushed the awful truths—that Aimee was wearing pedophile pants, that Jesus knew we were liars—to the far recesses of my brain as we walked toward the Salvation Army wearing dirty clothing from Value Village. My heart was pounding out of my chest. I tried to distract myself by focusing on the chances of catching a disease from the mothball-scented sweater I was wearing.

Then I saw an actual street kid with a dog and something occurred to me. "Aimee." I stopped. "Aimee, let's borrow that dog. We'll look more legit." I gave the kid five dollars and in exchange got ourselves one last prop—a dog on a rope.

Aimee must have seen the guilt on my face. Just before we entered the building, she stopped.

"Besides cab money, do we have money?"

I shook my head.

"Do we have a home?"

I shook my head.

"Do we want to go home?"

I nodded.

"Do we have some other way to get home that doesn't involve telling our parents we're morons and letting them lord this over us for the rest of our lives?"

I shook my head.

Aimee nodded and opened the door. "You do the talking."

"Hi." I was trying to look very, very homeless. Homeless and maybe even drug-addicted. I slumped my shoulders and pulled at my gross sweater.

"Hello!" The Salvation Army greeter almost squealed with excitement. Clearly a do-gooder thrilled to help the impoverished. "Your dog is adorable. What's his name?" The guy was skinny, blond, and well-dressed. I was mortified.

"Uh"—I started picking at my nails—"Sandy. His name is Sandy. That's right." I scratched my hair and faked a nervous tic. I watched his smile get nervous and I liked it. He tried to make the liberal "Don't worry, I think you're just like me" face. "Sooo . . . we heard you guys did this free-trip-home thing?"

He nodded and pulled a giant black binder out from under the counter. "Good choice, girls. Going home is the best choice. Getting help! I always tell people, 'You have to want it!'"

"Yeah." I reached down to pet the dog and some tiny bug on it bit me. "We want it."

He handed us a pair of forms. "Just fill these out." They weren't really detailed: name, age, reason for travel, destination address, Social Insurance Number.

Social Insurance Number?

"Hey, this isn't going to go on any sort of permanent record, is it? Like some government record future employers can access? Why do we have to give our Social Insurance Number?"

"It's just to make sure we're sending you to your actual home. Don't worry, we don't keep any of the info."

We gave the sheets back to him and he retreated to an office for a few minutes. When he returned, he was holding ticket vouchers in his hand.

"You have the tickets HERE?!" I was shocked. This was organization at its finest—and for hobos, no less.

"Yes, we do. It's a pretty streamlined program. I've given the airline your info. You can head down to the airport right now."

It was raining. With no umbrellas, Aimee and I dragged our bags across the tarmac to the airplane and climbed the slippery stairs up to the plane. It was Halloween, so the flight attendant at the top of the stairs was dressed like Freddy Krueger, and the pilot waved us aboard in a *Scream* mask. We plopped down in our seats wearing our beautiful new, wet Club Monaco clothes.

"This is definitely the plane we crash in." I sighed. "I can't believe the crew dressed up."

"I can't believe we told the airline people we were dressed as schoolteachers for Halloween."

I stuffed a bag under the seat in front of me. "If I eventually do die in a plane crash, and it isn't this one, I'll be really pissed off."

I pulled out Radiohead's *OK Computer* and loaded it into my Discman, determined to run the little power left in the batteries dead. I put my ear buds in and turned on "Paranoid Android."

As we taxied through the darkness in the rain, I looked around the cabin. The overhead lights only highlighted the fact that we were in a metal tube. A baby a couple of rows ahead stood up and faced me, face purple from screaming. I waved and made a silly face, but he kept screaming. What an asshole. I looked back at Freddy Krueger the flight attendant, showing us how to do up our seat belts. There he was, doing all the hand motions in a fucking Freddy Krueger mask to the Radiohead sound track in my ears. Aimee had already fallen asleep against her window. I shut my eyes, listened to the music, and relaxed as the plane started moving. I opened my eyes again and watched the rain passing through the flashing lights on the wing of the plane. I thought about when Aimee almost choked to death on the beach. I thought about Jake and Gryphon. I thought about our meat-and-potatoes van and the curse it probably carried and would continue to carry. And I thought about the Salvation Army. Then we sped up and took off into the sky, and I took my terrible horrible with me.

HOW I MET YOUR FATHER:
WHEN THE CHILDREN ASK, THIS IS WHAT I WILL HAVE TO TELL THEM

As I'm scowling at my reflection in the point-of-sale screen at the diner, Dave the manager says, "You look fucking hot."

The day before, I had all my hair cut off. It's a very, very short haircut, and I'm still in a state of shock. I'm feeling less Jean Seberg or Audrey Hepburn and more Michael Jackson.

"Kelly, I have the perfect guy for you!" Dave says.

"I don't know." I sigh and touch the inch-long strands on the back of my head. I fake-smile at myself in the screen, just to see what happiness with this haircut would look like. "Will he care that I look like a white Wilmer Valderrama?"

"Kelly, I want to date you, but since I can't, I want my friend James to date you. Someone needs to date you."

I nod. "Fine."

I'm making someone a cappuccino when a guy comes up to the diner counter.

"Can you pass me a spoon, please?"

I look in his general direction but don't really focus on his face, because I don't give a shit. I'm making a fucking cappuccino. "Uh, no," I say. "I can't." Just to let him know he's interrupting my grind-tamping rhythm. But because I'm only 50 percent asshole, after a second I take two steps to the cutlery, grab him a spoon, and turn around. And he's gone.

That was your father.

Your father asked for a spoon to get "a better look at me," which he confesses later that night. He was tall and had nice eyes, very boyish looking, which I liked.

"A better look at me"? I find myself weirdly flattered to hear this news.

"I'm sorry I was short with you about the spoon," I say, sipping the ice cream float I made for myself. "I consider myself a deeply disturbed girl these days, and I was recklessly and rudely sarcastic to you."

He shrugs. "You *were* kind of a bitch."

"I have no other option," I say, leaning my head back a little, trying to make my hair appear longer. "I work in a diner to stay alive."

"When I finished school, I worked in the Middle East for a year to pay off my student loans. I'm not trying to one-up you, but I'm pretty sure that's worse than this diner."

Nothing he says can faze me. "I have nothing. I have no hair. I'm not even allowed to have a cat in my studio apartment."

We're both depressed and lonely and it's love at first sight.

At home later I check my messages. My fuck buddy called.

"I heard you were with some guy at the diner tonight."

And that was the end of my fuck buddy. Kids, I'll explain that another time.

• • •

"Can we get really, really, really drunk together tonight? I feel like we'd be good at that." I ask your father this over the phone at 9:30 A.M., and by 9:30 P.M. we're sitting in a downtown pub, really, really drunk.

"I like hockey. But I hate the way hockey players talk."

"Me too. The worst."

"On *Oprah*, this woman said she was so upset because her husband called her a bitch a year into their relationship. I was like, *It took a whole year??* You called me a bitch yesterday, and that was the first time we met."

"But you *are* a bitch."

"And she wasn't?"

"Probably not, if it took him a year to say it and she got so upset that she was talking about it on TV. Probably not."

"I hate people."

"I hate people."

"Can we go to a park and have sex?"

We pull into the parking lot of the park and start kissing in the car.

"It's too cramped in here," I say, breathing heavily between kisses. "Let's get out."

I open my door and stumble around to the patch of grass in front of the car, sit down, then lay flat on my back in my peacoat. Waiting to be taken. I'm so drunk. I never have sex with strangers. Ever. I can't even focus my eyes. All I can do is lie there thinking about how bad I am. I am *sooooo* bad. I am a desirable woman.

"WHAT ARE YOU DOING?" I shout.

"Looking for a condom."

"I have a ton!" Really, I don't have sex with strangers. But I always carry condoms, because they fill my purse with the feeling of potential.

He comes around and stands above me, taking off his pants. I start to shimmy out of mine. I'm not trying to be sexy; no need for seduction under these circumstances. He lies down on top of me and a physical heat wave explodes through my skin to my core. This is followed by a squeak of a giggle, because he has the biggest . . .

"FAGGOTS!"

Wait, what?

"COCKSUCKERS! YOU FUCKING GODDAMN ASSHOLE-EATING MOTHER-FUCKING COCKSUCK-ERS!"

"Hold on. What the fuck is that?" I say to your father, not even whispering. I'm suddenly sober.

"It's my cock, babe," your father says, clearly still in the zone.

Though I'm not sure how, because—

"YOU FUCKING BUTTHOLE FUCKING FAAAA-AAAAAAAGGGGGS!"

I look up and a group of guys are screaming at us from a truck, twenty feet away.

"No," I say when it hits me. "Is this a gay pickup park?"

Then something else hits me. A rock.

The guys in the truck are throwing rocks at us.

Your father doesn't even notice. He's too far down the rabbit hole. Until—"What the fuck?"—a rock hits your father in the head.

"Oh my God." I wince. Back to whispering: "We're being gay-bashed because of my haircut."

I don't even think about the hate crime in progress. At this point I'm so angry at my hair, the hate crime seems loathsome but inconsequential. This stoning won't last two years, but that's exactly how long it's going to take before I stop looking like Matt LeBlanc.

Your father sits up and the truck drives away. I pull my pants up.

"Oh my God. This is some kind of gay park?" he asks me.

"I think they saw my hair."

A look of shock washes over his face. "They thought you were a guy?!"

I nod and light a cigarette. I'm, like, three minutes ahead of him.

He says, "We were gay-bashed for having straight sex. This is amazing."

"No, it isn't," I whine. "I shouldn't have cut my hair."

Your father helps me up and we walk back to the truck, matching black peacoats and dark hair.

"They thought I was a tiny gay man," I lament. "A bottom too."

Your father stops me from walking and holds my face in his hands. "You are so beautiful," he says. "You are the hottest chick ever. I've never been this hot for anyone." We kiss, and then he holds me, and I look over his shoulder at my reflection in his car's window and I see myself smiling with my stupid short haircut. That's what happiness with this haircut looks like.

And that's how I met your father.

LIFE WITH
HARVEY

"So, later this week you need to pick up my new Grand Cherokee and get rid of this weapons charge. It's bullshit! I'm allowed
to carry hunting arrows wherever I want. On set, in the mall,
wherever. Call Paul Zuker, my lawyer. He's in my address book,
under *L* for *lawyer*."

My boss, Harvey, sits beside me in the passenger-side seat of
his Land Rover. While I drive, he casually looks out the window
tapping the beat of Queen's "I Want to Break Free" with his
toothpick. Harvey is a TV producer. He dyes his hair black,
wears a plain black baseball cap, black T-shirt, black jeans, and
black shoes *at all times*. He has murdery ice-blue eyes; I think his
entire black costume is designed to accentuate those eyes. Some
people just naturally look suspicious, but Harvey seems to try to
make himself look suspicious on purpose. Like if *Saturday Night
Live* were costuming a "casual murderer" character and came
out with Harvey, people would say, "Whoa! Laying the murdery
vibe on a little thick, don't you think?"

"You've got him filed under *L*?" I ask. "Under *lawyer*?" I
always have to check his directions, which makes it sound like

I'm terrible at my job, when the reality is that my boss, Harvey, is kinda fucking crazy. I am called an "assistant." I make two hundred dollars a day, straight pay, to do things like picking up toothpicks or getting a plate of food on set that has never been touched by tin foil. This is a much more voyeuristically satisfying job than barista or video store clerk. My boss just wanders around the set all day, watching people work, so I get to do that too. Until I figure out where I belong—and I definitely feel like a film set is my place—this will do. I hope I belong somewhere.

"Yeah. *L*," he says, jamming the end of the toothpick in his mouth. A certain type of person uses a toothpick, stores it behind his ear. It really has less to do with oral care than with sending a visual cue to let you know they'll go 100 percent cowboy on you if provoked. "Also, I need to pick up some new arrows. Can you make sure you write this down when we stop, Kelly? *Arrows*."

"The police didn't give back your other arrows, like you thought they would?"

"Nope. They sure as hell didn't. That girl from the Gap got them all riled up! I have every right to carry my arrows in there. Why? Because I didn't have a goddamn bow. Such horseshit. Suuuuuch yuppie Gap horseshit. You know what I did, Kelly?"

"You brought hunting arrows into the Gap."

"Yes. But you know what I really did?"

I don't guess. I just look at the time on the clock: we're late. If I shut up he'll get through his speech faster.

"What I did, after all that yuppie Gap horseshit?" Harvey claps his hands together loudly. His eyes are darting as he adjusts himself in his seat. "I threw out all my favorite black Gap tees because I couldn't look at them anymore."

"Boom," I say. "For real, Harvey."

"What?" Confused, he puts the toothpick behind his ear and

momentarily stops fidgeting, locking eyes with me. Those murdery eyes with nothing behind them.

"Never mind, Harvey."

I've been with Harvey for a few weeks. He's a nice guy. I organize the time he has with his son. I drive him around. I answer his cell phone while we walk together. I order his food; he chooses good restaurants, which helps. And I take notes on everything he says. He's eccentric. Which to me means crazy . . . but with money.

I acquired the assistant position with Harvey while I was living up north near the Yukon with James. He was doing some environmental work up there and I decided to join him. Not to do environmental work, but just to hang out after getting fired from the diner. (Why? Long story, but let's say I got fired for switching shifts so that I could have weekends with him.)

"This is dumb," I told James over the phone. "Why am I looking for a dumb job down here, when I could get a dumb job up there and save money on rent by living with you? I don't need to be here to work in a diner and write. I can work there in a diner and write, right?"

"I'd love it. But it's a shithole up here, Kelly."

"Please, tell me all about it," I said, muting the *Felicity* marathon on my precious nineteen-inch TV and sitting down on my musty old LSD-patterned carpet.

He launched right into it. "First, I want you here. Second, this place starts with a 'Fort.' Any town that begins with 'Fort' is guaranteed to be a shithole. We're in the middle of the highway. It's a pit stop to nowhere. If you don't own a giant truck here, you're no one. *And* I just saw a golden eagle on the side of the road eating a moose asshole."

"Babe," I said, staring at desperate-faced Felicity on my TV screen. (I feel no bond to her and her collegiate whining. I never had a dorm room; I did the short haircut before she did. I'm a take-charge girl.) "I'm sitting here unemployed, eating a burrito on the floor of my rental, which is a converted suite in the garage of a Polish couple's house. I'm cool with shitholes. I'll be there next week."

On my first night near the Yukon, we met up for dinner with some local hotshots at a weathered Outback Steakhouse. We wedged ourselves into a threadbare booth with the couple, who looked like Loni Anderson and Burt Reynolds.

James and Loni exchanged a bit of small talk, while I sat mesmerized by Burt's furry upper lip. His luxurious mustache reached out to embrace his nose hairs to form a nose/lip carpet of impressive proportions. I guessed he had to be at least 60 percent Greek. All of a sudden the carpet spoke.

"There were a couple of grizzlies playing with a bale of hay in my yard," Burt said, fondling the edges of his lip hair. "They were tossin' it up and throwing it back and forth like it was a ball or something."

"Wow." I wrestled my gaze up to his eyes. "That's really so cool that you saw that."

Burt turned to me like he hadn't noticed me at all before that moment. It was as if I'd just sat down at the table and I hadn't been sitting there through our bloomin' onion or potato skin appetizers.

"Actually," he said, leaning across the table, "the last thing it was was *cool*."

I gasped, almost audibly. He mocked my *cool*. God, that was mean.

James put his hand on my thigh to steady me. "So, what did you do?" he asked Burt.

"I fucking shot them. I just opened up the window and shot 'em. *Boom!*" Oh, he was mean. Not just harsh mean, but might-just-shoot-me-dead-right-there-at-the-table mean. I sat back in my seat, squinting in confusion at the spectacle.

James leaned forward. "What did you do with them after you shot them?"

"I left them there. Then the coyotes came, and I fucking shot them too."

What? I sat back in the booth, squinting even harder.

Burt stopped rubbing his mustache to emphasize the severity of his own personal martial law. Loni nodded to me, letting me know that Burt spoke the truth. I was horrified.

Steeling myself, I unclenched my hand from James's knee, leaned forward, and peeled a piece of the bloomin' onion off with my bare hands. I wanted Burt and Loni to see I could be a bit of a savage myself.

Loni twirled her Chardonnay. "Well, our neighbor's dog kept coming over, so I shot it."

I laughed. Loni and Burt both gave me a stern look. My arm hung in midair, hand squeezing the oil from the onion.

"You didn't *seriously* kill all those animals?"

Loni sipped her white-lady wine, looking at me over the brim of her glass. After a long pause she said, low and slow, "It was an annoying dog."

The next day I was on the couch watching *Rosie* at two thirty in the afternoon. The sun had just set as James rushed into our little apartment, out of breath.

"So I was out in the field today to check up on some excavation with Burt and Burt pulls up in his truck and he's like, 'Hold on a second, I need you to help me,' and he pulls off into the bush. I follow him and when I get to the back he had fucking *dead coyotes* in the bed of the truck and I had to help him throw them into the bush and pretend I didn't give a fuck!"

I muted O'Donnell and faced him. He was half-laughing, half in shock. I was confused.

"What? Coyotes in the back of the truck?"

"He had a whole bunch of dead coyotes in the back of the truck."

"Oh my God," I whispered.

"And he didn't tell me and he pulled over, all, 'I need you to help me,' and he fucking opened the tailgate and there's all these dead coyotes and I had to throw them in the bush!"

"Oh. My. God."

"I know. Then he starts asking about you as I am throwing dead coyotes into the bush. What do you do? Do you have a job here? And my head is just spinning because I've got dead coyote paws in my hands and we're talking about something *totally normal*. It was a weird and abrupt change in conversation, to go from dead animals to you. So I tell him you do odd jobs, but you're a writer and want to be a screenwriter, and he says he has a friend who works on a TV series in Vancouver who needs an assistant."

"Burt has a friend in entertainment? What kind of entertainment? Rodeo?"

"The guy hunted with him or something. Anyhow, he wants you to meet him."

"Cool. Way cooler than throwing dead animals into the bush."

"Do you want to move to Vancouver?'

I did. I left James up north, we went back to our weekend rendezvous, and I headed down to Vancouver to meet Burt's friend, Harvey.

"Come on," Harvey says. "Someone's got to write this shit down. This shit is brilliant."

"Okay." We're sitting in Harvey's Land Rover outside of a television executive's office building. Harvey's meeting started inside ten minutes ago.

"Picture a movie about a man who loses his leg to cancer, and then he finds out his arms are really strong; he has long arm muscles or something—longer than most arm muscles . . . He's much stronger than he thought, and he becomes a wheelchair racer. That'll get viewers going."

Okay.

"Also? I was thinking about a story about an orphanage in Germany that sells kids to China. Everyone still hates those motherfuckers. You writing this down?"

I add it to my list, which now looks like this:

TO DO

1. Pick up new Grand Cherokee
2. Call Paul Zuker the *L* lawyer, weapons charge
3. New arrows to kill things, or shoot at plastic deer

STORY IDEAS

1. Leg cancer/mutant strong arm hero wheelchair man
2. Bad German baby sellers to China

After I've finished my notes, we walk into the building, fifteen minutes late. I pretend I'm writing things down in my notebook and take my spot in the corner of the conference room, scanning the crowd. Harvey always takes me into meetings, to show off, but I actually love getting to see all the different aspects of television-making, like how these execs like to sit around and talk about nothing. He sits down across from Lois, an executive for a big-name cable company. Lois wears her hair tight and dark blond. She's about fifty, and her skirts are always slit up the middle. From the front, when her legs are together in the hole of the skirt, her bottom half looks like a giant naked vagina. She looks vaguely pleased. "Harvey, the show came in second last Sunday."

"Second? We came in second? Okay, second is pretty good." Harvey pulls a new toothpick from his shirt pocket and nods to me. The nod means nothing. It's just a thing he does to make himself look more important. I nod back and try to look busy. This is basically my first paid acting gig.

"Yes, well, you came in second to *The Sopranos*, so . . ." She laughs. The whole room laughs. I laugh too, and I'm shocked to realize I'm actually proud of Harvey. He is the executive producer of a TV show that came *second* in the ratings—after THE SOPRANOS.

Harvey says nothing, looks at me, looks at Lois. "What the fuck is *The Sopranos*?"

After the studio, Harvey tells me we have an important meeting and directs me to a house in West Vancouver. We pull up to the garage of a house that is perched on the side of a hill. It doesn't look like the right spot for an important meeting, but I sit in the driver's seat as Harvey opens his door and gets out of the Land Rover. "Don't look out the back window," he says. "I need to change."

Two minutes later, Harvey comes around my side of the car with his arms outstretched, like a mini Elton John displaying his outfit before his birthday party. He is now wearing a full Ferrari-red car-racing jumpsuit. Like a mechanic. His eyes look much less murdery and piercing than before, but they are still very, very sparkly.

"Let's roll," he says.

He knocks three times and the garage door slowly opens to reveal a tiny, old Italian-looking man. (Dark hair, olive skin, spoke fluent Italian. He was at least 300 percent Italian.) Mr. Italy is also wearing a Ferrari jumpsuit, similar to Harvey's but definitely not more expensive.

"Heeeeeey!" says the old man, stretching his arms out to Harvey. They punch each other on the back mid-hug to remind themselves of how masculine they really are in their matching red jammies. The garage is walled with mirrors. And right in the middle sits a Ferrari. It was like a ballet studio, only instead of a ballerina there was a car.

Our important meeting was just Harvey getting in a jumpsuit to talk to his mechanic about his Ferrari for half an hour.

"Kelly, you see this??" Harvey points inside the hood, not really caring if I see anything.

"Yeah, I see it." I raise my hand and point vaguely toward the car, as if I've spotted something under the hood.

Harvey looks satisfied. "What a life!" he says with a smile.

My job is to do everything Harvey is too lazy to do for himself. On set that afternoon, I do what I spend most of my on-set days doing: nothing. I roam around the huge fake Yukon town outside Vancouver waiting for him to ask me to find his keys, or just call me in to listen to him talk about the time he dated Liz Hurley. I eat a lot of craft service (mostly maple-dipped doughnuts). When I'm not doing that, I walk down to the stream and throw rocks into it. As much as I love to see Harvey praised for playing runner-up to *The Sopranos*, I would not want his version of his job.

When the boredom threatens to break me, I decide to visit Heather, the young female lead, in her room.

"Want to play Tetris?" I ask her. We play a lot of simultaneous Tetris while I pick her brain. Maybe I could learn to memorize lines. Actors really do make a lot of money per minute of actual work.

"Acting on camera is easy, right? I'm pretty sure I could do it." We're sitting across from each other on her stiff chairs, staring at our Game Boys, our feet on the table.

"Oh, you could totally do it. You know, I get these massive panic attacks, and I do it every day. It isn't that big a deal at all. You just have to look natural when you say the lines."

"You get panic attacks?" I peer over my Game Boy. Her round dollface betrays not a ripple of reaction.

She sighs. "I went to a club last night and froze. I panicked from all of the people. I peed my pants a little. Okay, a lot. But it was dark."

"I get the pee thing. I get it. Doesn't the acting freak you out?"

"No."

"And it's good money."

"Great money, bad hours. But the hours are worth the money."

I liked the idea of acting. I liked the idea of a lot of things.

"Harvey told me you're a writer," she says. "Have you written a screenplay or something?"

I look up from the Game Boy and we make eye contact.

"Have you heard of Robert McKee?" I ask her. She shakes her curls no and reaches for her Master Cleanse cayenne juice, staring at me as she takes a gulp. I look up at the ceiling for effect, as if I'm collecting many important thoughts. "He's this big-time script doctor guy who does these traveling seminars about how to write a screenplay. Like the math of a screenplay? I went to his seminar and smoked cigarettes with him a lot. He had some good stuff to say."

"Did you write a script?"

I sigh and look at her. "I have nothing to say yet. I tried. I don't have a story. I'm just putting these little stories on the Internet on my GeoCities page." I didn't know how I was going to become a writer, professionally. At this point, I figured self-publishing was better than rejection letters. And I figured they'd all be rejection letters, because I didn't go to university.

"What's a GeoCities?" She looks confused, and I don't feel like explaining the Internet.

"Whatever. I'll write a screenplay one day." We both sit there in silence, and then I start my game back up.

"Are you still living in the Travelodge with the rest of the crew? Is it okay?" she asks. I lie and nod yes. It's actually very boring and I'm very lonely. Last night I wrote about how I'm sure Britney Spears could be cognitively challenged and no one would know, because she wasn't in the regular school system (to post the next day from work, where I had Internet access); I made a sandwich on my new sandwich grill, which I set up beside the bed; and then I watched the first episode of *Malcolm in the Middle*. When it was over, I waited in the hall for someone to come out to talk to. It took five minutes, but finally a PA came out and he happened to have just watched the same show. We both agreed it was a great pilot, and then I went to bed. Just as glamorous as I'd hoped.

"It's great," I say, smiling at my reflection in the Game Boy screen. "I have a maid and I make a thousand bucks a week. Couldn't ask for more."

Midafternoon. I carry Harvey's grilled vegetables and meatballs into the field, where he is shooting arrows at a plastic deer. He usually gets a PA to remove the arrows and reposition the dummy deer. He says he couldn't bear to accidentally shoot an arrow into a woman. I've pulled a table and a few chairs for him out there, as a makeshift office in a field—which is great today, because Harvey isn't alone.

"Kelly!" Harvey slaps his thigh and puts his bow and arrows on his desk. He's standing with a man I've never seen before, a man who looks like a sixty-year-old red-haired Kevin Kline.

"This is Bryan. He wrote the episode we're shooting. Kelly's Jewish."

I shake the writer's hand. "I'm not Jewish," I mutter to Harvey. I don't think I'm even 5 percent Jewish.

"Harvey tells me you're a screenwriter." I want to die. He's telling screenwriters I'm a screenwriter? Instead of dying, I pass Harvey his food and cutlery.

"Oh. Well, no. I mean, I write, but I haven't written a script yet." Please stop asking me questions about me. I don't know what I'm doing yet! I'm the arrow shooter's assistant.

Bryan furrows his red brow, and I spot little dandruff flakes there. "Are you going to film school?" he asks.

Oh God. I involuntarily roll forward onto my toes, clasping my hands together. I realize I'm trying to appear larger, like some sort of animal tactic, to stop myself from feeling so small and unsuccessful. This instant realization only makes my subsequent facial expressions and movements more awkward to complete.

"No." I pull my mouth to the side and slam my heels back into the soft ground. "I'm not going to film school."

Bryan nods, then sweeps his arm dramatically in the air. "It was raining when I left Los Angeles this morning. It isn't raining here. Odd, since it's usually the other way around."

I look over at Harvey to make sure he has everything he needs for lunch, hoping I've forgotten something so I can leave. Bryan continues the dramatics in a gray suit that's straight out of 1986. Of all the three hundred or more people here, he's the only one wearing a suit. It's like he's forgotten he's writing for a show set in the 1800s and shot in the middle of nowhere on a small western boomtown set. Instead he's dressed like a rich guy from *Down and Out in Beverly Hills.*

"The rain was so beautiful in the Pacific Palisades. Have you been to the Pacific Palisades, Kelly?" The sound of my name forces me to look away from the flakes on his shoulders and back to his face. Bryan gently bats a fly away from his head.

"No, I haven't. I've been to LA. But I haven't been . . ."

"*Oh!*" He clutches his chest and puts on his Ray-Bans, leaning onto Harvey's makeshift desk. I look down at Harvey; he has an entire meatball in his mouth. "OH, IT'S DIVINE!" Bryan continues. "The mist, the smell, driving my car through the winding hills with the green, slick, lush forests passing me by . . . Heavenly."

An indifferent-looking PA comes over the ridge of the hill. "Bryan, I'm ready to take you down to the set."

"WONDERFUL!" Bryan shouts, stepping away from the desk and leaning so close to me I fear I may inhale his shoulder flakes. "I hope to see you both later at the Sutton," he whispers. "And you must see the Palisades in the rain, Kelly. You must." He wags a finger at me and walks backward toward the PA, who is mouthing, "*Kill me,*" at me over Bryan's shoulder. I watch them walk across the field and then look down at the bow and arrow at my fingertips, wondering if I could.

As they disappear beneath the ridge, I turn back to Harvey. "Harvey, that guy was so LA."

Harvey grabs a napkin and wipes a lather of grease and sauce from his meatball-filled face. A crumble of ground beef drops from his mouth. "Hey, I'm LA too!" he says.

It's raining again. It's five in the afternoon. Every day at five o'clock, Harvey plays life-sized chess in a West Vancouver mall with the Persians. He's never late for this. The Persians are all at least fifty. They do not make eye contact with me. They offer me their seats. They are polite and soft-spoken, wearing modest robes and headdresses that are the antithesis of Harvey's black uniform. I was embarrassed at first to loiter around a large group of men in the middle of a mall, straddling chess pieces as they moved them around a painted floor. But now I just pretend they're all handicapped people and I'm the charge nurse keeping them safe. I wait for calls on Harvey's cell phone. I stare at mall people. I kill time.

"Hey, Kel," he shouts to get my attention. The sound echoes through the marble mall as he stands between a giant bishop and an eighty-year-old Iranian in a light-blue robe. "There's no way we're the only Jews in here, right?"

"I'm not Jewish," I mutter. "Harvey, we have to leave now if we want to get over the bridge and to the Sutton Place for drinks."

Harvey claps his smallish hands together and points at the old Iranian. "I'll get your queen tomorrow!"

"Harvey, why do you like hunting so much?" I ask as we hit traffic on the bridge. "I mean, do you eat the meat?"

"What are you?" he asks, digging away at his teeth with a toothpick. "Some animal activist?"

"Well, no. But if I weren't so selfish and lazy, I would be an activist for something."

"Oh, *something*." He chuckles.

"Yeah, probably hungry or homeless kids or the elderly. Something, though. Not animals. Maslow's hierarchy stuff. I'd start at the bottom."

Harvey tucks the toothpick behind his ear. "Huh?"

"Never mind. Do you think I should act or write?"

"Act. Hands down. More money. Get on the screen."

"But I want to write."

"Then why the shit are you asking?"

Harvey knows big people. He takes me for drinks with a couple of directors, Michael and Christopher, and of course dandered Bryan. I take fake notes for Harvey. They talk about actors: Milla Jovovich (very easily directed), Benicio Del Toro (a genius).

Michael asks if I'm an actor.

"Yes. Well, I *can* act. I've been trained. At the Citadel Theatre school when I was a child." Dear God, shut up. *Trained?* Please stop asking me questions about myself.

"Any film?"

"No."

"Did Harvey find you in film school?"

"She's not in film school," Bryan says, pinching his eyes closed for effect and putting his drink back on the table. His hand twirls out, palm up. His fingers flitter as he speaks, like he's typing in the air. Bryan is my favorite.

"So you're an enigma! You're cute, you can act, but you don't?" Christopher says, grinning to himself.

"She should be in movies. She's got the big head," Harvey says, sipping his Coke.

"Big head. Yeah, I've heard that. Big head, short body." *Shut up.*

Michael shoos Harvey off with his hand. "Forget Harvey, he's fucking with you. You should get Harvey to put you in his show. You'd be great! Hey look, David is here! DAVID!"

"Yeah, maybe." Shut up, Kelly.

I excuse myself and go to the ladies' room. I walk by a table of beautiful girls.

"Look at her sweater," the one wearing a fur-and-denim

jacket says loudly enough for me to hear while she points at my rayon sweater. It's a bit of a weird thing, being me—the girl in a rayon sweater who lives at a Travelodge and spends her nights on GeoCities writing short stories—in a place like this. A place where a grubby-looking Benicio Del Toro is sitting at a table I'm about to pass, surrounded by beautiful, young, leggy girls. Still, he looks at me longer than he should, causing one of his leggy girls to sneer at my rayon sweater, again.

When I return, I'm pretty sure David is talking about his new sci-fi where gooey people get plugged into walls or something. It sounds retarded.

I tell Harvey I'm leaving.

"What? Truly? Is it because I keep teasing you about being Jewish? I was just doing it while you were gone."

"I'm tired. It's eleven P.M."

"Okay. Everyone, Kelly is leaving. Say good-bye."

"Good-bye, Kelly."

Bryan leans over, takes my hand and kisses it.

"You are a great writer, Kelly. You will be great. I'll see you next time."

Full of shit, all of them. Bryan hasn't even read my thoughts on Britney Spears.

As I walk away, I hear Harvey. "Hey! My show came in second last week! Some show called *The Sopranos* came in first. You guys ever hear of that?"

I wince.

Lovable dumb fuck.

Tonight, leaving the Sutton Place for the Travelodge feels more dramatic than it has any other time I've made this trip, which is a lot of times. Tonight, it feels symbolic. It feels like I'm in a 1990s indie film, some role Parker Posey took that no one ever noticed.

I finally realize what I want to be: the guy with the twirly hand. I don't want to be the anxiety-ridden actress or the producer's assistant. I really do want to be Bryan, dandruff and all. To swoop into another country, wearing the wrong outfit, just to watch my writing come alive. To be dramatic about everything for a living and not even care about my flaky scalp.

I drive through the rain, opening the window and feeling the mist. I pass the wet green trees and pretend I'm fabulous Bryan in the Pacific Palisades, all the way back to my sandwich grill in the Travelodge.

THE BACKUP
PLAN

Weeks after having my first kid, I had a realization.

Everything had been smooth sailing: I was twenty-three and was in a great three-and-a-half-year relationship with James. That is, until I watched Oprah. There's a good reason a lot of men don't like Oprah: she's an instigator of change. Change is rarely something people greet with a hearty "Oh, this will be great! Can't wait!"

Oprah's guest that day was this fifty-year-old widow who didn't know how to manage money, or write a résumé, or *anything*, because her husband had managed everything while he was alive. Her only job until his death was the kids.

I panicked. "James!" I cried. "If you died, I'd be single. I'd be a single mom. What the hell would I do for a living? Become a waitress? I can't be a single mom waitress! I'm not Rosie Perez." I paced around the room, then went over to the couch, where I began frantically folding tiny baby Onesies. But they were all so tiny and easy to fold that I finished immediately, and that left me with nothing else to focus on, and I started in on James again. "I can't work any kind of job that involves a schedule. And my high school diploma is only good for entry into two professions—waitress or janitor. How good is your life insurance?"

"I don't know," he said nonchalantly. "I think you'd get, like, fifty thousand bucks or something." Then he turned on the blender to make a goddamn smoothie, as if this wasn't the worst news I'd ever heard in my life.

I walked over to baby Salinger in her swing and started cranking it maniacally, like some methed-out baggage handler.

"That isn't Space Mountain, Kelly. Stop cranking," James said.

I had a high school education and I had just had my first child. I'd watched enough Lifetime to know this put me in a shit position. I was one dead husband away from landing flat on my back turning tricks, or dead in a bathtub in Detroit.

I grabbed my keys, headed for the door, and shouted:
"I NEED A BACKUP PLAN!"

I drove over to the grocery store and picked up every information booklet from all the post-secondary education and vocational schools in the city.

I had to get myself a profession. But not just any profession. Here's what I needed:

1. Something that didn't take very long to train for. James could die anytime.
2. Something cool. I just don't think I could ever do a secretary/admin job. Sorry, all you struggling admins, but I've done it, and I'd rather shovel horseshit. I mean, I'm just no good at it. Nowhere near as good as you are.

The local technical school had the fastest programs (less than eighteen months) and promised the highest-paying jobs for its graduates (because they got to do, you know, technical stuff). I sat down in the grocery store café with the senior citizens and flipped through the pages, looking for something that seemed right for me.

DENTAL ASSISTANCE

Let me be clear about something. There's nothing more important to me than dental health. I'm a clean girl. I've had talk-too-close-gross-people near me and I've smelled decay. I would never, as an alive person, allow someone to smell decay on my breath.

But there was no way I was doing teeth. I dry heave when I floss my *own* teeth. Don't get me wrong, I won't judge you for your bad teeth. Rather, I blame your parents for not providing you with the structure any child needs to learn about oral hygiene and follow through on all that. I just can't touch teeth myself. I can't inspect them, I can't pick or scrape at them. I mean, if you ever want me to run away screaming, drag your nails across a chalkboard or scrape at my dry teeth with something metal. If I were a dental assistant, the first time I peered into a mouth full of decay, or leftover food, I'd barf right into it.

MEDICAL LAB TECHNOLOGY

Working in a lab, on the other hand, didn't seem so terrible. I loved my microscope kit when I was six. How would it feel to be the first person to find out someone had brain cancer? Awesome or horrifying? I might want to find out how it feels to see the cancer first, to sit back in my chair and think, *By GOD, I'm the only one who knows!*

I know, I'm a terrible person. But I'm sure there are lots of terrible people like me in labs thinking the exact same thing. Labs, after all, are for doctor rejects. For people who like to work alone. Who really grows up and wants to dip little slips of paper into test tubes full of pee? Who wants to cut into slabs of old ladies' shit looking for parasites? Freaks, that's who.

I couldn't spend my early days as a widow hanging out with freaks and old-lady shit.

REHABILITATION ASSISTANCE

Now this? This looked good. Maybe I wouldn't even have to go to school. I'd watched plenty of rehab shows. I was drunk for two years once. But then I read the description of the program:

Medical advances permit a growing number of children and adults to live successfully with disabilities. Under the supervision of an occupational therapist or physical therapist, the therapy assistant helps clients with injuries and disabilities regain their physical, mental, and social abilities, allowing them to be active participants in society. Assistants also support the clinic's administration by managing therapeutic supplies and maintaining equipment.

Oh, shit. This was, like, helping accident victims cope with their newfound paralysis? Welcoming them into the world of wheelchairs? Helping them learn how to bathe themselves?

For some reason, this was the one that looked good to me.

In hindsight, it probably was a hormonal decision. I had just become a mother. Teaching adults how to do basic stuff, like wiping their own asses—it was pretty much the same as raising a baby, right?

• • •

"Are you nervous?"

James turned into the school parking lot. Sal was sleeping in her car seat in the back of the car. I was nervous.

"No! *Pfft*." I waved my hand in the air and fidgeted with the leather handle on my bag of books. "It's going to be fun. I'm totally going to reinvent myself." I was speaking to James, but I was really just talking to myself. The classes were at night and on Saturdays, so James would be able to watch Sal while I was at school and I could be with her while he was at work.

"Being a student will be great! I'm going to get discounts on everything, and I get to sound young and stupid. And I need a little competition in my life again. Sal is no match for me right now. I can beat her in pretty much everything but bodily fluids, and even then, if I really put my mind to it, I could totally beat her at crapping my pants. Volume-wise, anyway." James stopped the car near the front doors, not believing my spiel at all, and I looked at all the other students walking through the main doors, like suburban androids.

"I'm really proud of you," he said. "This is a really responsible thing for you to be doing. You'll still be able to write."

"I know." I nodded. "See you at five." I kissed him good-bye and took one last look in the rearview mirror at Sal sleeping before I headed into the school, as a girl preparing to be a widow.

My backup plan for James's demise was really coming together.

The room was filled with a mishmash of characters: Slacker teens whose parents were forcing them to go to school. Smart teens doing an eighteen-month program so they could make decent money while they decided what they *really* wanted to do with their lives. A few women in their fifties whose children had just moved out of the house. A rodeo clown. And me. I've always had the potential to be a good student, but I never really worked for grades in high school. I mean, getting good grades so I could go to another school and then work for the rest of my life just wasn't the greatest incentive.

The courses were basically all biology and kinesiology, so I sat in the back row beside Melanie, a fifty-year-old mother who'd probably watched the exact same episode of *Oprah* that I had, and I resolved to become a machine, to remember every last bit of information I learned.

I would let no one get better grades than me—not those little teen bitches, not that rodeo clown. So I studied extremely hard and ended the program at the top of my class, with a 98 average. My reward? Not a trip to Amsterdam, as I was hoping, but the chance to choose where I'd do my practicum—a month-long trial run, broken up between two facilities. Most trainees were assigned to their facilities by an instructor, based on their strengths and weaknesses. I would get to be trained wherever I wanted and have the joy of working there for free. The instructor made a very big deal about my accomplishment, as teachers often do, and pulled me up to the front of the class. And while the other students rolled their eyes and clapped, I awaited my prize, like I was on winner's row on *The Price Is Right*. I was going to choose my placement right there, in front of my classmates, who had won NOTHING.

My instructor gave me my options:

"Okay, Kelly. You can choose from the Rockyview General Hospital burn unit, a senior care center, a sports center, or a brain injury care home."

Holy shit. What was this, *Sophie's Choice*? My instructor stood there smiling, waiting for me to choose, but my stomach was dropping like a bad Chinese meal. This was terrible!

"Um, just give me a second," I said, and ran through my options like it really was my Showcase Showdown.

Who would choose the burn unit? No one in their right mind. Jesus Christ. Fresh burn victims? I couldn't imagine the mental and physical torture the patients go through. There was no way I could deal with that. As it was, I was already only one mental break away from closing myself in the garage and letting the Pontiac Sunfire run. Sports center? Nope. Not interested in hearing jockwads reliving how they fucked up their knee playing tennis. If I had to listen to a bunch of hockey players talk all day, I'd light myself on fire.

Soooo . . . it was looking like seniors and the brain injured for me.

At least neither of them would remember me when I left.

The brain injury center was run outside a hospital. Every day the clients were bussed in to the center, where they had private rooms to work in.

On my first day, I stood in the lobby and watched as they were led, or wheeled, in. If it wouldn't have been so insensitive, I might have thought it looked like kind of a zombie parade, but of course I didn't think that because I'm not a sociopath. I'm not saying I had no empathy for them. I had the MOST empathy for them. I've just always naturally turned the worst things into comedy for myself. It's a coping mechanism to keep myself from crying through the majority of my life. I wouldn't be there if I didn't want to help rehabilitate these people, and if I wasn't so scared of becoming a single mom waitress.

Once they were all wheeled in, I just stood there uncomfortably, not knowing where to go or who to look at. Eventually some competent staffers started fanning out among them, taking each wheelchair and wheeling its occupant into the big room off the lobby. So I looked around, saw a wheelchair with a woman who looked like she was sleeping with her eyes open, and grabbed her wheelchair. She had beautiful hair.

"Hey! I'm Kelly."

"Margaret, this is Kelly," said Ray, a nursing aide.

Margaret woke up from her open-eyed unconsciousness and looked at me. I could feel she was smiling, though her face didn't move.

"Hi," I said again, as Ray started pushing her chair down the hall.

Ray lowered his voice. "I'll have to clean her up before you work on her. The people at the home are supposed to change her before she comes in, but they never do. They left her feeding tube in three times last week. They are assholes. Margaret had a severe stroke two years ago, one of the worst I've seen. No kids. Her husband is still around; he comes in and talks to her and drinks rum. They liked their rum together."

The phrase *no kids* hit me in a way it wouldn't have before I had a kid. I suddenly thought about having no kids and being old and stroked out in a hospital, and it felt way lonely. But what a selfish ass I was—glad to have kids so that I wouldn't be alone when I stroked out?! Shit.

I followed Ray, a sweet and portly blond man with a constantly flushed face, to Margaret's room and helped him move her from her chair to the bed. Moving wheelchair-bound people is an art. It's all about the angle of the chair beside the bed and the angle of the lifters to the bed. The trick is making the move as swiftly as possible. I was nervous. I hadn't really touched many people in my lifetime, I realized, and I definitely hadn't touched someone with paralysis. I was pretty proud that I could disassemble and reassemble a wheelchair in a couple of minutes, but I was scared to touch people as part of the job, and that was embarrassing.

Moving patients in the hospital was immediately different from the classroom exercise of moving classmates from chairs to beds, for several reasons:

1. Though Margaret probably weighed an actual 140 pounds, when we picked her up she magically weighed around 300.
2. When I lifted her from her chair, the waft of feces and urine was so strong I had to struggle to keep myself from dropping her and running.

"Are you comfortable with helping me change her?" Ray asked.

"No." I smiled. And I retreated to the corner of the room as he pulled her elastic pants down and undid her adult diaper. My first thoughts: *no bikini wax, atrophied thighs, but all around a good body.* I immediately hated myself for thinking it, but thanked myself for not saying it out loud. I was *way* too unprofessional to be in there. I was a crude and terrible person.

Ray called in another aide, a no-nonsense older woman. He turned to me. "This is going to take a while to clean up properly." Oh dear Lord.

"Okay, I'll go find someone else to work with." And I left the room, as relieved as if I'd just made parole or was a dude in *The Great Escape* or something. Instead, on my first day, I ended up working with Roger.

As she was leading me over to Roger, Nancy, a stout, polo-and-khaki-wearing soccer-mom type, gave me fair warning. "When he calls you a bitch, you have to tell him it's inappropriate," she said. "He can't call you names."

Roger was missing the left front part of his forehead, all the way back to where his ear would be. His brows and eyes were intact, but his eyes were floaters. He was dark ginger, with a mustache, and his head rolled around constantly on his neck. Nancy told me he had short-term memory problems and anger issues. Oh, and he might be blind, but they weren't sure.

"Not sure? What do you mean you're not sure?"

"When he's tested he gets everything wrong. His eyes don't move in response to stimulus. But he can find objects when he wants to. And he's talked about things around him as if he can see them."

"So, what do you think—he's messing with everyone?" Suddenly this was exciting.

"We don't like to think so."

Well, I did. I liked to think he was messing with everyone— because *he was missing half his brain*. I already loved Roger.

We walked up to Roger and his half brain.

"Roger, this is Kelly. She's going to be working with you today."

"SHE'S A BITCH FROM HELL!"

Roger jumped back in his chair—jerked back, really. He kinda stunk, and his sweater looked like one a kid in my fifth grade class had back in 1987. I was in love with Roger— seriously.

As the therapist was reprimanding Roger, I went through the list of activities I had to do with him that day. Nothing too hard—just a few hand exercises and then some memory games.

As soon as Nancy left, Roger lolled his head my way.

"Kelly, can I get a coffee? Two creams, one sugar. Don't be a bitch about it."

I leaned over, making sure I was out of my goody-goody therapist's earshot, and whispered, "I'm kind of a bitch about everything."

It took him a second, but his head stopped rolling and his eyes stopped floating and then his eyes started moving as though he was reading text. Then it came out:

"BAH!!!!!!!!"

Roger banged both his armrests and bellowed the loudest barking laugh I'd ever heard. It bounced off the ceiling tiles like piñata candy bouncing off a tiled floor. There was one tiny mouse of a woman in the corner, half her body paralyzed, the other half recoiling from the noise. "Oh my goodness, oh my goodness," she whispered, like the little girl in *Annie* with the voice of Piglet in *Winnie the Pooh*.

"BAH!!!!!!!!!" he screamed again, beating his legs and kicking his chair.

Shit. Nancy was coming back over.

"Is everything okay?"

"Yeah, he's laughing. Is that cool?" Jesus. People were so uptight about noises.

When Roger finished his coffee, I sat on a bed and he in his wheelchair in the exercise room. We were knee to knee. I held his hands and did the physical therapy exercises and stretches I'd learned in class over the last few months. This was a lot different from doing hand exercises with my classmate the ex–rodeo clown. For one, Roger's hands were rock hard—I could barely move his fingers. The ex–rodeo clown's hands were totally normal, except for the great amount of shame they held in them.

As we worked, I asked Roger questions.

"Where are you from?"

"I was in Bosnia and my head blew off."

Oh, wow. What was this guy, a genius? Sure he was off topic, but of course I wanted to know how it came to be that he had a giant hole in his head. And I really couldn't stop looking at it. Where the doctors had stitched his forehead together, they'd obviously shifted some skin from his scalp down to his brow, so he was growing a few sprouts of hair down there, too far down his forehead to make any sense. I wanted to pull them so badly, but I also didn't want to go to jail for assaulting a man with a brain injury.

"You were in the army?"

"Canadian army."

"Oh. Well, where did you grow up?"

"Edmonton."

"Me too!"

He didn't seem very interested, but he didn't seem upset either, and I figured all my questions were basically memory exercises, right? So I kept going.

"Where did you go to school?"

"Strathcona."

"Strathcona Composite? Roger. You did not."

"I did!!" He nodded furiously.

"I went there too."

"Oh," he said, unable to register the coincidence, or maybe not even giving a shit. Note: He *was* missing half his head.

"What year did you graduate?"

"Nineteen ninety."

"I was nineteen ninety-five." We didn't overlap at all. How weird was this? We walked the same halls. We might have had the same locker in the burnout hallway by the silk-screening and photography rooms. Was he hot when he was in high school? I didn't think he was my type; he had a mustache, plus he'd joined the army. I can't imagine anyone who attended my high school joining the army. But I was the class of Pearl Jam and he was the class of . . .

"What kind of music do you like?"

"Metallica."

"What's your favorite album?"

"*Master of Puppets.*" There you go.

"Do you listen to it at home a lot?"

No answer. More head rocking.

"Where do you live?"

Roger yelled at me. Just a loud sound, another bark. I'd agitated him, and immediately I realized why. He had short-term memory issues. He didn't *know* where he lived. And he was pissed. I'd be pissed too—everyone *would* be a bitch from hell if they couldn't remember anything post–*having their fucking head semi-amputated when they were twenty-four by a piece of shrapnel in a country half a world away.*

I pulled back and just worked away for a while on his hands, which had really soft skin, though the nails and cuticles were a mess. My only regret now is that I didn't give him a manicure.

When I heard some other patient crying, I realized that Roger had gone silent, and it bugged me.

"What do you think I look like?" I asked.

Roger stopped with the head rolling.

"Blond," he said. "Green eyes. Big tits. Nice makeup." It was cute—he was imagining me as Pamela Anderson.

"What am I wearing?" Looking back, this seems like an inappropriate question, and maybe it was, but I was honestly just curious. And my curiosity paid off.

"Burgundy sweater. Black jeans. Chuck Taylors."

"Oh my God! You can totally see me."

"Nope."

"Yes, you can! You just described what I'm wearing."

"You're a cunt! And a bitch from HELL."

Was he mad because I was talking too much or because I knew he could see me? Roger had suddenly become the most interesting person I'd ever met. Was he fucking with everyone?!

I wanted him to like me, to tell me he wasn't blind. I wanted him to like me enough to confide, only in me, about his non-blindness. "Do you hate me?"

"NO."

"You can see, though, right? Tell me you aren't blind!"

"BAH!!!! BAHH!!!! BAHH!!! BITCH!!!!" Roger was going nuts. Suddenly, I remembered I was supposed to be a professional. Which seemed dumb, considering I wasn't getting paid. In my view, that nonpaid status gave me license to do some of my own investigating on the job. I was a student! I was there to learn! What if I discovered that some brain injuries cause people to fake blindness, call us bitches, and fuck with us?!

But I needed to stay there in order to learn more about my patient, so I stopped with the inquisition, which was causing Roger to go mental anyway and causing everyone else to stare at us.

Okay, then. "Let's play Trivial Pursuit."

"Okay."

Roger kicked my ass at Trivial Pursuit all afternoon. His long-term memory was intact. Roger was a goddamn genius at Genus Edition, particularly history and arts and literature, which I found impressive—for anyone, not just this guy.

That night, I burned a copy of *Master of Puppets* for Roger. I brought it to him the next day and put it in his backpack. He seemed a little ambivalent. I was expecting him to be excited about it. I knew he didn't have the album. Was this part of his brain injury? It was confusing—he showed so much affection for the album before. Why not now? Was it because he didn't have a CD player? WTF?

The next day, Roger didn't seem to recognize me, even when we worked together.

"You want a coffee?" I asked. He just rocked in his chair, no answer. He didn't even mutter *bitch*. Maybe he was mad at me,

I mused. Maybe I'd gone too far. I can imagine NO ONE had ever questioned the blindness. Holy shit—I was *insane* for asking him if he was faking blindness! BUT at the same time I had just given him his favorite album. Shouldn't he have been a little happy about that? I know guys are confusing communicators, but a guy with some of his brain missing is even more confusing.

We went through his exercises with little talk that day, which is probably the way it's supposed to be. Boring. The same was true of every day that followed.

Nancy would check in on us, and apparently I was doing everything right, but to me it felt like the first day was right and every day afterward was wrong. Nancy's appearances became less regular after one of her teens accidentally lit himself on fire and she had to take leave. I wish I was kidding about that.

But, as far as Roger goes, I couldn't help feeling we still had some sort of familiarity. Roger seemed to enjoy my company; he would stop rocking when I got there, or at least slow down, and he stayed calm until I left.

The center ran a music therapy class once a week. Roger refused to go. He hated "Itsy Bitsy Spider." He hated the clapping.

"BULLCRAP!" he said. It wasn't, really. It was just a woman with an acoustic guitar. I left Roger comfortably in his room and went in to join the crowd in the large lunch area, another room attached to the kitchen. We sang the stupid happy children's songs and clapped and laughed a lot. I looked around the room and smiled, seeing everyone in the group so happy, showing exactly who they were before their accidents. Smiles penetrate though the broken mind, the broken body.

But Roger never came along, which made me sad. At first I didn't blame him, but the class was so positive that I started to feel like he was really missing out.

One afternoon, the music therapist was packing up her guitar when one of the younger guys yelled:

"JONI! 'BOTH SIDES'! NOW!"

Everyone went quiet. Another guy started nodding vigorously.

The therapist pulled her guitar back out and started strumming.

But now old friends are acting strange,
They shake their heads, they say I've changed
Something's lost but something's gained
In living every day

The guy who had requested it was Brandon, a twenty-two-year-old who'd had a kayaking accident the year before. Brandon didn't talk or make facial expressions. He sat wide-eyed, staring to the left, mouth open and unchanging. His body was in one of those twisted positions, stuck like a statue. His face looked nonstop horrified. In his room, his parents had hung photos of Brandon before his accident; he didn't look like the same human being at all. The boy in the photos was a young Ben Affleck—in his EMT uniform at work, on a hike with his dog, smiling—not a crumpled statue with wide, horrified eyes, but a "normal" young man.

Until Brandon asked for "Both Sides Now," I'd heard nothing from him. But when the therapist started to sing, he started to cry. Other patients started crying too, but their cries sounded sad in a familiar way. Brandon's cries were guttural. He couldn't move his mouth or tongue; he just moaned. It was terrible. It was beautiful.

I knew then why Roger never came to music class. This was fucking traumatic.

• • •

After music class, I walked over to Roger's backpack, which hung from his wheelchair, and opened it. The Metallica CD I'd made him was still in there. I'd thought for sure he'd been listening to it, but suddenly I remembered that I'm an idiot. *He has no short-term memory, Kelly.* He wouldn't even remember where his backpack was.

I walked up to his caregiver, who was the typical Tobias Fünke look-alike, as 65 percent of caregivers are.

"Why didn't you give him the CD I told you about?"

"What CD?"

"I told you, I put it in his backpack. It's a Metallica CD I made for him. It's his favorite album. You're his caregiver. What's wrong with you?"

Then I broke down.

Trying to collect myself, I walked into Margaret-with-the-beautiful-hair's room. She was alone and laying on her bed. I shut her door.

"Sorry, Margaret. I just need a second."

And I leaned against her wall and cried.

Roger didn't have his dad with him, like Brandon did. He didn't have photos on his wall. He didn't like being bathed, so people skipped out on washing him. Roger's caregiver was a dumb fuck.

I wasn't going to be able to help him. I'd never be able to help any of these fucking people.

Margaret reached her arm out. I looked up, feeling stupid. Then I walked over and took her hand. Earlier that week, I'd helped roll her onto her side and hold her as an aide changed her diaper. It was only fair that she see me cry.

"Ahhhh, I'm an idiot," I said.

Margaret moaned some words I couldn't decipher.

I smiled and wiped my tears.

"I wish we could have a rum together," I said, pointing at her feeding tube. "If I had some, I'd pour it in there."

She laughed and coughed and got some tears in her eyes.

I never found out if Roger got to listen to his CD. I hope he did. I hope he didn't cry, and I hope that every woman he meets is still Pamela Anderson.

"James, maybe I'm doomed to be Rosie Perez after all."

"You aren't."

"Can't you just see me? That Strong Single Mom who works with accident victims or dying people all day and has these emotional moments, then at the end of the pilot episode she comes home to an empty house and some dirty latchkey kid and you find out she's a widow, and everyone is all, 'Awwwwwwwwww, she's just as damaged as those people'?!'"

"I'm not dead."

"Well, when you are, I'm going to be that girl!"

"Better than being a waitress. And you'll make thirty dollars an hour."

"Waitresses make more than thirty dollars an hour."

"What waitresses?"

"Well, I don't know. Naked waitresses, maybe."

"Rosie Perez NEVER played a waitress who made more than thirty dollars an hour."

Next it was the senior center, which was beside the freeway. Somehow I convinced myself that that would be less upsetting.

Wrong again, Florence Nightingale.

It started out okay. I spent the first couple of days feeding Mildred. She was the nicest woman there. Quiet, sweet, beautiful, and not a sloppy eater. She didn't eat very much and she liked me to dab her mouth after each bite. I'd stare at her mouth, at the comb of wrinkles that led down to her lip, the long downy hairs on her face, and listen to the shallow and short breaths she'd take. I'd try to breathe like that. In–out. In–out. So. Quick.

Feeding people wasn't actually part of my job description. As an occupational therapy assistant, I was supposed to be teaching people how to feed themselves, or giving them devices, like spoons with special graspable handles, that would help them gain independence and feed themselves.

But Mildred was ninety-six. Why should she have to feed herself? Was she about to move out and get an apartment? Was she heading out on a backpacking trip through Japan to sample beer this summer? No, so I fed Mildred.

One morning I walked into her room to pick her up for breakfast, and her bed was being stripped.

"Hey," I said a little brightly. "Is Mildred already in the dining hall?" Please let them just be doing laundry.

"She's gone, Kelly."

"So I should just meet her down in the dining hall??" I said, peering out from behind my denial.

That was their cue to reassure me that Mildred was fine, that she'd had some weird burst of energy that morning and wanted breakfast a little bit earlier than usual, that she'd woken up twenty years younger and swaggered out of the place in high heels and red lipstick, that she'd just gone to live on a beautiful farm in the country. But no. She'd died.

I was fine for the first few seconds. Then I went all Kathy Bates—not Kathy Bates from *Misery*, but Kathy Bates from *Fried Green Tomatoes*.

"What are you going to do with her sheets and art? Her pictures?! Don't take the stuff off her walls! She just left!"

I decided not to get close and bond with a senior citizen again.

Of course that didn't work. Because I'm an asshole who cannot stop talking.

The next woman I was assigned to had dementia. She was convinced that we were in an English teahouse.

"'Tis two o'clock, m'dear! Get m'hat out! GET M'HAT OUT!!!!"

It was nine A.M. and Doris was already a full day's worth of crazy.

"*JOANIE!*" She called me Joanie. "Joanie, what are you doing here?"

"I came for tea."

"No, what are you *really* doing here?" She gave me the squint eye and leaned toward me with her hand on her hip like some elementary actor.

"I'm earning my diploma as an occupational therapy assistant."

"Why?"

"In case my husband dies and I have to raise my daughter alone. I need some sort of security."

"Is he dying?"

"No."

"You're an idiot, Joanie. I've always told Harold that. ALWAYS!"

And she left.

I was an idiot? I thought I was being responsible.

"Wait." I followed Doris down the hallway. "Doris, what do you mean I'm an idiot?"

"EXCUSE ME?!" Doris whipped around. "Excuse me, but WHO DO YOU THINK YOU ARE? Why are you TALKING TO ME?? *Police! POOOOOOLICE!*"

Okay then. Never mind.

• • •

I'd been in the palliative care center for an entire month. I liked the routine the patients had: breakfast, recreation, exercise, lunch, nap, dinner. The palliative care facility was a less depressing pill to swallow than the brain injury center. These people hadn't had their lives cut short. There were no accidents, and the overall feel wasn't as dark, though it could still get dark.

I generally tried to get into the senior center early and get out before sundowning began.

Sundowning is the therapy word for a whole mess of confusion, mood swings, and emotional turmoil that people with various stages of dementia tend to experience in the late afternoon. It's bizarre that it's a circadian rhythm thing, but I saw it with my own eyes. At around four o'clock, even the most rational of the folk with dementia tend to lose it a little, and like almost everything I experienced in this environment, it's upsetting to watch.

But after an entire month of seeing it, the sudden confusion and noise from the sundowners became my Pavlovian cue: the crying and sometimes yelling signals that my workday was done. My last afternoon, at around 4:30, I was on my way out of the building when I heard somebody crying. I can handle my daughter crying, my own crying, my friends crying—but senior citizens crying? I don't have the strength.

I followed the sound, and soon I came upon Peter. He was crying quietly and pushing his walker into the corner of two intersecting hallways.

He was pushing his walker into a wall and crying.

I'm no animal, so I stopped.

"Peter?"

"Yes? WHAT IS HAPPENING?"

You guys have to understand. It wasn't just Peter and me in the hallway. There were people *everywhere*. Other seniors, staff.

It's a busy corridor. But Peter's little scene was falling on deaf ears, not just because of all his near-deaf friends, but because the hearing staff wasn't listening.

"You're fine, honey. Come this way."

Peter shook his head but allowed me to lead him away from the corner. I walked with him down the hallway, totally unable to believe that I was the only one who would help him.

"We're going to get you back to your room," I said.

"My room is gone," Peter whispered.

"No, it's this way."

"It moved. Where is Catherine?"

Catherine was Peter's wife. She lived in the building next door, a basic senior center. This was a palliative care facility. The last stop. Catherine was fully capable of looking after herself, but she was no longer able to look after Peter.

I could have romanticized the situation a million different ways and depressed the shit out of myself, but I chose not to.

"Catherine isn't coming today," I said. "It's Thursday. Catherine plays bridge on Thursdays, remember? Look, here's your room!"

"Ah yes, ah yes," he said, though I don't think he really recognized it. I think he was just trying to hide his confusion. He was a sweet man.

"Are you okay now, Peter? Do you need anything else?"

He looked into my eyes and patted my hand. "God bless you," he said.

After I left Peter's room, I decided to say good-bye to Dean. Dean was the one with the Werther's Originals in his room, the kind with the chocolate in the middle. He was one of my favorite patients.

I knocked on his door.

"Hello?" I heard, a little weepy.

He was crying. Fucking sundowners.

"Dean? It's me."

"Oh, hello. Sorry, I'm a mess. I don't know what's wrong."

"Do you need anything?"

"I don't think so."

"I just wanted to say good-bye. Tomorrow is my last day. I was thinking I could come back and visit, or maybe work here part time—"

He interrupted. "Don't ever come back to this place. Ever."

I sat down.

"Why?"

"You don't need to be in a place like this."

I wanted to talk to Dean, but I didn't know where to start. You can't talk about the weather or bullshit like that with people in a place like this. I think the reason most people avoid visiting these guys is because it's impossible to spend any time there without thinking:

Wow, this really fucking sucks. This place really, really fucking sucks. You've lived your entire life free to do what you please. You've had a family, a home, a yard, and now you're HERE. And you're paying A LOT OF MONEY to be here! You're stuck sharing a room with some other old man you don't know. You eat shitty food in a loveless cafeteria. You have a bed that, chances are, someone else pissed and shit and died in. If you get stuck in a corner of some hallway, people ignore you. And now you're going to die in this building with a view of the freeway. Instead I said,

"Uh, so, tell me about your wife. We've never talked about her."

Dean looked up and tears filled his eyes. "Elizabeth!"

He stared into my eyes, moved by something I couldn't pinpoint. The silence was kind of extreme.

"I'm sorry," I said. "I shouldn't have asked about your marriage. It's none of my business."

"No, no, it's just . . . I haven't said her name in years."

My stomach hit the floor.

I have zero experience responding to this kind of human intensity. I'm used to "I didn't get any sleep last night," or "This coffee is gross," or "Mondays, right?" I have no experience in *a ninety-one-year-old man breaking down in front of me over the love of his life whom he lost four years ago, after spending a lifetime with her.*

Dean shimmied over to his closet—without his walker, so I knew he meant business. He opened the closet and took out a large box from a shelf. He brought it back to the desk where I was sitting and placed it before me. A photo album.

We spent the next two hours poring over his life, from birth until his wife's death.

"I haven't talked about this in years."

At one point, Dean's roommate appeared in the doorway.

"GO AWAY, ANDY!!!" Dean shouted.

Andy hobbled away, no questions asked.

Two hours after my shift ended, my family was at home, wondering where I was. I was sitting in a facility, listening to a man I barely knew recall his life, talking a mile a minute as the memories rushed back. I barely understood what he was talking about. Trips, people, children, cars, pets, homes. He was painting the picture of his life for me, quick as his tongue could move.

I got home late. When I saw James, I broke down.

"Don't die," I begged him. "I can't do that job. I'd rather be a waitress. I'd rather shovel shit. I can't do enough for them."

"You don't have to."

"I could have stayed all night, all year, and I'd never be able to do enough."

"You don't have to."

I went up to Sal's room and snuck in. The room had that sweaty, sleepy kid smell that you want to bottle up and huff in your car when you need a hit of oxytocin. I stroked her ringlets and thought about her life. If she'd ever be ninety-four. If she'd have a view of the freeway.

A week later, I graduated at the top of my class. I listened to Dean and decided not to take the part-time job at the center where he and Peter lived. After all, my husband wasn't dead. I didn't need a backup plan quite yet. I stayed at home and had more kids with the husband who didn't die. I made James get better insurance. I pushed all three of my little kids around the zoo in strollers. I don't worry about being a single waitress, but I still worry about not doing enough for people, and when I drive past palliative care centers, I pretend I don't know what's going on inside.

AN OPEN LETTER TO THE
NURSE
WHO GAVE ME AN ENEMA
BOTTLE AND TOLD ME TO DO IT
MYSELF WHILE I WAS HIGH ON
MORPHINE

Hello, Nurse,

I don't expect you to remember me, given that you work in a busy emergency ward helping many dying or seriously dismembered people each evening, but I came in one late November night in 2007 with severe abdominal pain.

The relentless agony of my abdominal pain was almost on par with the time I was giving birth and the head of my child got stuck in my vagina and I pictured all the women giving birth in the 1800s, in their cabins with babies stuck in their vaginas, dying by candlelight. So I would like to thank you for the morphine. It stopped my screaming and gave me a decent "just peed in my pants" buzz, about the equivalent of a fifteen-minute post-joint mellow. I would also like to thank you for the blanket you gave me when I got the chills. Offering an old, hair-tangled elastic so I could pull my hair from my sweaty face was a lovely gesture, the slight scent of Shalimar so soothing. I am nothing if not appreciative for the good things you did for me.

That said, I'm writing to clarify a point of hospital policy. You see, I'm not 100 percent certain whether protocol dictates that patients give themselves enemas, or whether nurses are supposed to administer them.

I ask because, if questioned, let's say, by a stranger on the subway, "Suppose you go to the hospital and need an enema; who would give it to you?"

My guess *would have been* a nurse.

You see, I'm still not even certain why I had the enema.

I loathed having to admit to you and the ER doctor that I had pooped that morning.

Regardless, you handed me the Fleet enema bottle and said the words I will never forget.

"The bathroom is down the hall."

"Pardon me?" Of course, dear nurse, it wasn't that I hadn't heard you. I merely wanted to be quite sure you weren't being comical. I was, as you know, under the influence of a heavy narcotic.

"The bathroom is down the hall. You take the top off the tip—it's lubed—you bend over, squeeze, and hold in the water for as long as possible. Then sit on the toilet and let it out."

"Okay." It was at this point, as I took the bottle from your hand—which was firm and resolute in its intention to pass it to me—that I realized you were absolutely serious.

I shuffled down the hall, bottle in hand, waiting for you to call out to me, waiting for me to be wrong about what I was about to have to do to myself, but you never called out to me. I'm a nervous wreck when it comes to attempting new things, but the morphine certainly took the edge off having to put a bottle of fluid up my ass in a public washroom. Also, I really don't like feeling mortal, and poo is just one of the obstacles that gets in my delusional ways. I'm a clean freak. I don't use public washrooms. I don't poo.

Whether it was standard procedure to have patients give themselves enemas, or merely you taking a break to grab an egg salad sandwich and deftly using my morphine-dazed state to your advantage, I will never know.

Nurse, I remember the moment quite well: standing bent over in front of the toilet, my one hand propped against the wall, the other gripping the bottle, poised to insert it into my asshole. Yours was a Herculean feat, getting me into this situation, yet you . . . you managed to do it simply by giving me the tool and your meager directions. Let us agree that without the morphine in my system, *you* would have been giving me that enema. I would have been lying sideways on a bed, iPod blaring, knees to my chest, trying not to imagine looking at my own asshole through your eyes, concentrating on something like the failed series *The Cosby Mysteries*.

In the cold, but thankfully private, bathroom, I took a good long look at myself in the mirror, and thought, *Crunch time*.

Fortunately, you didn't lie when you said the tip was lubed. Also, it was thoughtful that the bottle and fluid were heated a little. That might have been protocol rather than a sweet gesture on your part, to help enter my part with relative ease and less constriction. Nonetheless, it made the event more comfortable.

As the bottle squeezed empty in my hand, strange sounds erupted in my body. Clugs and squeals. This is where you failed me, dear nurse: you see, you weren't precise in your instructions. At this point I realized I had no idea *how long* I was supposed to hold the water in. I stood, half-naked in mid-squat, clenching my ass with as much tension as one can feel under the influence of morphine, and I realized that I had no idea whether "as long as possible" meant seconds or minutes. But perhaps I'm being too hard on you, because really, the morphine had robbed me of any concept of time.

I inched my way over to the toilet, wondering how long I could possibly hold the water in. For a moment, it occurred to me that gravity could help contain the water in my butthole. When I put my head between my ankles, however, I found I was utterly unprepared for the head rush and morphine spins that resulted.

I fell.

As I fell, a spray of water erupted from my body and spattered to the floor. Not much, but certainly enough to make me ashamed. Me, being a girl who did not want to tell you I'd already pooped that morning. I couldn't stop the ejection. So I gave up, got up, and voided into the toilet.

I can't claim I was spry in my movements, given the morphine. I'm not sure how long I sat on the toilet wondering if I was done, because it certainly seemed as though a lot more went in than came out. And like I said, you weren't very clear about how long this entire thing would take.

I may have blacked out, as I can't recall exactly what state the washroom was in after my fall. But I did my best to clean up the mess with the dry, unabsorbent paper towels available to me in the bathroom.

When I emerged, I walked back to my gurney and pulled the curtain. You arrived within a few minutes.

"Do you feel better?" you asked, and emotionally I don't think I did. You probably noticed this by the tone of the low yes

I grumbled as I tried unsuccessfully to mount myself onto the gurney bed, like it was a tiny toy horse. At last, I lay facedown on the bed with one leg hanging off, turned my head, and looked at you.

I could read nothing on your face. Were enemas not your forte in nursing school? Were you a deviant? Were you put on earth to help me find my inner animal spirit? I will never know.

What I do know is I had just gone against all of my moral excellence in that emergency-room public washroom. And because of that, my pain was gone. For that, I salute you.

I know that you probably understood how phenomenal your immediate effect on me was, what with the cessation of the pain that was as agonizing as my baby's head being stuck in my vagina, but I doubt that you imagined how your actions would shape me in the days and years to follow. I'd like to quickly tell you how this experience had a positive effect on my life:

The following week I visited my family doctor. When he entered the room and asked,

"What's new?" I responded: "Life changed for me when I gave myself an enema while high on morphine in a public washroom." And I have been a favorite patient ever since. He makes extra time to see me for last-minute crises with my children, and that really saved my rear the last time Henry had strep throat. You see, I'm now an infamous self-administering enema giver. That's *clout* in the medical world. And it's a skill I won't forget about.

The ability to give myself enemas has continued to come in handy. I had my third child in August 2008, and the week I was due I gave myself several enemas at home to prevent the feared "shit while I push the baby out" every pregnant woman (and her partner) dreads throughout the final days of her gestation.

For those reasons and many more, nurse, I'd like to thank

you. Whatever your reasons may have been, I am a better person for having given myself an enema while high on morphine, for unknown reasons, for undiagnosed pain, in the filthy washroom of a hospital, on my birthday.

Yours,
Kelly Oxford

MY ZOO

Kids are animals.

"Juice!" eighteen-month-old Henry yells from his car seat as I buckle him in. "Juice! JUICE! *JUICE!*" And he happily hands me a piece of snot, like it's payment for all the things I've given him.

They grow up so fast, people say. Not because children actually grow up fast, but because we mentally block out most of this nonstop shit show.

"Mommmmmyyyy?" whines three-and-a-half-year-old Sal. "Mommy? Can we go to McDonald's?"

"Juice!" Henry is fucking relentless, straining the neck and head that are so uncertainly attached to his little body, struggling to liberate himself from his car seat. His eyes are bugging out and his mouth is pulled all crazy as he peers into my bag.

"CRACKER! CRACKERS! *CRACKERS!!*"

I pass him the crackers and juice box, then bend down and wipe his snot onto the driveway.

"McDonald's, Mom? I would really love a nugget," Sal says, smiling sweetly.

"We're going to the zoo," I reply, thinking about how much I love McDonald's and how I've slowed way down because I don't want the kids to turn into those fat babies on *Maury*.

"Okay, wait a minute," Sal says. "Do we have chicken at home?"

"Yes."

"And fries?"

"Yes."

"And apple juice?"

"Yes."

Sal claps her little hands together. "Okay, well, when we get back home, let's BAKE-IT-UP-BUDDY!!! GIVE ME A SMACKERINO!" She leans forward for a high-five, like she's my drinking buddy or some kind of embarrassing uncle.

I pull away from the curb, thinking about how much easier that would have been if I'd been alone. I would have basically just gotten into my car and left. I wouldn't have Henry's snot on my hand. I wouldn't have had to stop to plan dinner or dole out any snacks.

An empty apple juice container flies onto the passenger seat.

"APPLE JUICE!!" yells Henry from his car seat. "MORE!"

"Henry, I'll get you apple juice when I'm not driving. At the zoo. And no throwing in the car. I'll totally crash and we will all die because you were thirsty for boxed juice. That's embarrassing. Frankly, I'd be totally pissed off if I died because of that."

I see Sal turn to her brother in his car seat. "What color is apple juice, Henry?"

"RED!" he shouts, sticking his tiny legs out straight. Henry shouts at everything.

Sal shakes her head and puts her hands on her hips. "Hen-*ry*! Apple juice is yellow!"

Henry looks back at her and shouts, "RED!!!"

"OH NO!!! HENRY, MY LITTLE BROTHER—ARE YOU COLOR BLIND? Apple juice is yellow!" Her hands fly to her cheeks, sick with fraudulent concern.

"Sal," I say. "Calm down. He isn't color blind."

Henry shouts: "RED RED RED!!!!!!"

Sal composes herself, looking for all the world like the mother of a child who's been stricken with cancer. She presses on, trying to make a firm diagnosis. "Okay, so what color is the train Daddy takes?"

Henry screams at the top of his lungs, his chin still tilted forward, lips jutted out like a little hound dog baby: "PUUUUUUR-PLLLLE!!!!"

"Henry!" It's exactly one minute into our day trip, and I'm trying not to lose my shit. "Stop shouting please!"

Sal gasps to herself and whispers sadly, "*You are color blind*, Henry."

"PUUUURPLEPUUUURPLEPUUUURPLE."

"MOM, HENRY IS COLOR BLIND!"

"JUICE MOMMA JUICE JUUUUUICE!!"

"YOU GUYS!" My eyes flash to the rearview mirror, then back to the road.

That's when I see the police officer standing in the street in front of me. I look at my speedometer; I'm doing three times the speed limit in a school zone. *Crap.* That's another thing that wouldn't have happened if I'd been driving alone.

I pull over and roll down my window, hoping the kids will still be screaming so he will hear my misery. Only now, of course, they've suddenly gone completely silent.

"I can't believe I just did that," I say to the officer, passing him my license and registration.

"MOM, ARE YOU GETTING ARRESTED?!" Sal shouts from the backseat. Henry stares at the uniformed officer, like he's a Catholic looking at Jesus Christ himself.

"You were doing almost seventy in a school zone, ma'am." He looks pointedly into the car at my kids.

"The crazy thing is I drive through this school zone twice a day, at least. And I *never* speed through it." I'm lying. Of course I speed through it, but usually not much over the limit. The children's park is far off the road and behind a giant fence. Kids need to learn how to cross the street. I'm providing a public service. I smile a phony smile. "Thank you so much. I've really learned a lesson today." I take the white ticket from the officer and reach back to put it in my bag.

Henry points to it: "BLUE!"

Sal looks at me, sadly shaking her ringlet-covered head. "Can glasses fix color blindness?"

I pull into the zoo parking lot just as the sun comes out from behind the clouds and a swan flies over the river.

"YAY!! We're here!!!" Sal cheers.

"LOOK! We got a great parking spot," I cheer. Neither of them cares; kids don't give a shit about good parking until you're halfway across the lot and one of them can't walk anymore because their "legs is dead." Maybe I had to get that ticket, I think, in order to score this amazing parking spot.

I get out of the car and walk around to Henry's door. I open it up, unbuckle him, and then, when I reach behind him to pull him out of the seat, I feel it.

Oh God.

I look him in the eyes. He looks me in the eyes.

"Henry?"

"Poop," he chirps. "POOOOOOOOP!!!"

He shit. It's exploded out of his diaper and gone up his back and all over the car seat behind him. It must have *just* happened, because I hadn't smelled anything. Today, I notice, Henry's shit actually smells kind of good, and I recall that he didn't eat meat yesterday, only strawberries and raspberries. Which explains how he's managed to shit in his pants like that.

Sal would have NEVER shit in her seat when she was his age. Henry fucking hates me! He shit in that seat to spite me. I pull my hand out; three of my fingers on my right hand are covered in shit. Shit studded with tiny strawberry and raspberry seeds.

"MOM!" Sal takes off her seat belt and scoots across the backseat. "Mom, you aren't supposed to touch poop, remember?!" She tries to get a good look at my shit fingers. Henry looks guiltily at my hand, then suddenly starts to point and shout at my fingers: "BROWN!"

Sal's bottom lip tucks under her top teeth. Her eyes go wide, and she claps her hands together. "Buddy! You aren't color blind!" And the weight of the world is off her big-sister shoulders.

Then the second bad thing happens: I realize I don't have the diaper bag.

"Sal, pass me that napkin on the floor." I'm scrambling. What can I wash my hand with? I have nothing! *It's just shit,* I tell myself. *It's just fruit that has passed through his body. It's all organic and natural.*

"That is so *grossss!*" Sal says, eyeing the raspberry seed stuck to the tip of my index finger.

"I know." I am almost dry heaving.

Henry starts to squirm in his seat. I'm worried he'll fall out, and the shit will go everywhere. "APPLE JUICE!!!" he wriggles and shouts.

I wipe the chunks of crap off my fingers with the napkin until they're vaguely clean, then stuff the crappy napkin into a paper lunch bag on the floor. "Sal, pass me another napkin." She passes me another one. I say a quiet prayer that I have a wad of napkins from the McDonald's drive-through in my purse. Fat *Maury* babies be damned—this is a sign that God approves of fast food.

I try to spit into the only napkin in the car, but I'm totally dry from panic. I put the napkin in front of Sal's face. "Sal, spit into this. You have more spit than me." She obediently spits into the napkin and I use it to wipe off my shit fingers again, tiny seeds and all. I put the napkin in the bag. I buckle Henry back up, trying not to use my right hand at all. "APPLE JUICE!!!" he shouts, right in my face. What is this kid trying to do to me? He shits in his seat, and I'm convinced he's done it on purpose because I haven't given him his second apple juice.

"Sal." I turn to her. "We have to go home. I'm sorry. There is poop everywhere. And even if I had the diaper bag, I couldn't leave the car seat all poopy like this in the car while we're at the zoo."

At first Sal looks sad, but then she assesses the situation rationally. "Yeah, this is bad. You need to clean up this poop, lady!"

I pick up the bag with the shitty napkin and throw it into a nearby garbage bin. I smell the fingers on my right hand. Terribly shitty. With my left hand, I grab a box of apple juice for Henry. His terrorist tactics have paid off. I use my left hand to poke the straw into the box, and as I pass it to him I say, "You really deserved to have me do that with my right hand."

I turn to Sal, who's waiting patiently in her car seat. "Sal? You want a juice?" I ask.

"Not until you wash your hands."

As I drive home—clean hand on the steering wheel, shit hand on the passenger seat—I lament the day as it now stretches out before me. I will have to strip Henry down, scrape shit off his seat and his clothing, wash him, wash everything his shit touched, and make lunch.

I slow down as we pass the police officer who had given me a ticket in the school zone. We are going the wrong way for him to get us, but still. Coming toward us, in his line of fire, is a woman in a minivan. She's speeding and yelling at her children in the backseat. He's totally just tagged her. I suddenly feel a horrible glee . . . pure joy. It isn't just me! I'm not the only one in this mess called Motherhood.

I look in my rearview mirror and watch her getting waved over. I'm elated. I slow down and watch as the police officer walks over to her window. Fifteen seconds later, still reveling in my happiness, I glance back again. He waves to her and she drives off.

SHE. DRIVES. OFF.

"WHHHHHHAAAT?!?!" I shout, slamming on my brakes as I watch the speeding minivan lady in my rearview mirror DEFINITELY leaving without getting ticketed. THIRTY MINUTES AGO, I WAS THAT SAME LADY, AND I GOT A TICKET. WHY WASN'T I WAVED OFF?!?!

I try to calm myself down, but I can't. I pull over.

"Mom, why are you stopping here?" Sal asks.

"I need to think, Sal. I CAN'T THINK AND DRIVE!!" I take a few deep breaths, and those deep breaths bring forth a great realization. I realize that I will never let this day go. I will be angry about it forever. I will be angry about the two-hundred-dollar ticket and the shit on my right hand forever.

If I don't do something about it RIGHT NOW.

I make a U-turn, pull up to the police officer—doing exactly the speed limit—and open my window.

"Hi." I'm smiling. "I just saw that."

He approaches the car. "I'm sorry?" he asks.

I look at his badge. "Officer Morton? I saw you NOT give that woman a ticket. You waved her away."

He realizes what I'm getting at and thinks he knows where I'm headed, but he doesn't.

"I want you to take my ticket back," I say, holding it out the window with my left hand. "It's not fair that she got off, and I got a ticket."

He laughs. "I can't do that."

"Then why did you let that other lady off, and not me?"

"She said she wasn't paying attention because her kids screamed and scared her."

My mouth drops open, and I make one of those choking/clearing-your-throat sounds. "When is that NOT happening in a car with children?! If that excuse is valid, you will NEVER ticket someone with kids in the car. When I drove past you, my son, Henry, was yelling for apple juice, and my daughter, Sal, was borderline suicidal because she thought her brother was color blind, so I WASN'T PAYING ATTENTION when you caught me speeding!! I just didn't try to use all that as an excuse."

"Sorry, I've already written the ticket."

I take another deep breath, then sit there quietly, trying to compose myself.

"You gonna get arrested now, Mom?" Sal asks.

I look at my shit hand on the passenger seat and decide: I'm not going to give up. I *can't* give up. Not now. Not with this shit hand.

"Ma'am," Officer Morton says, crossing his arms lightly. "You can contest the ticket in court. The date is on there, but right now I'll have to ask that you move along."

That's it. I've had it. Speech time. "Today was going to be a great day. I was taking the kids to the zoo. I LOVE THE ZOO.

You know why I'm not at the zoo right now? Because I got to the zoo and I went to take my son out of his car seat and I stuck my hand in his shit! He shit his pants and it went everywhere. I-HAVE-SHIT-ON-MY-HAND!!!!!"

Officer Morton stopped smiling and looked at my left hand on the wheel.

"NOT THAT ONE!" I shout, adrenaline pumping as I raise my right hand. "THIS ONE!! I have SHIT on my hand and I got a ticket and I didn't get to go to the zoo!"

Officer Morton looks around, then says, "Give me the ticket." Using my left hand, I pick it up and pass it to him. He tears the ticket up and leans toward me with a serious look on his face.

"No one gets a ticket on my watch when they have shit on their hand."

I pull into the driveway and turn around to look at Henry and Sal in the backseat.

"Mom! Can we have chicken and fries still?" Sal asks.

"Sure. I just have to clean up first. And Henry's probably uncomfortable." I look over at Henry, who's smiling and biting his apple juice straw. He's totally oblivious to the fact that he's got shit all over his back, or that I'm about to carry him to the backyard and hose him off, like an elephant.

"Can we still go to the zoo today?" she says, unbuckling herself.

"Nope, not today." I get out of the car, cross to Henry's side, and open the door. Sal stands in the backseat, beside Henry.

"Please can we go today?" Sal whines.

"We can go tomorrow," I tell her. "First thing in the morning. I can't wait to go."

"Me too," she says. "Animals act crazy. I want to see what kind of crazy things the animals do."

VEGAS

AT MY FUNERAL

1. Stuff my bra for me.
2. Play the "Game Over" theme from Super Mario Bros.
3. Have George Clooney and Ryan Gosling dance me into the room, like Bernie in *Weekend at Bernie's*.
4. Put pins in a map and yell, "Now you can go anywhere you want, baby," like Cher in *Mask*.
5. Play the videos of North Koreans crying for Kim Jong Il and pretend it's for me.
6. Hire Richard Marx to sing "Should've Known Better."
7. Put an unlit cigarette in my mouth.
8. Have Channing Tatum lap dance my casket.

This list is kept on my computer, in a folder marked IF I AM DEAD OPEN THIS along with my passwords and a bunch of notes reading, "Don't be sad, I'm in Heaven now. Ha ha ha!" So far, Clooney and Gosling have not yet confirmed, but Marx is standing by.

I don't think I'm going to die soon, but I finally feel like I'm growing old. Like, I know there's a Lil Wayne *and* a T-Pain, but somehow I thought they were the same person. You can be sure you're getting older when your finger isn't on the pulse of pop culture but you're sure it is. Getting old is when your complaints are so genuine that a friend can't console you.

I'm getting old and I hate it. I want to take charge.

"Angela," I grumble into my iPhone as I toss some magazines aside to search for my iPhone. "I need to start working out. I know I said I'd never work out, but I need to. Where is my iPhone?!"

"Are you talking on your iPhone?" I can hear her smiling.

"Yes. Yes, I am talking on the phone I am looking for."

"Kelly, you don't need to work out. You've never weighed a lot except when you've been pregnant. And even then you were the cutest pregnant ever."

"I don't want to lose weight, but my body is at least 78 percent fat. I sit all day. And the pregnancies ruined my stomach skin. It's all smooth when I'm vertical, but when I bend over"—I stand up and lift my shirt, bending forward to let my skin go slack—"my stomach looks like Mickey Rooney's face."

"Can you get that fixed?"

"If I can, I will. Trust."

"Well." She sighs into the phone and starts nervously stuttering some sounds the way moms try to spit out one kid's name but start with the names of all their other kids. "Wh— M—Uh— I-I started working out last week." My mouth falls open. One friend does not seek out a better body without notifying the other friend. This is friendship treason.

"And you didn't *tell me*??"

"Kelly, you said you'd never work out!"

"You said YOU'D never work out!"

There's a beat. Both of us breathing into our iPhones. We've never had a fight. We've never done anything terrible to each other in the eighteen years we've known one another—just like we've never exercised in the eighteen years we've known each other. I wait for her to apologize.

"I'm doing Tracy Anderson's Method mat workout," she whines slowly, confessionally. "It's on YouTube, but I'm going to order the DVDs. Gwyneth Paltrow does it, Jennifer Lopez, Kelly Ripa . . ."

"BYE!!" I hang up on Angela and start pawing through my closet to find my workout clothes. Thirty minutes later, I come up with a pair of black athletic shorts and a tank top. If it takes me thirty minutes to find my workout clothing, I figure, I'm not working out enough. (Note: I'm *never* working out.)

I open my computer, find Tracy Anderson's videos on YouTube, and start the program in my bedroom with my laptop open on my chair. I'm finally using that fifteen-year-old yoga mat for something besides building forts with the kids. Tracy is on my screen doing repetitive arm lifts and twists, and for the first minute I'm thinking, *Gwyneth's arms look that good from* this *easy shit?* But by the fiftieth arm lift and twist, I can't feel my arms and my shirt is so drenched in sweat I look like a landscaper from the Valley.

I smash the space bar with my useless arm to stop the video, then use the side of my hand to change it to a dance cardio video. There is Tracy, a smiling Bratz doll, telling me I don't need to know how to dance to follow her moves, but by the time I've figured out how she is doing what she's doing, she's on to the next move and I know she's a bald-assed liar. I'm out of breath, stomping across my floor, fully aware of how much I look like Shrek (not even Fiona), and praying no one comes home early to see this and mock me for the rest of my short and winded life.

A couple of minutes later, I'm two full moves behind her, and

I realize I can't do cardio. I bend over and look at my computer screen as my legs push their way through some palsied Boyz II Men cross steps. By 3:24 P.M. my ears hurt and I've gone deaf. I'm not sure about the possible medical causes—maybe it's the 78 percent body fat—but I sincerely go deaf when I do cardio, so I've always avoided it because hearing is rad. Then I look down at my shrunken apple stomach and summon some last refuge of energy.

Tracy is now erotically swaying her hips, giving me a pep talk: "Remember, this is a performance."

"Quit fucking me with your eyes!" I yell back.

"When you don't think you can do it, remember, you can," she says.

Fuck you, Tracy, I can, I think. I dig deep, I can barely hear as I jump from one foot to the next, my arms in the air punching around like I'm in a club. I can't feel my body at all, but suddenly I'm able to do it without wanting to quit. This must be the "zone" people talk about when they work out. I bet this is how dogs feel all the time.

I get through the last minute of the video by imagining Drake in the corner behind me, holding a golden chalice of cognac, saying things like, "You thirty-three? No way, girl! DAYUM DAT ASS!!" and totally asking me out on a date and then showing up as his character from *Degrassi*, Wheelchair Jimmy. If Drake asks you out on a date and shows up as Wheelchair Jimmy, you're the one. But I know I'm probably way too old for Drake. I'm *old*.

The next day, I give Angela the update. "I worked out yesterday, and I ordered the video program," I say like I've just become a professional bodybuilder. I'm all about taking charge of my life, and this counts now that I've remembered my body is actually a part of that too. I take this kind of thing very seriously.

"So did I." So does she.

"This is so great. We're going to be so fit in ninety days."

"One of my coworkers doesn't like Gwyneth Paltrow's body."

"I'm so glad I work from home so I don't have to hear crap like that," I say, staring at the wall in my bedroom, totally alone and bored. "I love Goop's body. Hold on, I just got an e-mail." I check every e-mail instantly, as though something incredible could happen at any moment.

I pull my phone away from my ear and click on the e-mail. It's from a friend:

Did you know that David Copperfield is a fan of yours? He just tweeted that your tweets are his favorite. That's so weird.

Incredible.

I get back on the phone with Angela.

"Angela? David Copperfield is a fan of mine. I should come up with a funeral request for him. Maybe he can make my body disappear and save my family the cremation fees. Tell me how many times you do her arm video tonight. I think I'm going to double up—my shoulders look great."

I check my Twitter account, go into my @ replies, and see this:

@kellyoxford, @alecbaldwin, @pattonoswalt, @rainnwilson RT @molsen23: @d_copperfield Whose tweets do you look forward to the most?

I follow Copperfield, then direct-message him.

"Thank you! You have any magic going on?" I hit send and then realize that he can't read my totally sarcastic mental intonation of "You have any magic going on?" I'm a fucking idiot.

He responds immediately, and earnestly, with a series of DMs.

He's performing at the MGM Grand in Las Vegas, he tells me, and if James and I are ever in the area he'd love to give us a private tour of his museum.

I immediately fire back, no hesitation, because I'm already imagining David and me in a helicopter, laughing together as monuments disappear below us. "Is the first weekend of May enough notice? Can we bring our friends? They are a couple. Where do you recommend we stay? At the MGM?" I hit send without rereading. I'm an insane person.

He replies: the first weekend of May works, and he'll set us up with rooms at the MGM Signature Suites.

I call Angela. "You and Matt are coming with James and me to Vegas to see David Copperfield and go to his secret museum."

"WHAT?" She laughs, knowing I'm for real because I'm always for real.

"Angela, I need *adventure*. I don't want to die without magic in my life. I'm aging. First weekend in May. It gives us a few more weeks of Tracy Anderson before we have to go sit beside a pool."

"It's not enough time. I wasn't prepared to get into my bathing suit so soon."

"Have you looked at your arms lately, Ang? Mine are insane. This program has FAST RESULTS. You should double up too. We're all going to Vegas."

At six A.M., three weeks and nineteen sessions of swearing and dancing with Tracy Anderson later, my mom stands in our doorway in her flannel pajamas. She's agreed to stay with the kids, even though she thinks David Copperfield is "kind of dark."

"You do realize it's the Black Lilith Moon this weekend," she says, widening her eyes for dramatic effect. "It's the supermoon, *and* it's the Black Lilith Moon," she says with premonitory fervor.

"It means all of your fears will rise within you. LOVE YOU!" She shuts the door.

James and I land in Vegas a few hours before Matt and Angela. There are dozens of islands of conveyor belts in the baggage claim, carousel after carousel. I've never seen so many black bags in one place. It's like some weird Christmas movie where the elves only make suitcases.

The place is wall-to-wall people. Babies crying, one-hundred-year-olds breathing from oxygen tanks, addicts gambling their change at ringing slot machines. People from India, Australia, Ecuador, Wichita, and all of their internationally corresponding smells. *Man,* I think, *Vegas is crowded,* but then I notice that most of the walls and ceilings are mirrored, and I realize it's probably an eighth of the crowd I think it is. The crowds are already driving me crazy, but I try not to complain, because whining is the mark of an old person. When I was younger, this kind of mayhem would have fired me up. Now I just want someone to pick me up and carry me the fuck out of there.

We grab our bags and tread over the dirty carpet, weaseling our way through the slot machines, old people, and Chinese tourists to the exit doors beside the taxi stand. I'm immediately assaulted by two forces: the heat of the Nevada sun and the three hundred people ahead of us in line for a taxi.

James looks at me; our eyes lock. "For real?" I mouth to him as a sweaty fat woman brushes past my bare arms, leaving her body liquid all over me.

"Let's go to the limo stand," he suggests, like some sort of wealthy genius. We get in line for a sedan. There are only two people in line ahead of us, and for an extra fifty bucks I'll get to avoid another person close-standing near me and sharing their personal humidity.

Our driver is Pasqual. "Can I smoke in here?" I ask. I recently started smoking more than casually again—you know, just so I can feel young and stupid and unable to develop cancer. Plus, I'm working out now, so I'm even.

"You can pretty much smoke anywhere in Vegas," Pasqual says as he drives the car farther away from the airport and closer to the Strip, which is basically three blocks away. "Did you see the line up at the taxi stand?" Pasqual states more than asks. "Fight weekend. Crazy weekend. This is going to be one crazy weekend," he repeats, like my mom just called him about the Black Lilith Moon, trying to scare us back to Calgary.

"Are you meeting friends in town?" Pasqual asks. I feel like he's asked this question too soon, but I guess that's what people do in Vegas.

"Our friends are flying in from Vancouver in an hour to meet us," James says.

Matt and Angela have been friends of mine for almost twenty years, and friends of ours as a couple for the thirteen years James and I have been together. I met Angela at Mrs. Louie's Korean day care when I was two years old, but neither of us remembers that. We figured it out when we were eighteen and Angela worked at the Alternative Video Spot by my childhood home. This was way pre-Blockbuster. We bonded over *Kicking and Screaming* and *Party Girl* and *Dead Man*. Our love for broody '90s comedies and Jarmusch cemented our friendship. She started dating Matt, her best friend, soon after.

"You here for the fight?" Pasqual asks. Jesus, Pasqual is nosy.

"No," I say, blowing my smoke out the window and squinting into the sun. Maybe I'll start tanning again. "David Copperfield invited us down."

"How do you know him?"

"He's a fan of mine." I hear myself and wince. God, I'm an

idiot. It's lucky I'm a girl—I'd be such a dick if I were a guy. "I'm a writer."

"Wow." Pasqual turns around to see if he recognizes me and looks like he thinks he does, which is funny for the second he does it. "What have you written?" he asks.

"A few pilots for NBC and CBS. A book. I just sold a movie to Warner Bros. Actually, absolutely nothing I've written has been produced or published yet. I guess it's pretty much a bunch of bullshit . . ." I inhale more carcinogens, pretending they're reversing the aging process. I'm talking to Pasqual but also mastering the art of not wrinkling my face while I smoke. It's a fine art. "Right now I'm pretty focused on my body and not dying."

James pays Pasqual for our ride, then pays him a little more to go and pick up Matt and Angela while we check into the hotel. Our suite is in tower two of the MGM's three towers and there's a connecting suite for Angela and Matt. It's the perfect setup. We can have our own space but be neighbors. We'll be Chandler and Joey and they'll be Monica and Rachel.

We have a kitchen, living room, bathroom, separate bedroom, and a very large en-suite bathroom. I have no complaints, even if the suite is only on the third floor of a thirty-six-floor tower, because I'm a gracious person and this room is a gift. James goes for a walk to get some coffee, and I turn on Judge Alex on the bathroom TV and have a shower.

It's my first shower in Las Vegas, and I feel weird about it. I know this place is a desert. I feel terrible for using so much water, even though I know that's dumb, because there are thousands of people in this hotel alone, cleaning themselves or swimming in giant pools of water, lifting their bikini tops to reveal expensive boobs and downing shots of Patron. As I stand beneath the shower stream, though, those boob images are replaced with images of African children hand-pumping dead wells in the desert, and the water falling on me feels illegal. So I quickly turn the shower knob to the left and get out of the shower.

I look at myself in the mirror. I'm doing better. My stomach is flatter. My thighs are slimmer. But I still look like I'm more than 50 percent fat. Skinniest fat ever. No one can ever see this mess. I'm so glad I'm married. I hope James doesn't go first. I'll have to spend all of his death insurance money on fixing my body so someone else can see me naked and not be scared.

I wipe my hand on a towel, pick up my phone, and text Angela.

> KELLY: You're in tower 2 room 3-704.
>
> ANGELA: Thank you for Pasqual!! Just got here. He's nosy.
>
> KELLY: I know, right? Tower 2 room 3-704.
>
> ANGELA: We're in the lobby. They say we're in tower 3, penthouse suite 26-840. I think we have your room.
>
> KELLY: Weird. Double check. We should have rooms beside each other?!
>
> ANGELA: Tried to change rooms, they said it was pre-arranged by Copperfield this way.
>
> KELLY: We'll meet you in your room in 15 mins.

I quickly put on my bikini, clench my butt cheeks to scan for cellulite (tons), and throw a dress on as I walk out to meet James in the living room.

"Angela and Matt aren't in the next room!" I announce, hands on my hips like some old lady, except my dress is still over most of my face and my eyes are the only thing showing. James holds my cappuccino out for me as I pull the rest of my dress down.

"Nice look," he says. "Where are they?"

"Tower three."

"Why are they in tower three?"

"IN A PENTHOUSE SUITE on the twenty-sixth floor with a WAY BETTER VIEW THAN US!" So much for being gift gracious. Oprah would not publicly approve of how much this was irritating me, but deep down she would get it. She has taste, after all.

I decide this minor flare-up counts as my cardio for the day, and we should move on.

"Let's go get them."

James reaches over to push the button for the twenty-sixth floor in the elevator of tower three. Underneath the number 26 on the elevator button are the letters . . . *PH.*

"They *are* in the pent—"

"NO." I put my finger on his lips. "Don't say it out loud. It's not a big deal."

James says through my finger, "I'm not making it a big deal. It's just cool that they're in the penthouse."

I nod earnestly. "It *is* cool."

Matt and Angela open the door. "Angela!!" We hug. Over her shoulder, I immediately see a bed in the room and realize what's up: they don't have a suite. It's small. I feel a sad sense of relief and momentarily loathe myself. "Your room is so cute!"

Angela looks like an Italian Alexa Chung. Matt looks like Gary Oldman's son, Edward Norton, or Kip from *Napoleon Dynamite.* But Matt wears really nice French clothing and has a better jaw than Kip.

Angela breaks away from our hug. "Thanks for sending Pasqual for us!"

"Was he weird?"

Matt nods. "He asked if we wanted to have a *good time*. He really wanted to show us a *good time*. He told us he could get us *anything*."

Matt raises his eyebrows evocatively and walks over to the table in the corner of the tiny room, by the window with the incredible view. (NO BALCONY. *WE HAVE A BALCONY.*) He grabs his wallet and addresses James: "Come with me to Walgreens? I need booze and contact lens solution."

Angela's arms fly up in the air. "I did not leave your contact solution behind! It wasn't my fault!"

Matt shakes his head and I change the subject. Nobody really needs a contact lens solution argument.

"Angela and I are going to the tower two pool. Meet us there. Then COPPERFIELD." I run my hands over my thighs. "Time for bathing suits. I have to warn you, I still have cellulite. Tracy Anderson better not be full of shit."

The MGM Signature has a whole selection of private pools, separated from the main MGM party pool by concrete fences. They're available to rent for one hundred dollars an hour and are totally empty. From the other side of the fences, the towel boys manning these pools watch as I try three times to unlock the gate, without success. "Fucking card keys never work. I swear to God my body demagnetizes them." Finally, I shout, "I REALLY AM STAYING HERE. IN THIS TOWER! THIS ISN'T A GAG!" The towel boys pretend they can't see us, even though we're standing three feet away from them, separated only by the bars of the fence and prestige. "JUST OPEN THE FUCKING DOOR FOR ME!!" I yell, pushing on the door like an animal, like Mike Tyson might do in the same situation. I'm yelling *to* them, of course, not *at* them; I have no desire to engage in negativity with the people responsible for making my pool experience sublime.

Finally, I figure out the how-to-put-the-key-into-the-door diagram, because I've tried every other combination. I slide the card into the slot and the door pops open easily. Like a joke.

Angela and I trip into the pool area. I'm furious, but trying to act like a queen in my *Real Housewives of St. Barts* bathing suit cover-up and sunglasses.

"Towels?" the short young guy asks. I pull down my sunglasses and look at him, like a gunslinger in a saloon.

"I want a lot of towels." He laughs, but I repeat myself. "A lot."

He mimics my serious expression, then nods, passing me a dozen giant towels.

"Why all the towels?" Angela hops over a puddle of water as we cross the pool deck, headed for the chairs.

"Power. It was a power move, Ang. They thought it was funny that I couldn't get in, so when I got in I took all the goddamn towels. I'm full of power moves. This way, no one fucks with me." I always like to pretend I want to be the alpha of any new situation.

We pull all the empty chairs in this "exclusive" pool area into a circle and take a few in the first row that face the pool. The pool will be our TV. I stack up several towels on each of the deck chairs. "See? It's like a mattress to soak up our sweat. Or a fort I can crawl into to hide my bikini."

"Genius," she says, sitting down and testing her chair out with a few bounces.

As I watch her, I realize I'm getting hot standing there outside in my dress. I realize what's supposed to happen next. But I can't do it.

"I'm not taking off my dress, Ang, I can't do the bikini yet.

I really didn't have enough time with Tracy and Wheelchair Jimmy for this sort of thing."

She laughs. "You're FIIIINNE!! Besides, no one is here."

"I'm not fine. And those guys are here!" I point at the only other groups of people at the pool: a crowd of drunks and some skinny girls who are sitting across from us. I pull my sunglasses back down over my eyes and lean back into my power towels, for drama. "I'm old, Ang. I've had three kids. If James died I could never date again. I couldn't bear to have another guy look at my body in its weathered state. James is conditioned to love it no matter what. It's like he doesn't even KNOW any better anymore."

My mom was right about this Black Lilith Moon shit.

"My mom was right about this Black Lilith Moon shit."

"You're insane." Angela stands up off the chair and removes her cover-up to reveal a cute navy '60s-style one-piece bathing suit.

"Oh my God." I push my sunglasses back up and look at her like she's the sun. I want to stare directly at her, but her perfection might blind me. "You look GREAT. You're always thin, but you look ballerina-healthy great."

Angela sits back down and looks at me the way I look at annoying toddlers who aren't listening to me. "We look *the exact same*," she says slowly, probably hoping I'll listen and shut up. "We look the exact same, but you have bigger boobs."

I point at her. "Your stomach skin NEVER stretched out to here to make room for babies!!" I reach out past my body, as far as I can reach. I'm exaggerating, but barely.

"I'm like that fat Subway guy's 'after' body. JARED. I have Jared's skin."

"You do not! What are you wearing tonight?" Angela asks, getting comfortable in her chair.

"*I DON'T KNOW.* Maybe a pair of giant pants? I could wear a giant pair of pants and pretend I've lost a ton of weight, and when no one believes me I can just bend over and show them the shrunken-apple skin hanging from the middle of my stomach." I decide to leave my dress on. I'm dying in the heat, but it's better than admitting to the mess underneath. Drake would never holler for this ass—not yet.

A waitress appears. "Would you ladies like a menu?"

"NO!" I snap.

"WE WOULD!" It's Matt and James. They're carrying a Walgreens bag. Matt is eating nuts.

"Matt, what the hell are you eating?" Angela asks.

"Cashews," he says excitedly.

"Cashews are delicious," James says. God, they're not helping me feel any younger.

"Better question," James says, popping a nut into his mouth. "Kelly, why are you wearing that dress?"

I look down at the sweat-stained dress I'm trapped in—a swath of cotton, smothering me like a pillow. I just shake my head.

That's when I notice something: a glint from the waitress's midsection. A BELLY-BUTTON RING. The older waitress, wearing a brown bikini. The older waitress, who's fully tan, with fake boobs and a rhinestone in her belly button. Who is totally cool with wearing a bikini as her work uniform. She's had a kid. Only one—I can tell from her skin—but she's done it. I stare at the rhinestone in her belly button. I wish I could be so ballsy. Flickering light, catching the sun, and calling out: "LOOK AT ME! I AM A SHAM DIAMOND IN A BELLY BUTTON, BECAUSE THIS BELLY IS WORTH LOOKING AT!"

I hated that rhinestone.

"We just want chips, guacamole, and salsa," James says, passing the menu back. He doesn't even notice her rhinestone-worthy stomach. I've ruined him.

"Awwwwww, sorry, that's not on the menu," she whines sweetly, like she's talking to a kitten or a handicapped person.

"We can't just get chips and salsa? With a little guacamole on the side?" he asks. Belly Button shakes her head, as if a sad-face emoticon is the only thing registering in her brain at that moment.

James takes the menu back, looks at it for a second, then returns it.

"All right. We'll have the nachos with the chicken, onions, cheese sauce, sour cream, jalapeños, guacamole, and salsa on the side."

"Wouldn't you be so embarrassed if your mom worked here?" I say under my breath to Angela as the waitress walks away. I'm never catty. Cattiness is a girl-on-girl crime. I'm not biased; I have as much contempt for men as I do for women. I'm just being a regular asshole.

James and Matt sit down beside us. "Hey—we saw Pasqual at the drugstore!" James says.

"Yeah." Matt laughs, eyeing up my towel situation. "He's weird. He just yelled at us from across the street. Kel, why do you have all those towels?"

"We got them for you guys," I say, as if this should be obvious. "Take the top ones, I've already sweated through them. We should totally call Pasqual and let him take us on an adventure!"

"I don't think so," James says. "He's pretty intense."

"Intense?"

Matt exhales loudly, sinking into his chair and applying SPF to his nose. "In the car he told us he was an Ecuadorian gangster. He had to get out of LA."

"See?" I turn my face toward the sun. "That sounds like fun to me."

"I don't think we can handle Pasqual's kind of fun."

James takes off his shirt and lies back on his chair. Matt follows suit. I wish I didn't care about how my body looks. I can't believe these guys can just take off their shirts like that.

"I can't believe you guys can just take off your shirts like that."

"Whoooo!" the large drunk group on the other side of the pool starts to yell. I open my eyes and watch a dozen of them push the fattest, drunkest guy into the pool and run. My prediction was right: the pool has become our TV. James hops over to my chair and sits next to me to get a better view. The fat drunk guy surfaces, wiping his face. He's directionally confused, looking around, trying to orient himself.

"Oh my God, they're leaving him!" Angela clutches her chest as she watches the fat guy's friends all run away from the pool area.

Matt looks on, nibbling at a cashew. "He totally deserves it," he says casually, indicting the fat guy with no evidence. We watch him struggling against the water as he walks to the stairs at the shallow end of the pool. It's taking forever. His friends are gone, laughing and running through the gate, across the pathway and into the hotel. A seagull cries.

Angela continues to stare at the guy, who is now wincing and crawling up the stairs like some tipsy walrus mounting a barnacle-encrusted Gibraltar. "I would be SO mad if my friends did that to me." Duly noted.

James nudges me, pointing at my sweat-soaked dress. "Seriously, just take it off."

"No point. We have to go meet Copperfield's assistant soon."

"Copperfield is going to get you onstage and do something to you," James says with a smile. What a fool.

"James," I say condescendingly, shaking my head, "he can't call me onstage. He's a magician. Magicians can't get caught using friends in their performances or people will think they're shysters!"

"You and David are friends?"

"HA, HA, James. Of course we are!"

Rhinestone Navel arrives with the nachos, toppings on the side, and four tequila shots.

Staring at the twinkle tummy beside me, I press my point. "Like, right after we eat these, we have time to go change and meet her."

Turning my attention to the food, I immediately spot skin on the cheese sauce. I point to the sauce and ask, "Will eating that make you poo?"

Sadly, the waitress doesn't hear and walks away.

Angela eats a chip. "Eventually, it will all be poo."

I pick up my shot of tequila and push the rest toward my husband and wayward friends. "Let's do these shots. My mom would want us to."

We drink.

My goals for this trip are to take charge and feel young. So far, I'm one for two. My secondary goal is to get an amazing story about meeting David Copperfield. I'm hoping he does something crazy. Maybe he'll tell me a secret, or he'll enjoy our company so much he'll fly us all to his secret island, or, at the absolute LEAST, he'll make my extra stomach skin vanish.

"I don't need to feel old. Look at this hot body!" I say to James from the floor where I lay, straining to pull my black leather pants up over my skinny but pure-fat legs.

"Your body is the sexiest," he says, not looking up from his magazine.

"I know!" The pants finally make it over my butt ledge, and I quickly zip and button them up, sighing at the ceiling.

"NICE BAGS!" It's an hour later and the four of us are on our way through the hotel to meet Copperfield's assistant. Angela and I trail twenty feet behind Matt and James when we become subject to vocal assault from two guys who could have been Lil Wayne and T-Pain. I wouldn't know.

"NICE BAGS!" The guys whistle, catcalling as they walk toward us. They've just unwittingly passed our husbands, who ignored the catcalls, not even registering that they could have been for us. Total insult.

"He likes your bangs," Angela says matter-of-factly.

"No, Angela. He said nice *bags*."

"Why would he say bags?"

"Because they're Chanel? Black people *love* Chanel," I state, and quickly, because the guys are about to pass us. We keep our stride steady.

"Where you girls going so fast? Damn!" I look at the guys as we pass them. They're young. I wonder why they're talking to us. Are we hot? Would I have a chance with Drake? I mentally assess myself: I'm wearing a sequin top and sneakers with my leather pants. Every girl in Vegas wears heels and walks worse than a baby. So I went with sneakers instead of heels, to ward off a too-sexy look. I like to look pretty, but I don't like wearing clothing that makes people think about my vagina. Angela is wearing all black, leather jacket and flats, totally gorgeous, but not all think-about-my-vagina-y. We look more New York waiting room than Vegas Strip. So I'm shocked that these guys are bothering with us.

"We're following our husbands," I say to Lil Wayne as I point to Matt and James up ahead. For a week before we left, James and Matt had planned on wearing Tom Cruise's and Dustin Hoffman's suits from *Rain Man*. Unfortunately the tailors weren't quick enough on the suits, and they both ended up dressing like '89 James Spader.

T-Pain looks at them. "Husbands? How long you had that problem?"

I ignore. This could get ugly—at least if our husbands weren't in the middle of a heavy debate on the merits of the cashew. Lil Wayne and T-Pain are past us now, but I can hear they've turned around and they're looking at our asses as we walk away.

Then one of them—I don't know who because I refuse to turn around—yells, "PULL UP THAT G-STRING!!!"

"Why is he yelling that?" Angela asks.

"Oh my God, Ang! He said *G-string* instead of *thong*, like I do! Maybe he's old like us!" I've been trying to remember to say *thong* ever since I got mocked on my blog for saying *G-string*. I'm learning.

Again: "PULL UP THAT G-STRING!"

My heart nearly stops. I'm humiliated. So much for dressing like I don't have a vagina. I lean into Angela and start walking faster, whispering, "I'm wearing a G-string. It must be showing." I refuse to reach back and tuck it back in. If I do that, I'm letting him win. We keep walking, only now I'm outpacing Angela, pulling ahead of her as I think about Lil Wayne seeing my underwear. Why aren't Matt and James hearing *any* of this?

"PULL UP THAT G-STRING, GIRL!!" It's like I'm a deer or something. Prey.

"Wait, you're wearing a G-string?" Angela calls from a few feet behind me as she jogs to catch up.

Technically, it's a one-size-fits-all thong I bought off Shopbop. I got three.

"You know? If I'd been walking this fast a month ago, I would have been out of breath. Tracy Anderson is *working*."

We round the corner and see Matt and James waiting for us at the last moving walkway before we get to the fountain where we're meeting Copperfield's assistant. Angela and I stop beside them, and I finally have the privacy to reach back and tuck my underwear into my pants. I gasp, dropping my hands to my sides. "My thong isn't even showing!!"

"You're wearing a thong?" James says, shocked.

"We're going to race." Matt stretches his arms, paying no attention to the thong comment. "James on the floor, and I'm taking the moving walkway." He pulls off his loafers, then locks eyes with James. James nods and starts the countdown.

"Three . . . two . . ."

"WAIT!" Matt shouts, pointing at James's feet. "Take a step back. You're one step ahead of me!"

James grew up with three brothers. I'm happy when we're with his male friends, because then he doesn't need me to play along with this kind of shit. I've been thrown into walls while wrestling, almost drowned in Puerto Vallarta during a "swimming contest," and I've eaten six hot dogs in a row and vomited in order to fill his brotherly void. I don't want to race, even if I am wearing sneakers.

James takes a step back. "Okay, you're good now." Matt shakes his arms out.

"Three . . . two . . . one . . . GO!"

And they run. Angela and I casually get on the moving walkway.

James and Matt are running fast. Neck and neck. Matt's glasses fall onto the human conveyor belt. Angela ballet-runs ahead of me and daintily picks them up. The guys make it to the wall at the same time. They're out of breath, unable to talk. Angela steps off the belt and passes Matt his glasses.

I step off the belt, the four of us standing in the corner at the end of the hall.

"But if Matt is *running* on a conveyor belt," I ask, "he's not actually running any faster, right?"

We all sit quietly and think about that for a minute.

"Sorry," I mumble. "Let's go find the fountain."

MGM makes no sense to me. Vegas makes no sense to me. It's like being inside a giant mall, even when you're outside. A giant mall with casinos, a wonderland where you can drink and smoke wherever you want, 24/7. If society ever decided to get rid of people with IQs below 100, all they'd have to do is set up this sort of place on an island with no return transportation. It would be like Shutter Island for people who use *party* as a verb.

Still, we can't find a fountain. "I'm going to ask this guy where the fountain is," James says, heading over to the black-jack tables. On the way, he walks right past a *Ghostbusters* slot machine, which I VOW I will not put any money in, because I fear I'd never be able to stop. What would the machine do when you win $200,000? Would the Marshmallow Man bust through the place? Slimer? Would 1980s Bill Murray call me on my cell and tell me I'm wonderful, saggy stomach skin and all? I need to know. One dollar and I would be down that rabbit hole.

"Are you ladies excited for Copperfield?" Matt is grinning. He likes this stuff. He likes Masonry and druids, secret societies and conspiracies in general.

"I'll tell him you're a druid." I look for James.

Angela grabs my hand and looks me in the eyes. "Do not tell him Matt's a druid!"

"You can tell him," Matt says, smiling wider, molars showing. "Did you know Copperfield's island has a secret cave with psychic monkeys that he's taught to draw people's thoughts?"

"No, Matt. I didn't."

"It's true. And I read that he originally bought the island because he discovered a water source there that could be the Fountain of Youth."

"Matt, please don't mention this stuff to David," Angela flatly begs. "Do NOT talk about the Fountain of Youth or psychic monkeys that can draw your thoughts."

Behind Angela, I spot James, walking behind a blackjack table. He's in the inner circle of about a dozen blackjack tables. He's headed toward the big guy in the suit.

"Oh my God, did James just go into THE PIT to ask the PIT BOSS where the fountain is?" I'm calling it the pit, but I have no idea if it's called the pit or if that guy is a pit boss. I haven't watched *Casino* since the '90s.

Matt and Angela turn around to look. There's James, walking up to the big man in the suit. In one swift motion, the man turns around, grabs him by the elbow, and escorts him out of the pit. He releases him with no further incident, which doesn't seem very *Casino*.

James comes back like nothing happened. "Fountain's this way," he says, pointing.

I take his arm. "Why did you go into the pit?? That pit boss was pissed!"

"I don't fucking know." He shrugs. "I just wanted to find out where this fountain was so we aren't late for Copperfield."

"Well." I shake my head, coming up with the most insanely dramatic example possible, to keep him from wandering into dealer-only territory again. "If something were to happen in that pit tonight, or to any of those tables? Those videotapes will be pulled, and when they go through them and see you walk in there like some stupid, lost asshole, they'll think it was a scam! They'll run a scan on your face and put you on TV as a suspect, or show up in our room and interrogate you and cut off your fingers."

I see by James's nonreaction that he isn't worried about being interrogated by guys named Johnny Three Fingers. Then some sort of miracle occurs: I see a poster for Drake.

I stop talking and walk up to the poster. I put my hands on either side of Drake's face.

"DRAKE IS COMING HERE? *NEXT* WEEKEND!!!??" I'm devastated. All I want to do is go to a Drake concert and do my Wheelchair Jimmy dance move for him. And also go on a date with him. Maybe he'll be my second husband.

"Do you want to come back for it?" James asks supportively, like a decent first husband.

"Naw." I know that next weekend won't be my time with Drake. We wouldn't get a chance to talk, or get to know each other. He'd think I was too old for him or too married for him, or something. "It wouldn't have worked out."

David Copperfield's assistant Stacy is standing beside the fountain. I know it's Stacy because she's the only woman by the fountain without a feather boa, a necklace with a tiny penis on it, glitter, or a two-foot-tall beverage cup. Plus, she recognizes us: "Kelly! I'm Stacy, I'll take you up to David's SkyLOFT."

We pass the regular hotel elevators, where a girl in a wet bikini is waiting for someone to pick her up or dry her, and Stacy opens a metal gate to reveal another set of elevators. Everyone is talking, but I'm too busy imagining what this SkyLOFT is going to look like. I want it to be insane and have some sort of a retractable roof. I want to feel naive and awestruck. I want David to have falcons and be wearing all black. I imagine him serving champagne and some weird fruit I've never heard of that he's cultivated on his private island. I grew up watching David Copperfield specials. I know he can fly.

The elevator doors open to a large, round lobby. It's very dark and throbbing with intense trance music. I wish I was making that up. We make our way across the lobby and into a hallway that seems to go on forever. It's the longest, darkest hotel hallway on earth, with burly security guards in front of some of the doors. I look over at Matt, Angela, James, and Stacy, and the sight of the five of us walking down the longest hallway to this intense music sound track reminds me of some 1990s movie, but one where everyone dies. Involuntarily, I whisper to myself, "Going to meet David Copperfield to this intense music is intense," but they hear it and laugh.

And then it happens.

All at once, David Copperfield appears out of nowhere—he is a wizard, after all—in the hall in front of us. He's wearing a black shirt and has prayer hands raised to his face, like a goddamned life-sized cutout. He says, "Do I hear the sounds of laughter out here?" I'm frozen. I wonder for a moment if he'll start to pull an infinite amount of scarves from his throat. I would stand and watch him do that, in this hallway, with this music and no talking, forever.

No one says a word as Copperfield ushers us back into his loft, holding the door for us to enter. He is tall and broad shouldered and has the beautiful bedroom eyes of Osama bin Laden. The first time I thought about how beautiful Osama bin Laden's eyes were was in the middle of the night, and the next morning I woke up with the worst UTI of my life. I'm sure the two were connected. I should probably find some cranberry juice later. But David does not give off an evil vibe at all, not even a creepy uncle vibe. There are no falcons, no retractable roof, just a stunning bright white loft space and a child in the dining room.

"Water, anyone?" David, the perfect host, walks over to the open kitchen and grabs a few bottles of Fiji water as his beautiful girlfriend, Chloe, comes down the stairs. She is not Vegas, she's entirely French. Beautiful young woman, no makeup, long natural hair. She probably washes with Fiji water.

"I like water," Matt says, a hint of mystery to his voice. He's totally going to talk about the Fountain of Youth.

I realize I should probably play the perfect guest, and friend to Angela, so I introduce David to everyone before Matt can follow up about the water. "Thanks so much for inviting us. Our rooms are perfect."

Angela coos, "Your daughter is so cute. I can't even look at her, she's so cute." We all turn to look at Copperfield's daughter, and she begins to cry.

"Thanks. Come, let's sit down." David's arm extends dramatically, like there's any other way for a magician's arm to extend, and he guides us to the living room. Matt, Angela, James, and I all squeeze onto the white leather couch. David takes the modern white leather chair across from us, and Chloe perches on the arm of his chair, like some goddamn beautiful French angel gargoyle.

"How do you all know each other?"

"How much time do we have? Isn't your show in, like, ten minutes?" I ask, taking a sip of my water.

He turns to Chloe. "I think it's in four minutes?" She nods, then he turns to me. "I just wanted to say hello before I went on." I can't help but stare at Chloe and David. They look so young. I mean, I know she's actually young, but I have no idea how old Copperfield is, and he still looks young for that age. Matt's totally right about David's Fountain of Youth discovery, and now I so want him to ask about it.

"Short version: Angela and I were in a Korean day care together as toddlers, but we didn't figure that out until we were eighteen and she worked in my video store."

"What kind of video store?"

"It was called Alternative Video."

"Not a Blockbuster," David confirms.

"No. Way before Blockbuster," Angela says, making me feel old again.

"Angela would recommend videos to me. Diamonds in the rough. And then we started dating these guys pretty soon afterward."

"More diamonds in the rough." David laughs. Funny magician. "So I know Kelly is a writer. What do you guys do?"

Matt leans back. "I'm in health care."

David looks at Angela. "I'm a buyer. Shoes, clothes."

"Oh." David turns to Chloe. "Chloe is designing shoes."

Of course she is. She's perfect. She's a perfect shoe designer. I love Chloe, the same way I love Gwyneth Paltrow. Most girls choose to hate these types of perfect girls, but I love them the most *because* other people have chosen to hate them.

David looks at James. "I'm an environmental engineer. I'm a hydrogeologist. Ground water. I mostly clean up the crap that oil companies leave behind. Not physically—I'm behind a desk, drawing up the plans."

David leans forward, scrunching up his face, and for the first time I see lines. He seems very interested in this stuff, for a wizard anyway. "I have some water issues on my island."

Matt leans forward too. "I've *heard* about the water on your island."

Holy shit, Matt is going to ask about the Fountain. I can see Angela shifting her weight as she mentally stabs Matt to death.

David's assistant enters the room and David slaps his knees lightly. "Well, we have to get going. I have a show in thirty seconds."

David walks ahead of the rest of us down the dance-club-music-filled hallway. He weaves as he walks, from one side of the hall to the other and back. You know how there are those electric fish that dangle a light in front of their mouths to seduce prey? I feel like Morgan Freeman's freckles are kind of the same thing. But at that moment, I felt like a tiny fish . . . watching that light.

As we reach the gate, Matt speeds up his pace. He passes David and opens it for all of us, including one other person.

"Dude"—James grabs Matt's arm—"that was Evander Holyfield. You held the door for Evander Holyfield." I missed it. I didn't get to see the ear because I was mesmerized by Copperfield's seductive S-patterned walk and the thought of Morgan Freeman's freckles.

David does a few more weaves, then turns dramatically and waves, making fancy Osama bin Laden magician eyes. And then he's gone.

When I imagined this evening, I thought we'd be in the huge MGM theater with cauldrons of magician's fires, falcons, and stadium seating. Instead, Chloe leads us to a large, lounge-y room. Round booths and tables, the kind you imagine in every Las Vegas venue, except for the one where David Copperfield performs. We are seated front-row center. Our table touches the stage. We can see under the props. I'm already looking for mirrors. But I still know that David can fly.

"Do you know how he does all the illusions?" James asks Chloe as we take our seats around the tiny table. *God*, James. You can't ask that kind of thing right off the bat! I have no idea what the protocol is when you first meet a magician's significant other, but this doesn't feel right.

"We look like superfans," Matt mouths to James. Then his eyebrows shoot up. "They've got cashews on the menu, James!"

We order a bottle of wine and a bowl of cashews, and I'm almost done with my second glass before the show begins. And I have to pee. While I was digesting the fact that Copperfield was a normal, falcon-less dude, seemingly as normal as James, I had drunk my entire bottle of Fiji water. I followed it with two glasses of wine. And now my bladder is bursting.

David does a series of tricks in his act that drive me crazy because I just can't figure them out, which makes me think maybe his *normal guy* stuff is an act. The most impressive trick is one where he lies in a coffin-sized box. The box is then collapsed, getting smaller and smaller, until he is only a head and feet sticking out of a tiny box spinning in front of us. I'm horrified to the point where I don't even remember how badly I need to pee. With my hands at my mouth, I look at a grimacing Chloe, who seems equally horrified. She does fuck him, after all. Is this pure contortion work or is he a wizard? I lean toward the latter, because the only humans I've seen contort themselves like this are French Canadians or small Asian girls, and David is a Jewish man. He didn't grow up with a *ceinture fléchée* or parents who turned his toddlerhood into one long plate-spinning class. If I had the gift of wizardry, I would totally be living it up with falcons and shit. For sure.

"Is there a good time during the show for me to run out of here and use the ladies' room?" I whisper to Chloe as she sips her Pinot. She looks at me like I've said, "I've shit myself."

"Ahhhhh . . ." she hums, looking confused, but not "I am French and don't understand" confused.

"I just really have to pee. I don't think I can hold it." But Chloe is looking over my shoulder and smiling.

And then there is light. A spotlight.

And then David is standing behind me. He is in the audience, with his hand on my shoulder. I find myself involuntarily standing up. He's bringing me onstage. I look over at James, who is smiling and chewing cashews. "I told you," he mouths to me, with wet nut crumbs in the corners of his mouth, as I walk toward the stairs. Numbly I climb them, one by one, as I think, *Please do not pee yourself. It will be harder to lie about a rejected bladder-saving operation to a crowd of people than it was to a gas station attendant.*

David leads me to a spot on the left side of the stage in front of a small camera crew. I turn to look out at the audience; then I see the Plexiglas box with a scorpion inside. As David has me put on large rubber gloves, I wonder how large the human bladder is, my human bladder in particular. Judging by the larger outputs of urine I've had, I would estimate that mine is roughly the size of a medium grapefruit. When I zone back, I'm holding the Plexiglas scorpion box and David asks me to pick a card. I choose the ace of diamonds. David then asks me to put down the box and take off the large rubber gloves I've just put on.

"Now," he says, "pick up the scorpion." And suddenly I'm not thinking about my bladder. I realize I'm on a goddamn Las Vegas stage with a full bladder beside THE David Copperfield, and he's just asked me to pick up a scorpion. I look up and over his shoulder to the large-screen TV on the theater wall. It's me. I look small, and my arms look defined, but I don't look happy.

"You don't seriously want me to pick up the scorpion?" I ask into his mike, knowing it will get a laugh—and it does—but I mean it.

"Yes, just reach in and grab it," he says, cocking his billion-dollar eyebrow at the audience, winning himself an even larger laugh.

I look at the scorpion. I'm going to do it because Copperfield got a bigger laugh than I did, and that is just wrong. I'm going to be the goddamn hero today, David. *I* am. The crowd's laughter dwindles to nothing when they see that I'm raising my arm and reaching for the scorpion. Then, in a millisecond, it occurs to me: that little arachnid isn't moving. I haven't seen it move at all. Holy shit—it's totally fake. With the confidence of a drunk white girl dancing on a speaker, my hand darts into the clear box to grab the black scorpion. Someone in the crowd gasps: I'm fucking wowing them.

Then, just as I'm about to make contact, David grabs my arm to stop me. He smiles and shakes his head. The scorpion scuttles across the box and I remember how much I have to pee. David grabs the scorpion himself, pulls it out of the box, and holds it in front of the cards. The scorpion grabs my card, the ace of diamonds. I can't believe Copperfield subcontracts his card tricks out to insects.

After the show, I take the longest pee of my life and then we pile into a perfectly normal minivan with David and Chloe. A minivan, with toys stuffed under the seats, that will carry us to David's museum of magic secrets.

When we arrive at a large building in an industrial part of town, an entourage of people awaits us. Slowly and painfully, I climb out of the minivan's third-row seat and discover that there's no other way to climb out of the third row of any such vehicle. It's cramped and awkward and I vow never again to give my kids shit for being so slow. (Note: I do not own a minivan anymore. I own a Mazda with a third row. This is important for me to mention because of minivan stigma. I grew up in an Aerostar, I know. Minivan stigma is worse than Mazda stigma, and D.C. is probs not afraid of minivan stigma because he owns islands and can shrink in a box.)

"This is Homer," David says. "Come over here; we'll take a photo." David guides us to the entrance of the building, and we line up in front of the door so that Homer can take a few shots. I'm feeling out of place, but in a good way, as if Walt Disney himself were about to give me a private tour of Disneyland after hours. Like: What the fuck am I doing here at midnight, with a camera crew, my husband, and my closest friends, at a wizard's private museum?

Then we went inside.

"This was the store I grew up in, in New Jersey. Korby's." We were standing within an exact replica of his parents' store. It was totally, perfectly retro, right down to the original shirts his parents sold. It even had the store's original TV in the corner, which was actually playing an episode of *The Man from U.N.C.L.E.*

I think, *This is fucking insane.*

"Yes," David says, smiling directly at me. "I even have the original TV I used to watch while I sat in the store." Wait, I didn't say that out loud, did I? He was just working off my "This is fucking insane" face . . . I *am* the Helen Keller of body language. Right?

David leads us into the tiny change room and asks Matt to pull on a tie hanging on the wall. Matt is more than pleased to be the Macaulay Culkin to D.C.'s Michael Jackson. He pulls the tie, and the back wall is transformed into a secret door opening into a foyer, where Homer and the entourage are standing. They've somehow gotten in there without us noticing.

"Amazing!" I say. "How many Homers do you have?"

We walk through, room by room, and see that David has kept, stored, and itemized every piece of video, film, or paper that has ever mentioned him. He has saved every set prop, every costume from every tour, and thousands of magic kits—every single one that has ever been made anywhere. He has a puppet room with Paul Winchell's ventriloquist figures, Edgar Bergen's Charlie McCarthy, and Howdy Doody, who is horrifyingly uglier in person than he was on television. He has the gun that shot and killed Chung Ling Soo when he attempted (unsuccessfully) to catch a signed bullet that was aimed at him. He has every Houdini item you've ever seen in a book: Houdini's water torture cell, Metamorphosis trunk, magic wand, and Mirror cuffs. He has Jean-Eugène Robert-Houdin's original automatons, including *The Singing Lesson* automaton, *Pastry Chef of the Palais Royal* automaton, and his mystery clocks. (And, NO, I didn't know what those were before this tour, but now I can't imagine my life pre-knowledge of their existence.) To put this into perspective: he tracked down and purchased the actual counter from Macy's in New York where he bought his first piece of magic. It's like everything he's done, and everything he's ever wanted, is there. David's museum represents a manifestation of dreams, really, if you want to get deep about it. It's the sort of thing you expect from a billionaire. I've not been let down.

James can't stop touching things. It's making me crazy. I'm watching him flip the pages of Houdini's notebook and I'm totally wincing because there is no WAY he should be touching this shit. I steal a glance at the entourage, who are watching him closely. James clearly didn't hear a word I said about the pit boss. Am I being too naggy?

Then David puts his hand on my shoulder and nods. Again I wonder: Is he reading my mind? That would scare the shit out of me.

I walk over to Matt, who's looking at Doug Henning's jean jumpsuit.

"It's so tiny," he says. It *is* tiny. I couldn't fit into it if I did Tracy Anderson nonstop for the rest of my life.

"Matt? What did you say about those monkeys who read minds?"

"They're on his island. Apparently he taught them to read minds, and then they paint your thoughts. Don't you want to see them?!" I did my Internet research and saw NOTHING about mind-reading monkeys, so this is shocking. I'm usually quite thorough.

"I don't want to see them, Matt. I had one bad monkey experience as a kid. I couldn't deal with another. But if he taught *monkeys* to read minds . . . do you think he can read our minds?"

Then, from somewhere, comes a loud knocking noise. Steel. *Bang, bang, bang.* Matt and I tense up. Is this it? Black Lilith Moon–style *bang, bang, bang, bang.* On edge, frenzied from the noise, Matt and I look around and see it.

It's James, knocking Houdini's milk drum with a "Hmmm, how's this work?" look on his face. Engineer-turned-thirteen-year-old-boy.

"Now, this is the Blooming Rose Bush, created by Karl Germain and presented in St. George's Hall in 1906," David says, and like obedient dogs commanded to the alpha, we all flock to him. I'm freaking out. He can totally read my mind. I'll stand on the right if he blinks twice. He blinks once.

"Kelly, you just sit here." Oh fuck. Okay. That's it. David

guides me to a chair in front of a large ornamental antique-looking chest as I try not to think of things like orgies and his penis and what he might look like while taking a dump on a toilet. But now I'm totally thinking about where his penis might go when he's taking a dump on the toilet, because that's the WORST thing you can think about when you know that person is reading your mind. James is still looking at Houdini's keys. What is he thinking about? Oh God, if David can read my mind, then he can read EVERYONE'S mind. I know James is probably thinking about sex, or trying to dissect how all these tricks work. Angela is tallying up how much this stuff cost, what is pretty and what is pretty ugly. And Matt is thinking about how to woo David into spilling the beans about the Fountain.

David and I make eye contact. Oh shit, he knows I'm thinking about what they're thinking about.

"Angela, you sit here." David guides Angela to a chair. "And Matt?" he says. "Would you be so kind as to take this seat?" Matt basically skips to the plush chair David has offered him. Then David goes to the Blooming Rose Bush pot. He puts some soil into it and, of course, invisible seeds. *David? Can you hear me?* David looks at me. Adrenaline rush, like in seventh grade, when I asked Neil, a ninth grader, to dance with me. (He did, but there was another girl dancing with us in a circle.)

Suddenly, a bush begins to grow out of the pot. Dozens and dozens of fresh roses appear before our eyes while beautiful music plays and lights flash all around us. I know David is extravagantly generous with his money, but still, the outlay on fresh flowers appearing is flattering. He's bought at least a hundred Colombian roses for us and had one of his assistants put them into this magic pot for us, right? I'm more amazed with that kind of generosity than I would be if that pot were actually growing roses.

David grabs one of the roses and gives it to me. That's it.

DAVID, IF YOU CAN HEAR ME, GIVE ME A SIGN. Then it happens. Matt's chair falls backward, but not because he's lost his balance. His chair is spring-loaded, some kind of trick chair . . . he's shot across the floor. I lock eyes with David as he helps Matt to his feet.

Dear God. David, I'm sorry I thought about you sitting on the toilet. It's just where my mind went.

"My back hurts," Matt whispers as he leans into me in the back of the van. Guilt.

"You don't have to whisper, Matt. David can read our minds."

Matt nods. Nothing is too weird for him. "He does have heat sensors on his audience. He checks to see which illusions they respond to." Matt really does know a lot about Copperfield, and he's been injured in the line of duty, so I don't argue.

David turns around in the front passenger seat and says, "We're here. Would you like to have brunch with us by the pool tomorrow?"

Of course, I think without speaking, because I know he can hear me. James turns to me and gives me a great "WTF, why aren't you answering?" face.

"Of course," I say.

It's two A.M. The four of us walk through the lobby together, exhausted.

"James, I don't think you were supposed to touch that stuff."

"They didn't care. No one said anything."

"It's called a museum. Not an interactive museum." I hate when I'm old and naggy. I can't help it anymore. It's terrible. "Sorry. I hate me. Let's go up to our room for a drink before you guys go to your tower," I say to the others. "I still hate it that you're way over there. PS, everyone: David can read minds."

No one reacts for a second. Then Angela stops walking.

"Oh my God, you guys. WAIT. Wait. Wait."

"Did you forget something?"

She shakes her head no. "Give me your pen," she says.

She takes my Sharpie, then walks to the lobby desk and writes something down on a piece of paper while Matt, James, and I stand around like assholes.

"ANGELA, COME ON! I NEED A DRINK!"

She returns holding up a piece of paper:

"I've been thinking," she whispers. "When Matt and I checked in, they said the rooms were prearranged like this. Separated. Maybe they're his personal rooms? He has a SkyLOFT; why not some Signature Suites?"

She's right. "You're right." I grab her shoulder. I'm totally buying this theory. My mental compass is generally fixed some-where between *bullshit* and *fun*. "I'd do the same thing if I were a billionaire magician putting people up in a hotel. It's like having your own *Big Brother* TV show."

Matt agrees. "Totally. It's the only explanation."

"No WAY," James says. "That's illegal. There is no way he would bug the room. We're nobodies. He wouldn't bug the room for us. Who cares about us? Let's go."

"James! The people on *Big Brother* are nobodies! It's not about who you are, it's about watching how people work when they think no one's around," I say, following everyone into the eleva-tor bank. "Angela, I love you even more now. I didn't think that was possible."

James opens the door to the suite and walks right into the kitchen to mix drinks, like it isn't totally under surveillance by a wizard. Matt goes in next, and Angela and I follow . . . slowly.

"Well, hello, Emile Berliner." Matt chuckles as he puts his coat on the barstool.

"Who?" I ask, scanning the walls, vents, anything for mikes or cameras.

Matt leans forward conspiratorially. "He invented the micro-phone. That'll give Copperfield a good laugh when he hears it."

"Oh my God." James puts four glasses on the bar and free-pours vodka and 7Up into each. "You guys are being idiots. This place is not bugged."

"What's that?" Angela is pointing to a wall of cupboards. I see what she is pointing at: a tiny black wire sticking out from a crack between a pair of doors.

"Oooooh!" Matt walks over to the wire and picks it up, opening the door it's peeking through. "It goes up behind here. I can't see."

"IT'S THE SENSOR FOR THE REMOTE CONTROL," James says. "THE TV IS ABOVE IT." Then he drinks his entire drink and goes into the back room.

"He can't handle this, you guys," I say. Then I drink nearly my entire drink.

"I'm not going to get naked at all in my room. I think I already have, though, so it's probably too late," Angela says. Then she drinks her entire drink.

"I'd totally bug people if I were a billionaire. We should call Pasqual and have an adventure."

"Not Pasqual, Kelly." Matt shakes his head. Then he downs his entire drink.

"We should go back out. I don't want to stay in here," I say, collecting our empty glasses.

"We should go see some strippers. We're in Vegas."

And with that, Matt shoots up from the chair, and James emerges from the back room.

"Let's go."

"DO YOU WANT BOTTLE SERVICE?" a short, plump, chesty brunette yells over the music to us when we walk into the giant, glowing smut haven that is the Hustler Club. I notice it's wheelchair accessible. Bless Larry Flynt. "A BOTTLE AND A TABLE UP IN THOSE VIP BOOTHS?"

"SURE," Matt yells back.

"WOOP! WOOP!" the girl screams, and other B-list girls arrive excitedly. They turn on some glow sticks and begin dancing us to our table.

"What the fuck is going on? This is awesome," I whisper to James. I've never been to a "fancy" strip club, and none of us knows what bottle service is. When I was sixteen, I had to pee really badly while waiting to go into a Smashing Pumpkins concert. I used my fake ID to get into a bar to use the bathroom and didn't realize it was a dingy strip club. There was a girl on a pole, fully naked. She wasn't even on a stage. It was like someone's basement barroom with a naked girl in it. I had to pass her at eye level to get into the bathroom, wearing my silver leather jacket, pretending I wasn't surprised. When I was twenty-three, I went to Crazy Girls in Los Angeles and got stuck in a bathroom trying to keep a stripper who was OD'ing on heroin from swallowing her tongue. So my experience in strip clubs was limited, but pretty real as such experiences go. This time, I just want to feel like a baller. I want to be a strip club patron, not a lost child or a nursemaid to a naked vomiting girl on a bathroom floor. I'm not even sure this is fancy, but so far, with actual stages and a parade to our table, it is the fanciest I've seen.

We sit down in a large white booth, but we're pretty far from the pole and dancers. "Is it really fancier when we're sitting so far away?" I ask James.

"We don't want to be in Pervert's Row," he replies.

"James, no one calls it Pervert's Row," I reply, proud of my sudden PhD in strip lingo. "And I'd rather be close to the strippers than way up here!"

The waitress opens the drink menu for us and shines a spotlight on the options. Like most normal human beings whose parents couldn't afford sleepaway summer camp, when it comes to champagne I have no idea, so I just look at the prices. Ugh, this is not what I was hoping. The cheapest bottle is $150, so we order the second-cheapest bottle, at $300.

"What do we do?" Angela asks me.

I shrug. "I have no idea. Just watch? No, wait—I think we need to get lap dances." I look down at the stage below us and see a stripper climbing to the top of the pole, *two stories high*. "She is amazing!!" I shriek. "I want to be that strong!" I realize she's probably twenty-eight and an athlete. I mean, all of these girls were gymnasts. That's what gymnastics prepares you for: stripping, not the Olympics.

"Angela, I will never have a normal body again. Babies ruined me."

"You are dumb. Your body is great."

"You're my friend. You have to say that or I'll stop speaking to you."

A bullhorn siren goes off, and the same parade of glow-stick waitresses returns, all dancing toward us, holding up our bottle of champagne like an offering to the pussy god Larry Flynt. The lead waitress uncorks the bottle and squeals. Another puts a martini glass full of whipped cream on our table. A third girl puts a martini glass full of strawberries on our table and shouts, "DON'T WORRY, THEY'RE TOTALLY FRESH!"

The champagne opener is their leader. "Is there anything else you need?" she asks me.

I grab her arm and pull her onto the couch beside me. "Look, we have no idea what we're supposed to be doing here. We can get lap dances, right?"

She laughs, then sees I'm dead fucking serious. "Yes. Actually, the girls usually come right up and offer. But everyone is scared of you guys."

"Scared?"

"Yeah."

I look around at the other people in the strip club. They're all Vegas casual, touristy and totally drunk. A red-faced guy in a T-shirt is dancing with his pants half down. A bunch of stumbling Asian girls, wearing all the jewelry Forever 21 has ever made, are screaming and dancing at their table. Then I look at our group. We're totally deadpan. We're all wearing dark tailored clothing. We look like hot fucking narcs. Or Europeans.

"How do we do it?"

"I can send some up." She looks around. "Do those two look good to you?" I don't even look. I'm on a mission. "Yes. So how do we pay them?"

"Give them twenty dollars after they dance. If they ask for more, tell them to fuck off. You can also get a private room or booth. They're upstairs by the bathroom." Then she walks away.

I turn to Matt, Angela, and James.

"She's sending up two lap dancers for the guys."

Their faces fall.

"Right now?" Matt asks.

"Yes."

We're terrified. Two girls walk sexily to our table. One is tall and thin with no boobs. The other looks like a large-breasted teenage girl who wears Juicy Couture as formal wear. They give Angela and I tequila shots, maybe as a "We cool?" gesture before they ride our men.

The thin one mounts Matt's lap on the far side of the couch. I focus on the booby one climbing on top of James. She immediately puts one breast on either side of his face and slides down, slowly. His head reemerges from the top of her breasts, like a horrified baby being born. His hair, forehead, and then his wide, terrified eyes; he's looking right at me from in between her real boobs. He reaches out and holds my hand. Matt sits back impassively while his dancer rides his lap; he looks like he's reading Yelp reviews on his desktop. The girl reaches over and starts to stroke Angela's chest. For twenty bucks, I feel like the girls are really giving a good show. I wouldn't try this hard. Thighs pumping, hair tossing—it's athletics for sure. And then they're done. All at once they're trying to make small talk: "I like your shirt! My boyfriend would never wear that," or "Can I have some of your champagne?" I pass them the money and they leave, because I don't share my champagne with naked girls who ask me for it.

Matt leans over to James. "Did you get a boner? I didn't!"

"Nope, not even close!"

"Angela," I ask, "was she feeling your boobs?"

Angela looks traumatized. "She said, 'You can take off your shirt too,' and I said, 'That is way too complicated.' She said, 'My sister works here too,' and I was going to say, 'WHOA! Bad childhoods,' but instead I said, 'That must be nice.'"

Then it happens. While Angela tells the guys how traumatized she was by the girl's 100 percent flat non-boobs, I see a girl walk onstage to Skid Row's "18 and Life." She looks exactly like if Megan Fox and Christina Aguilera had a baby: Fox face and body, Aguilera thugness. She isn't trying very hard on the stage; there's hardly anyone there to tip her, so why would she? I like this lazy hot stripper the most.

I stand up and look at my crew, pointing at the stage. "I'm going to get that one and take her to a private booth to see what she does to me."

James sees her. "I'm coming too."

I drink three shots of tequila and sway to Skid Row. When she gets offstage, I walk up to her. I'm terrified, thrilled, and drunk. I feel like a Middle Eastern sheik or an old Mexican hobo.

"Can I get you in a booth with me?"

She smiles. "Sure."

The booths themselves are giant chair-and-a-halfs with six-foot-tall backs, all slightly turned into the outer walls so they're pretty private. She motions us to an empty booth.

"Do I just sit in it?" I'm really playing it cool.

"Yeah. You can sit together, or he can stand and watch, or whatever."

"We'll sit."

I slide into the corner of the velvet booth, and James sits beside me. He is sweating. We are not calm; the tequila has not worked. But this doesn't put our girl off. She pushes my legs apart and straddles one of them. I try to relax, or look relaxed, and shift position, resting my arm on the booth. Into something wet. I lift my arm out of the wetness. It's semen. I can tell it's semen. I just put my elbow into someone's semen. I am not going to look at it. Even when I get out of here to wash my elbow, I will not look at it. I will never look at it.

I look at James. I want to tell him there's semen on my elbow, but I don't want this trip to the strip club to be a total waste of seven hundred dollars. I see the tissue on the table in the corner and suddenly understand the difference between getting a private booth dance and getting a normal lap dance at the table in the main bar: in here, you can totally jerk it. Only I have no wiener to jerk.

The stripper grabs my hand and puts it on her perfect B-cup boob. And now I know why guys say, "I didn't know if it was real or not," because I can't tell if her boob is real or not. This is the first time I've ever touched a boob that wasn't my own. It's a *lot* like touching your own tongue after it's been novocained at the dentist. She's kissing my neck and running her hands all over my torso, my back and my stomach, when she whispers into my ear, "Damn, you have a tight hot body."

I pull back and look at her. "What?"

She stops her dancing. "Seriously, you have a really fucking good body. I've been doing this since I was sixteen. I *know* girls' bodies, and you have a hot body."

I turn to James. "DID YOU HEAR THAT?!?" I squeal. "SHE thinks I have a great body!!" This is one of the biggest moments of my life. For a minute, I forget about all about my semen elbow. Megan Fox just touched my three-baby stomach and told me I have a TIGHT HOT BODY. I get up and start jumping around. "Yeah! TRACY ANDERSON I LOVE YOU!" I pick my drink up off the little table with the tissue box and throw the whole thing back. I deserve it.

Then it hits me. "OH MY GOD, WHAT IS THIS?!"

That glass was not mine. I just drank someone else's old water. Maybe Semen Elbow's water. I have his DNA in my mouth and stomach and on my elbow. I throw the glass in the corner. "THAT WASN'T MY DRINK, JAMES, THAT WAS NOT MY DRINK."

I start spitting on the floor.

"Honey, what? It's okay." Megan pulls out her rhinestoned BlackBerry and starts typing on it with her superlong acrylic nails (French manicure, like all good strippers/OC housewives) while I spit in the corner.

James stands up. "Should I get you something?" He sees my panic.

I yell at both of them, because I feel like they just don't get it. "I JUST DRANK AIDS WATER AND I HAVE CUM ON MY ELBOW." James's eyes widen, but with confusion; he looks like he's on a game show where he has to beat the clock to complete a task but his brain doesn't yet understand what that task is. He rushes off, saying NOTHING, leaving me with a stomach full of AIDS and a stripper with real or fake boobs.

Megan looks up from her BlackBerry. "You want Listerine?"

I nod. "NOW. QUICKLY!"

We scurry out of the booth room to the row of hand-washing sinks outside the bathrooms.

"She needs Listerine," Megan says to one of the girls behind the sinks who washes your hands for you. (Fancy.)

"I DRANK AIDS WATER," I repeat to the hand-washer,

who looks at me like I'm mentally handicapped. "And I have cum on my elbow. Can you please wash it off for me?" I wash my mouth out with Listerine, over and over, spitting into the sink like it's curing me of the AIDS I've ingested. I can't believe I drank that water. I begin a mental inventory of everything I just caught: hep, hep, herp, AIDS, strep, influenza, SARS. This is the Black Lilith Moon stuff my mom was talking about.

Angela appears. "WHAT HAPPENED?! James just came back to the table and said the words *communicable disease* to Matt."

I shake my head. "It was terrible, Angela. I drank from a water cup. It wasn't mine. It was an old cup in a jerk-off booth. I have AIDS and I had cum on my elbow."

Angela's eyes open wide and she shakes her head. "NO."

"Yes," I say. "That woman washed the cum off my elbow for me. We should have called Pasqual . This would have never happened with Pasqual!"

"Oh my God," she whines, consoling me. "You totally have AIDS."

Megan goes back to typing on her phone. "You don't have AIDS," she says.

At six A.M. I crawl under the bedsheets, where no one can see me, and finally fall asleep. I wake up an hour later, at seven, and vomit across the room and into the bathroom. It's either the diseases or the drinks, but I'm vomiting everywhere as James lays passed out with his face in the pillow. When I was younger, I was able to drink tequila and fall asleep and wake up and eat eggs and wear makeup like a normal person and not barf at all.

I text Angela. "On floor of bathroom. Throwing up everywhere. I hate being old."

"Matt is sick too," she texts back.

I peel myself off the floor and brush my teeth. I avoid looking at myself in the mirror, but eventually I catch a glimpse of the monster. I look like I need a dollar sign in my name. I look like I had a terrible childhood. I look for a dent in my forehead. A few months ago I drank moonshine and I was so hungover and sick that my forehead actually caved in a bit, until I looked Cro-Magnon. I will forever rate my hangovers based on that forehead divot. No divot today.

I text Angela. "There is no way I'm making brunch with Copperfield."

She replies. "Nope."

James is awake when I walk back into the bedroom. He's wearing his workout clothing. "I'm going to the gym."

"Wait, what? I'm so sick I think I'm going to die. Why aren't you sick?"

"Do you think our tolerance levels are the same because we've lived together for thirteen years? It doesn't work that way. Do you need anything?"

I pout. "No. But you're forty years old, and I'm only thirty-three. I think having three babies come out of me really aged me. I'm, like, eighty in so many ways."

He kisses my plump forehead. "Love you. Go back to sleep. I'll get you Gatorade."

I fall back to sleep. At one P.M., I wake up and text Angela.

> KELLY: I'm scared to cancel brunch with Copperfield.
> ANGELA: He'll understand.
> KELLY: But he's Copperfield. No one cancels on him. I'm a jerk.
> ANGELA: You're sick.
> KELLY: Because I'm an idiot. Should I tell him I have AIDS?

ANGELA: No.

KELLY: He probably already knows, right? What if he thinks we're canceling because he really did bug the room and he heard us talking about it last night?

ANGELA: If he bugged the room he knows you're vomiting everywhere.

When I'm done throwing up for the fifth time, I realize I have to call Copperfield. This is a moment I could not have imagined happening. I am canceling brunch with David Copperfield because I have a hangover from a strip club where I probably got AIDS.

"Hello?"

"Hi, David?" Calling him David is weird.

"Hello! How are you doing this morning?" I figure he probably already knows, right?

"I'm not doing so great. Uh, we went to Hustler last night, and were out until six A.M. And now I'm totally sick and, well . . . I don't think I can make it for brunch. Unless . . . I, like, get better in a minute or something. I'm pretty sick."

"Well, that's no good."

"No, no. I mean, I just don't think you need to see me vomit. I'm totally embarrassed by this, by the way. Not normally my thing but, uh, Vegas."

He leaves a knowing pause. "How were the girls?"

"Huh?"

"At Hustler? Were they good? I haven't been there in a long, long time. You never know what you're going to get."

"Uh, there were a few good ones. Nothing that made me cringe or anything."

• • •

When we get to the airport that night, I feel better, but not by much, waiting in the baggage and ticket line in my hoodie and sunglasses, with thousands of other people in hoodies and sunglasses who'd also spent their morning in Vegas vomiting after spending the night in a strip club.

Matt seems exactly as hungover as I am, but he's limping. "Sciatica, from Copperfield's trick chair," he said. "Why would he do that to me?!"

The guilt eats me alive. "It was my fault, Matt. I'm so sorry. It's just that I needed to know if he could read my mind, and I asked for a sign and . . ."

". . . and then my chair fell?"

"YES. I'm sorry. I didn't mean to give you sciatica. It was totally my fault. Forgive me?"

Matt nods. I hug Angela. "That was fun. I won a little with the 'Great body!' thing, and I lost a lot with the dirty-water/hangover thing."

"Yeah, well, you'll have more time for Tracy Anderson before we go to his island."

"When we go to his island, can we find the psychic monkeys and the Fountain of Youth?" I ask.

"It's the only reason to go," Matt replies, leaning into his bag like a crutch.

"Maybe next time we'll find the bugs in the room?"

"There were no bugs in the room." James hugs Angela.

"I know there were no bugs in the room."

We say our good-byes to Matt and Angela, who head off to a different terminal. Angela had found eighty-dollar tickets to Vancouver on Singapore Airlines, which I was *sure* was a computer glitch. I figured they were going to end up in Singapore by tomorrow. We walk to our gate.

• • •

As our plane is boarding, I notice a tall black man. I notice him because there's a horde of screaming women chasing him and taking photos with their phones. Everyone notices him.

"OH LAWD!!!!! SWEET LAWD, HOLD ME NOW!" one screams, and I recognize the object of their *woop woop*s and *holla*s. It's Common. ID'ing celebrities is a small gift of mine. I pull out my phone and tweet: "Hey @common, you're on my flight. You're a huge fan of mine, right? Maybe I'll say hello."

I get on the plane and discover that James and I are sitting right behind him. I check my Twitter replies:

@kellyoxford ASK HIM ABOUT DRAKE
@kellyoxford IF DRAKE IS ON THE PLANE U GOT
    A PROBLEM
@kellyoxford ur an ugly cunt

I wonder why people would bring up my second husband, Drake. I Google and get the answer: Drake and Common are feuding. Common thinks Drake is a punk and Drake thinks Common is bashing him because Common is old.

I had NO IDEA about their feud. My finger has officially left the pulse of pop culture. This clinches it: Drake will never shout "DAT ASS" at me, because, quite frankly, if Drake is accusing Common of being old and out of touch, I'm going to be on Common's side of that. I get it. For that reason—and because I say things like "quite frankly."

I sink into my gross airplane seat and look at the top of Common's head. He's wearing a neck pillow. It would be funny if I played one of his songs on my phone full blast. I scroll through my list and land on "Come Close." I wait until I think he's fallen asleep, then stand up and reach into the overhead bin as an excuse to see if he is asleep. I see his face, eyes closed, relaxed and asleep on his neck pillow. Common looks so peaceful, like he's dead. This is as close to being Serena Williams as I'll ever get.

I sit back down. I don't have it in me to blast the song and wake him up, even if it means I won't be able to say I did that. Because I'd love to say I did that, but it seems stupid to wake him up. I reach over and grab James's hand. "Is my body really okay?" I ask.

He nods. "It's my favorite thing."

Maybe I'll get David to bring his psychic monkeys to my funeral. Maybe I'm over pulling up my G-string. Maybe I'm not growing old, maybe I'm growing up.

FROGGER

James crouches at eye level with the kids. His eyes dart back and forth, splitting his eye contact evenly among the members of our attentive brood.

"Remember, you're about to see everything that is wrong with the world."

He lovingly tucks Sal's hair behind her ear and stands back up. Seven-year-old Henry and two-year-old Beatrix stand to the left and right of him, nine-year-old Sal directly in front. We look at James's grim expression.

"Are we gonna be okay?" Bea asks.

"Of course we will, Bea." My nonchalance is in complete contrast to James's heat. He's at Cormac McCarthy–stage seriousness, like it's the end of fucking days.

Henry's stationary foot shuffling quickens. "What do you mean, everything that's wrong with the world?" he asks, both scared and excited, his eyes darting around the crowd, hoping to catch a glimpse of the something that's wrong with the world. Henry's thing is making life dramatic and as action laced as possible. "Like torture chambers and war?"

James shakes his head. "It's going to be disgusting." He throws the backpack over his shoulder. "I just need you guys to know that before we go in. I disagree with everything we will see." Then he exhales dramatically, pushing what sounds like all the air out of his lungs, as we watch and wait till he's done.

I clap my hands together excitedly, smiling.

"Ready to go to Disneyland?"

"Have a wonderful day," says the woman who just charged us almost $450 for our single-day passes.

"Yeah, right," James mumbles in reply. James had a lecture for us in the parking lot: "Good businesses don't charge fifteen dollars to park in a lot where the only place you can go is their venue, where they're going to charge you hundreds to enter." He had a few more on the freeway on the way there: "See how that guy is driving? Don't do that. He wants everyone out here to die. He's probably on his way to Disneyland to stuff his fat face with churros."

This is the kids' first trip to Disneyland. And it's my husband's first trip to Disneyland.

I've been here before, when I was twelve. When my friends were sneaking off and trying cigarettes and playing spin the bottle, I was at Disneyland with my parents, still two years away from getting my period. My sister and I were wearing matching home-sewn, florescent pink-and-gray fleece jackets. My little sister, that is, who'd already had her first period.

I had a great time in Disneyland, but I kept my enjoyment a secret. It was tainted by the fact that I was so old and dorky. I shouldn't have loved it so much. I shouldn't have loved the songs or had my name embroidered onto one of the hats with the ears. And I certainly should not have bought an autograph book and had Peter Pan and Goofy and Winnie the Pooh sign it.

James and I agree on every single thing we hate, except for Disneyland. Today was my day to change his mind.

My goals for the day were simple:

1. Keep everyone hydrated. Nothing is dumber than dehydrating.
2. Get Henry a corn dog. Henry's friend told him the portal to Hell is under the *H* in the Hollywood sign, so his main goal on this California trip is discovering that portal. His Disney goal is to eat a corn dog, because the same said friend told him that the corn dogs at Disneyland are "the best corn dogs in the universe."
3. Feed Sal. Sal basically wants to do what every nine-year-old wants: to consume as much as possible.
4. Introduce Bea to Belle from *Beauty and the Beast*.
5. Keep James from losing his mind in the crowd and 95-degree heat.

As soon as I see the turnstiles leading into the park, I realize my fatal mistake: I probably could have picked a better time for this trip than *spring break*. What a dumb fucking idea. "Hold hands with Dad or me while we get through this," I say to the kids, whose attentions are being pulled in a million directions at once. There are hordes of people and buggies and strollers, parents with kids on their shoulders, balloons, different songs blasting from every direction, as we become one with the sea of people trying to get through the turnstiles.

Having three children doesn't seem like it would be so different from having two, but when you're shepherding them through parking lots and the chaos of crowds outnumbered, you quickly realize you're way out of your fucking league. Imagine playing *Frogger* with three tiny frogs behind your frog and you can't control them with arrows. There is just no goddamn way you can get three kids to listen to you at the same time. If you like people who do stupid shit all the time, become a parent. You'll love it.

"There's Mickey the Mouse!" Bea squeals as we make our way under the train bridge and into a tunnel. I look to the right side entrance and see it: there he is, Mickey. But then I look back at Bea and realize something horrifying: she's looking to *the left*. At a completely different Mickey Mouse. There are two Mickeys, one in each entrance tunnel into the park. They're hidden from each other just slightly, so the kids don't notice, but *I've* noticed, and the illusion of his majesty is gone forever. I've just gone from a lifetime of fetishizing Mickey as a god to visualizing some vault teeming with a thousand empty Mickey costumes, strung up on hangers, chins dangling to their hollow mouse chests. Mouse skin suits.

The line to see Mickey is already stupid, a hundred people deep.

"MICKEY THE MOUSE!!!" Bea screams.

"We can't get a picture with him," I say, my newfound contempt for counterfeit Mickey showing just a bit around the edges.

"Awwwww!" Henry whines.

"Why not?" Sal sheepishly asks. Unlike twelve-year-old me, nine-year-old Sal understands that she really shouldn't give a shit. Just like me, however, she does.

I pull the kids to the side of the tunnel, so we won't get trampled by the mobs of eager families irately shoving and pushing their way through to the best day of their lives. James stands nearby giving me his "ABORT MISSION" look, but I want the kids to get a good look at one of the many Mickey Mice. "Okay, look at him from here." They already are, transfixed.

"Team," I say to the three sets of eyes that are not meeting mine at all, "we need to go and get our fast passes for the Indiana Jones ride. You guys want to go on that, right?"

"YEAH!" Henry and Sal shout.

Bea rolls her eyes. "I don't."

"Good, you can't go on it anyway. Let's go."

I pull them back into the wave of people, James trailing behind. As we walk past the line of families, I look at all the moms and dads waiting in line to get Mickey's autograph and photo and realize: They are *happy*, standing there in line. They're smiling. A few of them are *singing*.

"James, what are these people, handicapped? Who likes waiting in a line with their kids to see some dude in a mouse costume? I mean, I *was* one of those people, I guess. Before I got my period."

He nods. "They're totally handicapped. No need to talk about your period."

I wish I had more patience for stupidity, but I use it all up pretty quickly on my kids. I rarely say no to things that aren't death traps, but when I do say no, there is a reason: stupidity.

I can see James clenching his jaw as we move forward. "We need to get the fuck out of here," he whispers. "This was a bad idea."

"James, it's going to be amazing." I let go of little hands and throw my own hands in the air, clinging for dear life to my life-is-what-you-make-it, Pollyanna-till-you're-paralyzed smile. "It's Disneyland! Preplanned fun! We don't even have to think about entertaining!"

"CORN DOGS!!!!" Henry screams, running off and disappearing into the crowd toward a snack stand.

I look at James. "We can just lose him now, right? We don't really need him."

"Yeah, leave him," Sal says casually. "But maybe later? I want a corn dog too."

"MOM! THEY LOOK DELICIOUS!" We're barely within earshot of Henry, but as usual he makes it work.

"Henry," I say, jogging up to his dumb, smiling face. Not too fast—I hate running. "You can't run off like that. Do you want to be the first of the three of you to get kidnapped?"

"Mom, no one gets kidnapped in Disneyland. It's basically illegal."

"Dude, kidnapping *is* illegal. Not just basically."

Bea chimes in. "I would kidnap kids here, Mama."

"Twenty-four dollars?" James is grabbing his change and three corn dogs for the kids. "These things cost twenty-four dollars? We send that sponsored World Vision kid twenty-four bucks, it lasts him a month."

"They look delicious." Sal is a monster child. At nine years old, she's five foot four and thin, with a size seven foot. She is a human garbage disposal unit.

"AHHHH!" Henry says, the steaming tip of a corn dog hanging out of his mouth. "This is delicious."

"Uh, Mom?" Bea looks up at me, holding her corn dog. "This is too hot."

"I know. Just wait a minute, it'll cool down. Want me to carry it?"

"I'm not even hungry." Her eyes are wide, like she's surprising herself. "I want to see Belle."

"I'll eat it." Sal lunges for the corn dog.

Henry sees her and lunges in too. "No! I want it."

Queen Bea lifts her eyebrows, making her power move. Kids are so predictable.

"Bea, you're sure you don't want it?" I ask.

She nods. "Belle is all I want."

I turn to Sal. "Can Henry have it? He's almost finished his, and corn dogs was his thing. I'll get you something else."

"I saw a gift shop over there," she says.

"No gift shop!" James says. It's kind of our rule: We can go to the museum, the science center, the zoo, but we avoid the gift shop like the chicken pox. Gift shops are for suckers.

We aren't suckers and we aren't getting dehydrated. "Drink," I say, passing the kids their water bottles.

"Okay. Look, it's Disneyland. If things go well, meaning *if you listen . . .*" I pause dramatically, alpha-momming them into eye contact until they're hanging on to my words like I'm Oprah, ". . . we will go to a gift shop."

"Yesssss!" Sal says, under her breath, dipping her corn dog into the little container of ketchup. Out of the corner of my eye, I see some dubious-looking fortysomething guy standing alone against the facade of a building, watching her as she eats her corn dog. I decide to put my fear of creepy molesters to bed for the rest of the day. Even if I continue to check bathroom stalls before allowing my kids to enter them, I will NOT let myself worry about weirdo single men in the Happiest Place on Earth, not today.

"Sal?" I say. "Turn around and face the castle when you take a bite of corn dog. I heard it's good luck."

The crowd throughout Disneyland is thick and 85 percent gross. You have the locals (deadpan), the socks-and-sandals crew (Europeans), and the people dressed like they just walked off the set of *Roseanne* (small-town Americans and Canadians). Our group is the "normals," which makes up, perhaps, 15 percent of the herd. Of course that 15 percent can then be divided further into different subsets: overprotective parents, neglectful parents, teens on dates, adults on dates. It's just a LOT of people. We can't even get into the ticket area for the Indiana Jones fast passes without waiting in a line.

"I'll stand over here with Bea while you get the passes," James says, a continuing absence of Disneyland excitement in his voice.

"James, you should totally go on this ride with them, though. Indiana Jones is, like, meant for you. I'll stay with Bea."

"I don't want to do any rides." Crowd stress is really fucking ruining this for him.

"I don't want any rides either," Bea says, putting her hands on her hips briefly before taking James's hand again. "Dad and I are just gonna check stuff out and find Belle."

"Let's get on the ride!" Henry shouts, taking the final bites of his second corn dog and punching his fist in the air.

"We can't—look!" Sal points to the sign saying that the wait for the ride is thirty minutes. "We're getting the fast passes, so we can skip the line later."

"I'll be over there." James points to a wall.

"Dad and I will be over there!" Bea says, dragging James off through the crowd.

I pull out a bottle of water. "Here, Henry, stop punching the air and drink."

Henry pulls his fists in, loses the goofy smile, and shoots me his "Oh my God, Mom" squinty eyes. "Mom, I JUST DRANK."

"You're never thirsty. If I listened when you say you have no thirst, you'd be dead ten times over."

He grabs the bottle, takes a tiny sip, and our line moves forward.

I print out three fast passes from the machine. "Okay, let's go to the front of the line!" Henry punches the air again.

"Oh my God!" Sal spins around, a full spin on one foot. God, I miss involuntarily spinning around like an idiot. "Henry, the pass is for later," she clucks. "We come back to get on the ride, we get to skip the line—then and then only." Sal knows what a fast pass is. Like me, she's a researcher. She's my Cliff Clavin when I'm too lazy to deal. She's constantly schooling us with facts:

- *"Did you know that palm trees aren't native to California?"*
- *"Did you know that* Cali *means 'hot' and* fornia *means 'oven'?* California *means 'hot oven.'"*
- *"The orange scent on Disney's Main Street? They pump it into the air."*

"Hen, we have to come back at eleven A.M. That's when these passes get us in. We'll come back then and go right to the front of the line." We all walk to the middle of the park, not really knowing what to do next. Unlike families with ride missions and preplanned outfits and preparedness, we've found our way into this like we always do: by winging it.

Looking around, it seems like the most popular ride at Disneyland today is obese ten-year-olds riding in strollers. At times, the crunch sound of kids pushing candy and dry cereal out of Tupperware containers and into their mouths is louder than the Disney theme music coming out of hidden speakers. Adults leaning on benches throw back cups of cola as big as toilet bowls.

"Okay, James, I have a plan." I do have a plan, but James is focused on someone else's child, who's chasing a duckling that's following its duck mother. The child is about to catch it, and the happy parents are recording the whole thing.

"Hey!" James shouts, expressionless. The family looks at him. "If he catches that duckling, the mother will abandon it. So your kid may as well step on it too." James loves helping people.

He turns to me. "What's the plan?"

"Okay. If you don't want to go on any rides, I'll take Henry and Sal to Pirates of the Caribbean and the Haunted House. You can take Bea to Fantasyland. I'm sure you'll find a ride to go on."

He nods. "Hey, Henry, you okay?"

Henry is holding his stomach. He nods, then lets out a huge burp. "Now I'm totally fine."

Twenty minutes later:

"Mom, I'm going to puke."

In the darkness of the Pirates of the Caribbean ride, I can see Henry's glassy puppy-dog eyes. I've seen those eyes before. Henry vomits, a lot. At every party, every movie, everywhere he should be having a good time, he manages to vomit. I should have brought a bag.

"I don't have anything for you to puke in," I whisper, rubbing his back. "Lean over the side." Thankfully, with all his puking experience, he's gotten pretty professional about it. Never any noise or crying. It's 100 percent business. Also, it helps matters that we're in the back row of the boat and it's fairly dark. He leans over. I see his back heave a couple of times.

"Is Henry puking again?" Sal asks. "He really needed to puke at Disneyland. It's pretty much his destiny."

Henry sits back up. "She's right."

"Those corn dogs really were magical." I pass him a hand wipe for his face and give him his water bottle. "You're gonna be totally dehydrated now if you don't drink this."

"Mom?" Sal turns around. "This is kind of boring. Jack Sparrow is just around every corner making dumb faces."

"True." Henry nods.

Wow. When I was a kid, I was thrilled by this ride—and that

was pre–Jack Sparrow. Now, I'm a dyed-in-the-wool "I used to play with rocks and had the time of my life" type. God, I'm old.

We make our way back into the sun and heat and people.

"CHURROS!!!" Henry leans back in his wide stance and punches the air again.

That air punch is getting a little tired. "Got any other moves?" I dare him, and he starts in on the robot. He does a mean robot. At least I birthed one dancing monkey.

"Mom, can we *plllllease* have churros?!" Sal begs. It's a low whine, like she's asking me for the right to vote or the right to choose her own husband.

"Henry just barfed."

He turns his robot move on me. "I'm empty now. Clean slate. I can start all over again."

"Like when you shake an Etch A Sketch?" I ask.

"EXACTLY."

A text from James comes in on my phone. The kids edge closer to the churro stand, I follow as I text. Total text-walking asshole move.

JAMES:	We need to get the FUCK out of here.
KELLY:	What?
JAMES:	Now. Let's go. We're at the main middle-circle thing.
KELLY:	Wait, what is wrong?
JAMES:	There is nothing for Bea to do here.
KELLY:	There is nothing for two-year-olds to do . . . at Disneyland?
JAMES:	You can stay. I'm leaving.
KELLY:	Stay there.

"Mom? Churros?"

I look over at the kids standing in front of the churro stand. Henry is miming eating a churro. Sal is rubbing her stomach, giving me a thumbs-up, and smiling.

"Guys. Wait. We have to save Dad."

James is standing beside Bea. He's pale and it's 95 degrees and he's in the sun.

"Drink this." I'm already passing him his water as I approach. "What's wrong?"

"This place. This place is wrong." He keeps his voice down, for the kids, as Bea goes up against Sal and Henry on a "Who had a better twenty minutes in Disneyland?" conversation that will most definitely end in yelling in less than forty-five seconds. James puts the bottle up to his lips, and I notice a man staring at him. The perverts are out in full force today.

"Are you freaking out?" I ask James, because he's prone to just shut down when things get too stupid. Like when my mom had a "game party" and invited all of our extended family? Great-uncles, cousins, grandparents, and Risk, Jenga, Monopoly? After an hour I found him in the fetal position in Henry's twin guest bed, before anyone had to mortgage a railroad or anything.

James nodded. "This is just SO DUMB. The wait for the ride for Tangled is SEVENTY-FIVE MINUTES. There are families waiting in line with crying babies to go on an eight-minute ride. This place is like sports for fat people."

"James, that isn't even a ride. It's a line to meet Tangled."

"By God."

The kids are yelling.

"You are stupid! And YOU won't get a churro, EVER!" Bea shouts.

"Bea," I say. She looks up. "Don't call people stupid."

"Henry did it first," Sal says.

"Let's make this clear, you guys are *all* stupid. Just don't call each other stupid. Okay?"

James doesn't even notice. He's more upset now than he was this morning when he couldn't use his credit card at the gas pump because Canadians don't have zip codes.

"AND . . ." He points at the castle. "And that castle is *bullshit*!! It isn't even a castle! It's just an entrance to get into Fantasyland!" He sighs.

Aha! So he's *disappointed*.

I can see it all clearly now. James was *excited* to walk into the castle, until it let him down. Now I know there's hope for him. He just has to be wowed by something, or see the kids excited about something that's Disney-specific. Buying them more shit in the park will not count.

Then we notice Bea, who's standing there looking past us all into the middle distance.

"*Belle.*"

We turn. There she is, five hundred feet away, in her yellow dress and tall, dark bunhead hair.

"James." I hug him. "It's going to be fine. Let's go get in Dumb, Handicapped Parent Line to see Belle."

Bea is the only girl toddler who's not in full princess gear. But this doesn't seem to upset her. "Look at these kids," she says, too loud, in a kind of mocking wonder. "They are dressed like princesses in front of the princesses."

One of the moms, who's shamelessly wearing a professional-looking Snow White costume, totally breaks character to give me the evil eye. Henry agrees with Bea. "It's embarrassing!" he says to her, as one mother gets in line behind us, carrying a baby who doesn't even realize she's dressed like Cinderella.

We watch moms and dads fix hair and dresses as they make their way, one at a time, to meet Belle. And she doesn't even look like the real Belle. I mean, she has a dark wig on, but she isn't nearly as pretty. Bea doesn't mention that.

"We're next," Sal says to Bea, getting her excited. We push Bea forward, so that Belle knows who her target is. We've watched the films, but we have no idea how Method these theme park actors might possibly get. None of us wants to get trapped having a fake conversation with Belle about her crazy dad, or her favorite books, or how Gaston could get pretty gropey, or anything really. I can see that James has calmed down. This line wasn't so horrible, and we're about to make Bea's dream come true. It's our turn.

"Hello!" Belle says to Bea, and the four of us move forward with her slightly, then fan out, giving her space.

"Hi," Bea says.

"What's your name?"

"Bebe."

"What a cute name! How old are you, Bebe?"

"I'm two."

"Are you having fun today?"

"Yes."

Belle looks at us, and I suddenly realize we aren't meeting parenting protocol. I pull out my phone to take a picture of Bea standing beside Belle like a normal parent would.

"Would you like to come stand beside me and give me a hug so your mom can take a photo?"

Belle opens her arms wide and smiles warmly at Bea, like she isn't the thousandth kid she's hugged this week. I think about the germs on her dress, from all of the gross princesses who have wiped their hands and noses on her. I know she only has that one yellow dress. Belle was poor.

"No," Bea says. "Actually, I don't want to hug you . . . I want to meet the Beast."

"What did she just say?" I ask James. He puts his finger to his lips. International sign for "Not you. Not now."

"*The Beast?!*" Belle squeals, covering her O mouth with her white-gloved hand. C minus. Totally overacting.

"Yes." Bea repeats herself like Belle is a two-year-old. "I want to meet the Beast."

I can see that the other parents are getting annoyed with how long our photo session is taking. We definitely aren't following princess protocol at this point. They can fuck off.

"Well, Bebe, you are very brave, aren't you?"

"No."

"You must be, if you want to meet the Beast."

Bea gives her her best Gaston. "Bring me the Beast."

"The Beast is having lunch."

That's the best she can do? This woman does not have kids.

"Where's he having lunch?"

"In the castle."

"The castle isn't real," Sal says from the sidelines. In my head, I tag a "Bitch, please" to her sentence.

Belle looks at Bea. "I can tell him hello for you."

"Okay." Bea smiles at Belle, and walks back to us, shrugging her shoulders.

James picks her up and puts her on his shoulders. He's smiling. Kids can have that effect on you—pulling you out of your own headspace to save you from yourself. Reminding you that they're always able to steal 100 percent of your attention away from whatever bullshit your mind is running full throttle through the hamster wheel.

"Guess Belle doesn't eat lunch with the Beast," Bea muses.

Henry grabs my hand as we start to walk away from the princesses.

"Man"—he turns to me, shielding the sunlight from his eyes—"it costs a lot of money to find out everyone is lying."

"Drink."

I take the kids' water bottles out of my bag outside the bathroom where they've just emptied their bladders. If I make sure they all drink together, I can keep them all on the same pee schedule. That's important stuff when you travel in a pack.

"Okay. When I'm done counting, you're done drinking. Go!"

They drink.

"One . . . two . . . three . . . four . . . five . . . six . . . seven. Okay, seven is good."

"Mom, you are weird. But I know there's a method to your madness." Sal pats my shoulder and collects the water bottles, putting them back in the bag.

"Are you sure you don't want to go on the Indiana Jones ride?" I ask James one last time before we use our fast passes to cut in front of the eighty-minute line of a thousand people sweating in the sun.

"No, you go. Have fun." He kisses me. "Bea and I are going to climb the tree house."

Henry gets behind the fake steering wheel of our fake Indiana Jones Jeep and privately air punches toward the floorboards.

"You gonna drive this thing for us, kid?" an older, balding man asks, sweating through his brown polo shirt as he climbs into the row behind Sal, Henry, and me.

"Yeah!" Henry yells back, tossing Sweaty Polo a thumbs-up. The sound track to the ride begins.

"You trust him?" the man asks Sal, giving me that parent-to-parent wink.

"No." She laughs, and as we make our way through the ride I suddenly feel a weird sense of community with the other parents in our fake Jeep, helmed by my unskilled and vomit-prone son. All of us laughing and *whoa*-ing together. All of us spending more money than we should, gambling on a chance to create memories in this place built on make-believe. The best parts of childhood, adulthood, and parenthood are those pure moments of bliss, when you completely forget about your future and past and live in your moment. That, I realize, is why I loved Disneyland as a preteen: it was an escape from that time, from the fears of never getting my period, of being pressured into trying cigarettes, and of liking *Days of Our Lives*. That's why there are moms who are itching to dress up like Snow White for an entire day, in public, with zero shame. It's the best kind of lie. To stop thinking about the shit in our lives for a day and pretend that a princess is real, that the Beast is in the castle, and that they never take off their costumes or meet for some crappy cafeteria lunch and a cigarette behind the facade walls of Main Street.

The end of the ride is just approaching when the Jeep suddenly stops, the sound track cuts out, and all the lights come on.

Henry's hands fly off the wheel. "I didn't do it!"

"The ride broke down," Sal says, a slight worry in her voice.

I'm relieved. "I am so glad it didn't break down when the boulder was coming at us. At least we're near the exit."

Sweaty Polo Winker replies, "Yeah, but now we're stuck here, looking at the exit."

"We should just get out and go." I'm not even going to hesitate on this one.

Henry agrees with me. He starts fiddling with his seat belt. "Let's go, then."

"But wait!" Sal isn't unbuckling with us. "They told us not to get out of our Jeep until we're at the end. How will we get out of the trench?"

I look ahead and see three sets of emergency stairs up to the exit platform.

"We're only two Jeeps back from the end," I argue back. "We're gonna do this! You coming?" I ask the man in the sweaty polo shirt. He turns to his teen daughter, then back to me, nodding. "Let the boy lead. He's done a great job so far." Then he gives Henry the man-to-man wink.

I turn to Sal. "I know you hate breaking the rules, but we don't need to be held prisoner on a broken ride! Come on, it'll be fun to run to those stairs. We can pretend we're all Indiana Joneses!"

Polo Shirt is right on board with me, living the fantasy. "Let's go!"

And then, without notice, the ride starts up again.

"Oh." I'm bummed.

The Jeep pulls up to an uninterested ride operator, who presses a button to unlock our seat belts. It's like a slap in the face.

"We couldn't have done it anyhow," Henry says dejectedly.

"Oh, Henry, it's okay. Sal was right, it was against the rules anyway. But I would have done it!"

Sweaty Polo pats me on the shoulder. "You're fun. I would've done it with you. Good mom. Take care."

We wind our way out of the long ride area and out under Tarzan's Treehouse.

"MOMMMM! SAL!! HEN!!!" We all turn our heads at the sound of Bea's voice and see her and James, smiling up in the tree house. The three of us run up the stairs to them.

• • •

Henry and Sal are ecstatic.

"DAD, THERE WAS A SNAKE THAT POPPED OUT AND SCARED SAL SO MUCH!"

"AND THE BOULDER CAME AFTER US AND THE RIDE DIED AT THE END AND I AM SO HAPPY THAT DIDN'T HAPPEN AT THE PART WITH THE SNAKE OR THE BOULDER!"

"SOME OLD SWEATY MAN KEPT TALKING TO US!"

I pick Bea up and turn to James. "There are no people in this tree house. It's, like, us and Tarzan."

"Too many stairs. People don't want to exercise here. Most people here are physically incapable of climbing these stairs."

"You into it now?"

"Yeah, sorry about that. I was just freaking out. In a different headspace. Bea and I are having fun."

"Can we go in those giant teacups now?" Sal asks. "Like, from those dorky Disneyland commercials?"

"Sure," he says. "After Bea is done up here, we'll get some churros and go in the teacups." James is back. He's planning and ready for action. The kids run around the tree house, laughing and yelling, and James and I look out over the people walking below us, moving together slowly, like cattle. James reaches into the bag and gives me a water.

"Don't dehydrate like some dummy. Drink."

I drink.

EPILOGUE

KELLY: I might have talked about you in the book.

BEA: No, you didn't.

KELLY: I might have. Do you think anything can be perfect?

BEA: Yes.

KELLY: Like what?

BEA: Like watermelon, my birthday, your hair . . . sometimes.

KELLY: Right, sometimes those things aren't perfect.

BEA: No. Not always. Some things are always perfect, though.

KELLY: Like what?

BEA: You.

KELLY: Aw, cute. You're sweet. You don't know me at all.

BEA: Mommmmmm.

KELLY: No, seriously. You've only known me for four years.

BEA: Mommmmmm.

KELLY: I guess you also lived inside of me for a year and only a couple of other people made it through that.

BEA: Mommmmmm. But I really don't want to be in your book.

KELLY: Why?

BEA: I want to be in movies.

ACKNOWLEDGMENTS

THANK YOU:

James, for being base Maslow, always. The people who came out of my body, for reminding me we aren't born with thought filters: Sal, Henry, and Bea. My mom, for always asking me where I was with the book, and my dad, for never asking. Angela, for being extra eyes and a memory box of things I'd forgotten. Aimee, for living. My sister, Lauren, also for living but mostly for asking when the book parties would be. Kate Cassaday, for using a computer to edit—instead of a fucking pencil (who edits with pencils?)—and therefore uprooting her entire work process when I asked her to. Cal Morgan, for always being a talking head wearing a bow tie in my mind. Without Kate and Cal's (annoying) prodding (mostly Kate, super-naggy) and strong sense of humor (both equally funny—I'm a mom, I know how to word this), my book wouldn't be as good. Erin Malone, for being the woman in my corner holding the towel and spraying water all over my face. Jhoni Marchinko, for telling me all of this made sense. Molly McNearney and Jimmy Kimmel, for letting me live with them for twenty years. And finally my publishers, for being so smart.